GW00578163

With Resolve – With Valour

Volunteers of WW. II
On The Home Shores

By the same author

The Tree Climbers
(A Childhood In Wartime Brighton)

Bittersweet Seasons
1947 In Sussex
(With Wartime Excerpts)

Escape From Catastrophe
1940 – Dunkirk

Assisted by the author
Paraffin Lights – Water From The Well
By
Michael Butcher

With Resolve – With Valour

By
David J. Knowles

Published by
Knowles Publishing
18 Castle Avenue, Rochester, Kent

First Published 2002
Knowles Publishing – Rochester

ISBN 09534358 4 9

Front Cover Photograph

**Wartime Ambulance Service To Casualties At Farrindon Market,
London. Also Helping, A.R.P. Wardens, Police And Others.
(Photograph Hulton Getty Picture Collection)**

Back Cover Photograph

**Hop Picking In The Blitz 1940 – The Main Street At Marden, In Kent
(Photograph Kent Messenger)
As It Was Dangerous To Pick Hops In The Hop Gardens,
During the Battle of Britain, Some Farmers Brought
The Hops To The Village So That The Pickers
Could Be Near The Shelters**

Published By Knowles Publishing, Rochester.

Typeset by Academic & Technical Typesetting, Bristol.
Printed in Great Britain By Bath Press.

Acknowledgements

My thanks go to the following:

To Nikki Green of the W.R.V.S. in taking so much interest in the book and helping me by visiting people to get their stories of World War II. To Rowena Howse, the W.R.V.S. Archivist for all her help. My special thanks to my friend and author Michael Butcher, who allowed me to use pieces from his book 'Paraffin Lights – Water From The Well' about the 1930/40/50's, in particular about Sussex during the war. For my friend Mary Buck for her reading of the book.

Dennis Morgan for some lines from his book – 'Cardiff A City At War'.

Paul Tritton – the author of 'A Canterbury Tale' – for letting me use an extract from the book about the film of the same name. Also, some lines from her book – 'A Time to Be Born' – by Lois Lang-Sims and all the help given by the archives at Canterbury Cathedral.

Squadron Leader Beryl Escott with help with some lines from her book 'Twentieth Century Women of Courage. Roy Ingleton for some lines from his book 'Gentlemen At War' – Policing Britain 1939–1945.

Michael Hunt at the Ramsgate Maritime Museum. Mick Twyman of the Margate History Society for informatio. Tony Walters for information on lifeboats and allowing me to use lines from his book 'The Margate R.N.L.I. Station.' Steve Peak for lines from his book – 'Fishermen of Hastings.' The Railway Museum at York. The London Weather Centre. B.B.C. archives at Reading. The R.S.P.C.A.

The Kent Messenger Group for both their accounts and photographs about the people of Kent. Help from other papers include, The Evening Argus, in Brighton & Sussex, The Chatham News, The Coventry Evening Telegraph, Folkestone Herald, The Portsmouth News, Plymouth Evening Herald, Western Morning News, South Wales Echo, The Hull Daily Mail, The Yorkshire Evening Post, West Sussex County Times, The South Eastern Press, The Times, The Daily Mirror, The Southern Evening News.

The reference libraries at – Ashford, Brighton, Canterbury, Cardiff, Chatham, Coventry, Erith, Gillingham, Gravesend, Hastings, Hull,

Margate, Plymouth, Portsmouth, Ramsgate, Renfrewshire, Rochester, Southend, Strood.

For Trevor Harris and John Puplett for their help on the tug – *Challenge* and others tugs.

To Ron Hellyer, who in Chapter Seven gave me several pieces in his writing about the Fire Brigade – both auxiliary and full time, at Plymouth. I have written and telephoned him on many occasions. Many thanks Ron. Thanks also go to Danny Moynahan, of the Coventry Fire Brigade for all his information on the Fire brigade in the blitz.

To George Fearn of Coventry, for all information on his father Albert who won the George Medal and was written about in a special supplement in the Coventry Evening Telegraph.

For Christopher Hall at the Canterbury Library for help with photographs. Chris Robinson for his help on Plymouth and photos.

Kathleen Eneas, for her information about her father, Arthur Almond, in the Portsmouth Police during the war. Tony Ellis of the museum of Coastguards at Humberside as well as Chris Coleman, about his father Arthur in the Auxiliary Coastguards.

Julia Aries, the archivist at Glyndebourne, in Sussex and many more who helped with their stories, including: Jim and Elsie Denne, Ivy Kilminster, Georgina Merrick, Harry Tate, Ursula Hall-Thompson, Harry Philcox, Winifred Thorne, Dot Weedon, Dorothy Parker Albert Barnes, Robert Chown, Jim Peall, Phyllis Knott, Patrica King, Alan Rose, Ray Gallagher, Timmy Martinez, Maureen Andrews and her twin sister Joyce, the daughters of the late Alice Rawlings, Joan Goodyear of the Red Cross for her information on the late Dorothy White – George Medalist and a member of the Red Cross. To Jim Gardener on information on Chislehurst Caves. George Medalists Grace Rattenbury, Rose Ede, Maude Steele, Charity Bick and Betty Quinn. To Fred Roberts, Betty Rhodes, Joyce Burton O.B.E., Pauline Hollyer, Joe Nixon, Mrs.Piper for information on her father-in-law, Ronald Piper who was awarded the George Medal.

To Hubert Keyes-Evans, Mary Verrier, Naina Cox, Ernest Bowler, Mabel Siddall, B.E.M., Joe Pengally, Ken Searle, Les Greef, 'Babs' Davies, David Maclean, Eric Hart, Margaret Hall, Mary Cooke, Alf Glover, Charles Sweeney, Hugh Macleod, May Hewitt, Penny Summers, Laura Waterman, Fred Palmer, Sheila Lucas (stage name Sheila Ryan), Joy Turner, Marjory Manton.

My sincere thanks to anyone not mentioned here for their time and much appreciated help.

Contents

Illustrations

Parents, W.V.S. and other volunteers help to see the children off from Gillingham – in Kent 1939.

PATHOS

With Resolve – With Valour

Introduction

Having been born into a family with military connections – which go back through quite a few generations – my early years were certainly influenced by the 'soldierly talk' that took place at home, in conversations my father had with fellow army officers, who were quite frequent visitors to the flat we lived in, in my grandparents' house, in Brighton.

Father had been badly wounded at Mons in the First World War, and a promising career had been brought to an abrupt end. In 1937, the shrapnel, still embedded in his left leg, turned gangrenous and, in a life saving operation, the leg was amputated from well above the knee – forcing him to wear a stump type of false leg for the rest of his life. After this he became a frequent visitor to the army officer's hospital in Percival Terrace in Brighton – just near the seafront. His visits there were dual purposed – to receive treatment and, also, to visit fellow officers who were still recovering in the ward, where he had spent several months during the summer of 1937.

I was born in the spring of 1933 – blissfully unaware, of course, that this would be the year of the rise to power of perhaps the most infamous person in history – Adolf Hitler. My birthday is 20th April, the same day of the same month as the new chancellor of Germany – but there, I am pleased to say, all similarities end!

During the turbulent years of the 1930's, it became increasingly worrying to the population of Britain that there was a possibility that there could be another war with Germany. By 1937, this possibility was being considered by many as 'a probability' – or, in my father's words – "The Hun is definitely at it again – let's pray that I'm wrong!"

In 1938, after the Munich agreement, even some of father's most pessimistic associates at the hospital, had to agree that it certainly looked as though another war had been avoided and that there probably would be – 'Peace in our time'. However, even at this time, preparations still went ahead with plans for defending the home shores in the event of war, and father's attentions, knowing he would no

1

longer be a part of the armed forces, turned to what voluntary organisations there were, that would be essential in time of war and, whether or not he could be a part of any of these.

In early 1939, when the situation on the continent had once again worsened and father and his friends were by no means alone in predicting that war was – 'just around the corner,' plans started getting into full swing for eventually evacuating children, who lived in areas likely to be affected by air raids or even invasion, to safer parts of the country, in the event of this happening. Also, several voluntary organisations were getting 'geared up', so that they would be prepared to play their part in the forthcoming hostilities. These organisations included the newly formed Women's Voluntary Service (W.V.S. – now W.R.V.S.), Local Defence Volunteers (L.D.V.) – and the Home Guard, The Red Cross, The Auxiliary Fire Service, Air Raid Precaution (A.R.P.), including Air Raid Wardens, The Auxiliary Coastguard – (including the intriguingly 'Coast Watchers') – Fire Watchers and Roof Spotters, Land Girls and anyone else who volunteered or was there to help on the homes shores, in what was likely to be a bitter conflict.

At the launching of my book, 'Escape From Catastrophe – 1940 Dunkirk,' at the Imperial War Museum, in May 2000, it was put to me by some members of the W.R.V.S. and Red Cross, who were representing those distinguished services at the launching, that it would be a good idea to put together a book, similar to the Dunkirk book in format, about the voluntary services during World War II – in other words, using as many hitherto untold stories from people from all over the UK as I could get hold of – 'stories that need to be told before it's too late!' – As one W.V.S. lady enthusiastically said to me – meaning that I should start writing immediately!

So, I have done my best in putting together a book which, although only covering a little of a vast subject, at least gives some new light on the huge and essential parts played by so many voluntary organisations, including, as well, those members of the public who just happened to 'be there at the time' and, without hesitation, volunteered their help.

In writing this book, my own childhood memories have, of course, helped enormously. Although I was 'just' a child – I was there – I can remember the atmosphere. Also, I am lucky that in response to various local newspapers, throughout the UK, printing my requests for people, with wartime stories and experiences, on the home front, to write to me or telephoned to me, I have received some excellent contributions, and I am pleased to include many of these, never published before.

2

Also, and I hope the reader will forgive me here, I have included just a few pieces from books by other authors, with permission, of course, as well as including, what I consider to be necessary pieces from my own previous books, including about 'Dunkirk.' However, I feel that all the stories are well deserved to be read about, and, are also certainly tributes to those people who unselfishly were there to help others – during a time that should never be forgotten.

Chapter One

To Be Prepared.

By the time Mr. Chamberlain had formed a coalition ministry in late May 1937, the civil war in Spain had just entered its second year and the position, politically in Europe, was to say the least – 'giving rise for concern.' For some time now, during the unsettled 1930's – a decade which W.H. Auden was later to describe as 'the dishonest 30's' – the position on the continent, because of Germany's aggressive policies, had been drawing closer to hostilities breaking out for the second time in the first half of, what was to become, the most eventful century in history.

In the United Kingdom, many people hardly believed it possible that Germany could be in such a position again, so quickly, to be a threat to the hard won peace signed for at Compiegne – just nineteen years beforehand.

Because of this threat, people were beginning to think more seriously about starting up various voluntary organisations that might be needed – indeed, essential – in what would be a very different kind of war, on the home shores, to anything ever experienced before.

As far back as 1914, Sir Arthur Conan Doyle, the creator of Sherlock Holmes, and H.G. Wells – so well known for his futuristic writings – had suggested that local defence groups should be formed in various towns throughout the UK. This, of course, was at the advent of World War I. With World War II possibly 'just around the corner,' this idea, to many, seemed even more essential than at that time. However, the original idea hadn't gone down too well with some of the top brass, including Lord Kitchener, and, accordingly, in mid August 1914, a notice was circulated in the national press forbidding the formation of local voluntary defence groups. Nonetheless, a volunteer training corps was later allowed to be formed. This was heavily weighed down with restrictions – such as uniforms being allowed, as long as they didn't 'copy' the army. Also, any arms used, would have to be their own – they would get nothing from public funds!

By 1916 though, they were given official recognition and, although during the next two years all sorts of new ideas for this voluntary force

4

would be tried out, by 1918 the volunteers were viewed with a good deal of cynicism by many in 'high office' and, by 1920, the force was disbanded.

In 1931, because of the country's financial crisis, Ramsay MacDonald was chosen to head a national government; this caused many politicians to seek more extreme politics, with some, including Oswald Mosley, even turning to Fascism.

In the summer of 1935, eleven and a half million people voted in a peace ballot, conducted by supporters of 'The League of Nations,' and a majority of ten to one voted in favour of disarmament!

However, in September of that year, Stanley Baldwin's new 'national government' issued the first circular on air raid precautions, and many people, including my parents, found this rather disturbing – "I wonder what the hell really is going on?" – my father had put in his erratically kept diary at that time.

In the United Kingdom, in 1936, at a time when the Royal family were getting most of the public attention, the warning signs from Europe were, nonetheless, not being ignored and small national defence units were already being formed. A year later the first big appeal to the public for volunteers for the A.R.P. (Air Raid Precaution) was considered something of a joke, and not many people came forward. However, there were some, including my father, who were quick to voice their opinions of how essential they thought such voluntary services were.

At this time, my father, an ex regular army officer, seriously wounded at Mons in World War I, which had meant the finish to what could have been a promising career, was taking a very keen interest in all that was going on, on the continent – eagerly devouring all the latest news and frequently appraising situations with a 'military mind.'

We lived in Sussex Square, in Brighton – just a couple of hundred yards or so from the seafront. My grandparents owned number thirteen, a large elegant house that had been split up into four flats. My parents, my sister, Jill and I occupied the top flat. Sussex Square is one of the famous Regency squares in Brighton and Hove, and particularly notable because of the expansive and beautiful gardens that are entwined by the square and nearby crescents – which lead down to the sea. These gardens, which were open to key holders only, were where my parents spent many peaceful hours in their leisure times, and we children were fortunate that we had these areas, plentiful in trees, shrubbery and lawns, to play in.

Father now worked as a representative for a well-known firm of builder's merchants, and travelled to many areas in the country –

particularly in the southeast. He also, from time to time, went for treatment for his wounds to a 'military' hospital in Brighton. In early 1937, when 'war clouds' were beginning to gather on the continent, father was rushed to hospital in the middle of – "A night I shall never forget!" my mother later told my sister and me. The shrapnel remaining in his left leg had turned gangrenous and, during a life saving operation, the leg was amputated from well above the knee. Father spent several months at the Army Officers Hospital in Percival Terrace, Brighton – close to the seafront. All the nurses there were nuns – as an ex Sandhurst man and ex regular army officer, who had been 'wounded out,' he was entitled to be there.

During the summer months of 1937, we visited father frequently at the hospital – daily, in fact. The ward he was in had a good view of the channel, and he made good progress on the road to recovery. He told us that, in a way, he was in his element there – the conversations between himself and fellow officers in the ward mainly centred on the situation in Europe and, as he put it " – there were many discussions on this subject – some of them quite heated." He came home in the early August of that year and, because of his new disability, we moved from the top flat at number thirteen, to the one on the ground floor, which had recently become vacant – no stairs!

By this time, the possibility of war was very much on many peoples minds, and father turned his thoughts to the voluntary organisations that would be needed in time of war, and wondered whether he might be able to be a part of any of these, should the need arise. This was despite his disabilities, which, apart from only having one leg now, also included wounds in his left arm that had – 'virtually put it out of action.'

By early 1938 the situation in Europe hadn't improved in any way, and the threat of war was now very real. In the spring, Germany annexed Austria and Hitler was now giving his attentions to Czechoslovakia. Before this, on Thursday February 17th 1938, there was a London air raid practice. The Borough of Paddington experienced a theoretical air raid, lasting nearly two hours, when the Air Raid Precautions Organisation of the borough carried out the first trial exercise of the passive defence services to be conducted by a London Municipal Authority. There was no 'Blackout,' no aeroplanes were heard overhead, no searchlights were used or guns fired and, in the absence of any more spectacular features than a few fireworks, the demonstration attracted little attention on the part of the public. But varied personnel of about 200 helpers were afforded some useful

6

practice in the duties, which would fall to them in the possible grim circumstances, which the exercise suggested.

Other details, concerning this exercise, showed that some consideration was being given to the voluntary services in the event of war; it also showed that although volunteers for the A.R.P. were slow in coming forward to start off with – there was, at least, something happening!

Apart from the A.R.P. it was realised that volunteers would be needed in all manner of civil defence services – in particular, volunteers for local defence would be needed in all areas, possibly to be made up by older, retired ex-servicemen. But, although there was some enthusiasm shown by members of the public for such organisations, possibly to be called 'National Defence Companies,' there certainly wasn't a rush to join up and, even as late as the October of 1939, a month after war had been declared; what few volunteers there were, for what soon would become a necessary force, were extremely thin on the ground, and hardly even thought about by the government and the public alike. It would take the preceding days to Dunkirk to awaken everyone to the seriousness of the situation, and this would be the time when the local defence volunteers were formed, a little later to be called, 'The Home Guard.'

Well before this, in the spring of 1938, it was realised that all kinds of other voluntary help would be needed, and it was at this time that the idea of forming the Women's Voluntary Service took shape. The Home Secretary, Sir Samuel Hoare, had contacted the Dowager Marchioness of Reading (Lady Reading) and asked her whether she would consider starting a special women's service – "Something new" – with the aim, amongst other things, of helping to recruit women into the A.R.P.

Lady Reading was about to go abroad for a month, when Sir Samuel spoke to her about this, but, taking note of the urgency of his request, she cut this down to two weeks, most of which, whilst travelling on her trans-continental journey, she spent studying A.R.P. and other manuals – "To get a clearer idea of what was needed." On her return, she produced a memorandum for the Home Secretary, outlining what would be needed to create an organisation, which would work in association with the Home Office, the local authorities and the A.R.P. Hence, 'would be volunteers,' after various brushes with people who, at the least, could be described as being 'none to helpful,' and also, after coming up against a few 'brick walls,' the Women's Voluntary Service was born and was destined to play a huge role in the coming conflict.

7

One of the first of the many duties the ladies of the W.V.S. found themselves very much involved with, was helping in the evacuation of children who lived in vulnerable areas – in other words in the cities and towns most likely to be bombed – to safer venues. I must add here though that, apart from the 'official' voluntary organisations, many other people, who happened to be available, also volunteered to help with the evacuation programme, and some of these I have included in the book.

It was on September 26th 1938, when war was looking to be inevitable, that the Home Office officially asked the W.V.S. to give help to local authorities throughout the United Kingdom, to assist at the places that were scheduled to receive evacuees. But, of course, this was the critical time when the question of whether it would be war or peace, was very much in the balance and, all those who would be involved, voluntary or otherwise, were waiting tensely to see what would happen – 'Munich' was just around the corner.

The Air Raid Warden Service, that had been created in April 1937, were now on the alert and, on the 25th of September 1938, the day before the W.V.S. had been asked to help with the evacuees, the A.R.P. were mobilised – all of a sudden, there was a lot more interest in this essential part of civil defence, with many more volunteers coming forward.

In The Times on September 27th 1938, an article headed – 'A.R.P. activity, steps taken in all parts' – went on to say:

'Unabated activity in the preparation and perfection of plans for the passive defence of the civilian population, in the event of an emergency, was reported yesterday from all parts of the country. Thousands of people attended A.R.P. depots to be fitted with respirators, and in many places distribution has already begun. From an early hour A.R.P. officials were kept busy.

During the daytime most of the applicants were women, many of who brought their children, and rows of perambulators were a familiar sight outside many depots. In the evening, the rush of applicants was naturally much greater and many men went straight from their work to the depots.

Thirty five million gas masks are stored in depots in London, Reading, Bristol, Cambridge, Coventry, Nottingham, Manchester, Liverpool, Leeds, Gateshead and Galashiels. In London and many towns, trenches as refuges, are being dug in the parks and other spaces, and for this work the Ministry of Labour and the employment

8

exchanges are in need of more men than are available, and it is hoped that those who are ready and able to play their part in this urgent duty will get in touch with their local exchanges.

Leeds and Cardiff, for example are preparing shelters in the open spaces for a tenth of their population; the Birmingham and Swansea Police are taking a census of cellars that might be used in case of necessity and, in Hull, an appeal has been issued to owners of vacant land to place it at the disposal of the A.R.P. authorities.

Mr. Herbert Morrison M.P. Leader of the London County Council and chairman of it's A.R.P. sub-committee, issued the following appeal for volunteers in the London county area: "In these critical hours when our country, with the rest of Europe, is facing the finely balanced alternatives of peace or war, A.R.P. preparations are a matter of the greatest urgency and importance to every London citizen. So far as the London County Council is concerned the official organisation has moved forward with every practicable thoroughness and efficiency. I am indebted for their loyal and energetic support.

We are still, however, in need of the assistance of many thousands more voluntary A.R.P. workers." Mr. Morrison went on to say, apart from the A.R.P., volunteers were urgently needed for the Auxiliary Fire Service, both men and women; also, people were required for the Auxiliary Ambulance Service – especially for ambulance drivers.'

At home, in Brighton, most of the occupants of the houses in Sussex Square had the use of the basements to shelter in – when these tall and elegant houses had first been built, the basements had been used as servants' quarters, but now they were mostly used as flats in their own right. At number thirteen, we were fortunate that the basement had recently been vacated and was to remain so for several years. My mother had been quick to take advantage of this, and heeding father's advice to "be prepared!" she had 'hung' two hammocks across the basement hall for my sister and me to use in the event of any air raids. She had also put various old armchairs; she had 'mysteriously' acquired, beside the hammocks, as well a hefty old table and a cupboard for refreshments – all for the comfort of anyone else from the house sheltering with us. As father put it – "the refreshments will definitely include some 'Dutch courage' for the adults, as well as lemonade, or anything else for the children."

However, on the 28th of September 1938 everything was put on 'hold' for a while. When Parliament had assembled on this day, and after Mr. Chamberlain had been addressing the house for over an hour, talking about the current situation on the continent, a note was handed to him. He quickly read it, there was a pause, and then he told the house that Hitler had invited him to Germany for further talks, and he immediately left the house – soon to be on his way for that historical meeting in Munich.

On the 29th of September, my father had entered into his diary, along with various other comments, – "let's hope that the Czechs will get a fair deal out of these talks as well!"

Despite the fact that new peace talks were going on, throughout the country the preparations by some of the voluntary services carried on. In the Sussex Daily News that day, a headline to an article said 'Precautionary work goes on in Sussex.' The article went on to say: '– All the work in connection with air raid precaution in Sussex was in full swing yesterday when Mr. Chamberlain's announcement of a further conference with Herr Hitler, in conjunction with Signor Mussolini and M. Daladier, became known.

There was an immediate sense of relief from the tension, but, of course, there would be no summary suspension of the operations that were being carried on after so much preparation. The ultimate effect remains to be seen.'

The next day, the same paper told of the peace treaty being signed, but, also on the same page, it told of evacuation plans in the event of an emergency.

Back in Downing Street, that evening an ecstatic crowd cheered their prime minister – they applauded this momentous agreement and celebrated that it would be 'peace in our time.' However there were others who were annoyed at the betrayal of the Czechs, and these included two men who would be playing major roles when war was declared nearly a year later – they were, Mr. Duff Cooper, who had promptly resigned from the government, and Mr. Winston Churchill.

A lot of people now felt very uneasy about the 'sell out' of the Czechs – 'ashamed' would probably be a better word, and those with some military and political knowledge felt that the situation in Europe was, eventually, bound to get worse!

Up to this time my father's diary had been reasonably well kept, but it was soon to become very 'sketchy' – and then stop – which is a pity. None the less, after the Munich Agreement, he had written, amongst a lot of other thoughts and happenings – "I wonder who we'll sell out next to avoid war – I wonder what really will happen in Czechoslovakia now, and where Herr Hitler will have his eyes on next?!"

10

From the time of that particular entry in his diary, there was nearly another year of peace to go before war was declared but, in March 1939, Czechoslovakia was completely taken over by the Germans and with the Russians signing a pact with the Germans in August, things were looking distinctly ominous. Consequently people started viewing the situation far more seriously and it seemed that there wouldn't be 'peace in our time' after all – indeed, it looked as though war was just 'around the corner.'

Because of this situation, the Territorial Army now found itself 'flooded' with applications to join up. The only trouble was that the weapons they would be issued with would be mainly out of date and, thus, probably inadequate – so too, the uniforms!

Other essential services were also taking good heed of the situation – the fire brigades were now taking on more auxiliary firemen and firewomen, and the police would soon be taking on wartime reserves. As far as the police and police war reserves are concerned, I think that this would be an opportune place to put in a small piece written by the late Arthur Almond and sent to me by his daughter, Kathleen Eneas. Arthur was in the Portsmouth City Police during the war; he had been promoted to sergeant in 1937. In May 1938 the Chief Constable of the city police had sent him to a Home Office Anti Gas School in Gloucester, to train as an instructor.

In his writings, Arthur points out that – "In the event of an enemy air attack a system of air raid wardens would also be necessary to assist the police, whose numbers would be insufficient to cope with all the likely demands." These particular wardens were not to be confused with the A.R.P. (Air Raid Precautions) who, although working in close harmony with the police and air raid wardens, were a separate organisation.

Arthur went on to say – "In a garrison town and mighty port such as Portsmouth (and other towns and cities in similarly vulnerable positions) our A.R.P. recruits of those days, as well as regulars in the police and fire brigade and wartime volunteers to those services, included many old soldiers from World War I – and their keenness was marvellous! They were always ready with information about their actual experiences under gas attack in World War I, and were always ready to help and 'have a go,' at this time."

Whilst on the gas course, Arthur learned that he had come top of a promotion examination, and was now promoted to inspector. This spurred him on to get the required grade in anti-gas training and, on returning to Portsmouth, was detached to anti-gas training. This shows

11

that, at this time, although many people thought that 'not a lot' was being done in the way of preparation, should war come to the home shores – in actual fact, the police and other organisations were quietly preparing, so as not to cause any panic, for what could be the worst aspects of aerial warfare.

Fortunately there were no gas attacks during the war, but gas was always a real threat. I've included other pieces by Mr. Almond, later in the book.

The coastguards were also taking on more auxiliaries as well as volunteers who would play their part as coastwatchers – keeping an eye out for anything that looked suspicious or that needed help around the coastlines of the United Kingdom. Also, the R.N.L.I. – some of whose younger volunteers would be going into the forces – would fall back on 'retired lifeboatmen,' still very able and willing to take part during a period of time that promised to be full of activity.

I remember my father being told, by an uncle of mine, who was in the navy, about a friend of his who was in the coastguard and about all the extra duties the coastguards would have in time of war. I remember hearing bits and pieces of stories about looking out for spies landing on lonely stretches of the coast, and I found the whole subject intriguing and exciting. This is a subject of which very little has been written about, but, through the help of Tony Ellis of Humberside Coastguard and other members of the coastguard, as well as being allowed access to their wartime archives, I have been able to include several stories of this essential part of the security of the UK during those vital years. These stories appear later in the book, but I feel I should put in here about how they prepared for war.

In 1939, secret instructions were sent out to coastguard inspectors and district officers, which were not to be opened until receipt of the code word – 'GUARDIAN.' These instructions were that all coastguard stations were to be put on constant watch, employing extra personnel, if necessary, to report any warship, British or foreign, and any other ship not usually seen in the area, which was acting suspiciously – such as, steaming past slowly or dropping articles overboard.

Throughout 1939 the Admiralty and the Board of Trade, co-operated to bring the war-watching organisation up to a high state of efficiency. To supplement early instructions there was also advice on how to recognise spies, under the heading – 'Enemy agents illegally landing in the UK.' The coastguards and coastwatchers were told that spies may be dropped by parachute or landed on the coast in small boats, such as, rubber dinghies, fishing boats or even submarines. Also they outlined what a spy might look like:

(A) The spy will probably be a youngish man.

(B) He will have wet or sea stained clothing.

(C) He would probably be ignorant of his whereabouts.

(D) The spy will almost certainly be wearing civilian clothes, but they might have a queer cut.

(E) The spy may be carrying a wireless transmitter with him.

(F) The spy will be carrying a large sum of money in bank notes – anything from forty pounds to five hundred pounds, or even more.

These are shortened versions of the full instructional advice given to the coastwatchers; the instructions went on to say about looking for mistakes on forged identity cards and other papers. However more about the coastwatchers later in the book.

On the 25th of August 1939, on the continent, with Germany's intentions against Poland casting a dark shadow over the whole critical situation, Britain and Poland signed a treaty of alliance, but, even so, there were those who thought that we should – 'Leave well alone' and avoid war 'at all costs!'

At home, my father said to a friend he had invited to dinner that night – "I hope I won't have to say, 'I told you so,' and like Czechoslovakia there's going to be another sell out, after all the furore that that caused – I can't see how they possibly can!"

In the early hours of 1st of September, Germany invaded Poland – the writing was now 'firmly on the wall!' Consequently, later that day, the call up for the forces began in earnest, as did the official evacuations of children from London and other exposed places, likely to be the most vulnerable areas should there be air raids. To start with, these plans hadn't included the threat of invasion and many children found themselves being sent to coastal resorts, which would soon become restricted areas – places most likely to be in the front line in the event of the country being invaded. Also that night, the blackout began – even though war hadn't yet been declared. Mr. Chamberlain was still appealing to the Germans to withdraw from Poland, but it seemed that he just wouldn't commit himself. However, there were many in parliament who were getting highly fed up with all the dithering and, on the 2nd of September, they revolted! It was at this time that Mr. Chamberlain, at last, gave way, saying – "Right gentlemen – this

13

means war!" At the same time as saying this – there was a huge clap of thunder from a storm going on outside – "Perhaps rather prophetic!" – One member was quick to retort!

When it was later announced that Mr. Chamberlain had given Germany the ultimatum to withdraw from Poland by 11 a.m. the next day and that he would broadcast to the nation shortly after this, everyone prepared for the worst. At 11.15 a.m. on Sunday 3rd September, we knew that we were at war and, shortly after this, the first siren sounded – sending millions of frightened people to seek shelter from what they thought was an imminent air raid. It turned out to be a false alarm, of course – but it had alerted us, and there were many who prepared even more vigorously for whatever the coming days, months – even years, might bring.

Chapter Two

Evacuees.

When the first air raid siren sounded, minutes after Mr. Chamberlain's broadcast, we had hurriedly gone to shelter in the basement at number thirteen – but this, of course, was a false alarm and it wouldn't be until the following year that we would get used to the musty smell, of what father called – "The Dungeon," – and which he took somewhat longer than anyone else to arrive at, after each siren had sounded.

The immediate response to that first siren had had much the same reaction over most of the country, but despite the panic, there was also some humour. In his book 'The Gentlemen At War,' which is about the police force during World War II, and written by ex-policeman, Roy Ingleton, he says '– In London and all over the country policemen were throwing switches to sound the alarms, or taking to the streets, blowing lustily on their whistles and, in some cases, bearing cardboard notices on their chests advising the populace – 'AIR RAID WARNING – TAKE COVER.'

The situation was not without its humour, however. Sergeant Grey of the Metropolitan Police on the Isle of Dogs, remembers meeting one of his men coming towards him soon after the first sounding of the air raid siren, fully kitted out with his steel helmet, eye shield, gas-proof jacket and trousers, rubber boots and with his gas mask at the ready. It was a warm day and the unfortunate officer was perspiring freely. The sergeant gently led him back to the police station where a senior officer remarked – "For goodness sake, Constable, you frighten me! God knows what you'd do to the public!" Comical though this might seem in retrospect, this man was not alone and one air raid warden said, the streets were manned by war reserve policemen in full gas clothing, consisting of oilskin coats and trousers, rubber boots, helmets and respirators, and with warning rattles in their hands!

At home, in Brighton, for a while after this, we were on our guard – "prepared for the worst!" – Mother said ominously. But we soon got back to the old routines again and, for a time, everything seemed peaceful.

15

However, this certainly wasn't a time of inactivity for the preparations going on in some of the voluntary services, with recruiting now increasing dramatically in everything apart from the Local Defence Volunteers – eventually to be called The Home Guard. Volunteers for this section of civil defence wouldn't be called upon until May 1940 when Mr. Eden would broadcast to the nation, appealing for people to join.

Perhaps the busiest people in those early days of September 1939, were the members of The Women's Voluntary Services – their assistance had been 'officially' asked for in helping with the evacuation of children from the areas most likely to be bombed. Quite a number of the children had been sent to coastal towns in the south – proving that whoever had done the early planning, hadn't taken into consideration that these would be the areas most likely to be in the frontline – should we be invaded! Mostly though, the children, sometimes accompanied by their mothers, found themselves on the way to more distant pastures, such as the west country and, in particular, Wales.

There are many stories about the evacuees and the people who helped them – including those who shared their homes with them. Some of them, when they arrived at their destinations, found that they were being treated with indifference by those who took them in; a typical attitude being – "It's our duty to have them – so, we'll just have to, I suppose!" A few others, unfortunately, met with cruelty and abuse. Mainly however, the evacuees were treated with kindness and consideration and the worst part of the whole business, for those not accompanied by their mothers, had been the wrench of leaving their homes, their parents, other relatives and friends and everything else that was familiar to them.

Ivy Kilmister (now Luxton) of Chatham was just six years old when, with most of Glencoc School at Chatham, she was evacuated to South Wales. She and another girl, Mabel Fisher, aged five, had sat together on the train journeys; there was only one teacher in charge of all the children in their carriage. They had been warned that should they be 'machine-gunned' by German aeroplanes, they were to hide under the seats. "We spent the whole journey absolutely terrified and crying for a lot of the time – we felt completely lost!" Ivy told me. On arrival at their destination, a village called Brynmenyn, they were all gathered together at the village school and, with all the Welsh children from the school looking on, were split up and taken on journeys by taxis to whoever was going to take them in. No definite arrangements had been made for them, and Ivy and Mabel became even more terrified when a man looked into the taxi that they were in and said to the driver –

16

"I'll take these two." During the ride to wherever they were going they clung together, both felt a lot better when they stopped at a house where a lady appeared from within and quickly took charge of them. It would be several years before Ivy would see her mother again and, during the years that followed, the only contact with her would be when parcels arrived, from time to time, with a few articles of clothing and an envelope with half a crown in it!

One particular evacuation – this time of quite a large number of very young children, which I feel I should include here; I have already written about as a 'wartime excerpt' in a book I wrote about people returning to civilian life after the war – 'Bittersweet Seasons – 1947 in Sussex.' This Excerpt was about the evacuation of some very young children to the 'hallowed halls' of Glyndebourne Opera House in Sussex – which had ceased to have its opera seasons for the duration of the war. Julia Aries, the archivist at Glyndebourne, had sent me the details for what happened. These were in notes written by M. Fowler, who was part of the Glyndebourne organisation, and Monica Edwards, who was a resident of Ringmer, and also a voluntary helper at Glyndebourne Nursery School.

M. Fowler writes:

In 1938, with war clouds looming on the continent, the Glyndebourne Estate Office, without any prior consultation, was advised that preparation should be made for the immediate reception at Glyndebourne for 200 school children – evacuees! Two days of frantic preparation, including filling sacks with straw, to be used as temporary mattresses, followed.

However, things weren't needed – Mr. Chamberlain had arrived back in the country, waving that famous piece of paper and saying that it would be 'peace in our time' after all.

Because of this, Mr. Christie, the founder and owner of Glyndebourne, had given instructions to Mr. W.E. Edwards to act on his behalf in consultations with the London County Council, with the understanding that Glyndebourne would offer accommodation in the opera dining halls and other outbuildings for nursery-school aged children (babies not envisaged).

With the radio announcement, in 1939, of the government evacuation scheme being put into operation, Mr. Christie's London office staff, then mostly scattered on holiday, forgathered as arranged at Glyndebourne, while the small nucleus still in London, hastily packed up the contents of the office for a transfer to Sussex.

Mary Allen, the youngest and newest of Mr. Christie's London office staff and sole occupant of the Cockspur Street office, at the end of August when the war seemed imminent, remembers Mr. Edwards telephoning her and telling her to pack up such items as she could and come down to Glyndebourne, bringing the money and the keys. Mary remembers seeing vans piled high with furniture etc. Arthur Howell, one of Mr. Christie's Ringmer Motor Works staff, met her at Lewes station. She was welcomed and comfortably settled in at Glyndebourne by Mrs. Daniels, the housekeeper.

On September 1st, a mercifully brilliant summer sun bathed the countryside on that morning, as the front lawn at Glyndebourne gradually became covered with crawling babies and toddlers, as bus upon bus of London passenger transport disgorged its load. The children came from five different places – two day nurseries, one privately run babies home, a large L.C.C. institution for babies, mainly of unmarried mothers, and the nursery school attached to the Union of Girls' Schools Settlement at Peckham, each unit with its own matron or superintendent and assistant staff, and some L.C.C. domestic staff. Within the course of a couple of hours, the Glyndebourne population had been increased by 372 – 300 children and 72 adults.

All Mr. Christie's staff were brought in on some particular job – one on catering, another arranging sleeping accommodation for nursery staff. Mary was put at the disposal of the nurseries and remembers writing to a dozen or more parents. All took turns at nightly blackout and firewatching duties.

There is little point in lingering on the difficulties of those first few weeks; all evacuation schemes experienced similar teething troubles. Glyndebourne was greatly blessed by being able to call on Mr. Moores, the village grocer for immediate food, and Gote Farm for milk. The old L.C.C. cook managed to cope for this large number on totally inadequate stoves, and the nursery staff cared as best they could with make-do apparatus. Mr. Christie's office staff found themselves doing the most unexpected jobs, not least Rudolph Bing, the General Manager of Glyndebourne and the man whose job it was to select and seek the services of the singers in the operas, who was seen emerging from a Lewes store with a pile of children's chamber pots! Several of the nurseries had come anticipating that equipment would be awaiting them. Jock, the stage foreman, continued as a tower of strength throughout the nursery occupation. Teenage children from surrounding families (two on horseback, I remember) converged on Glynebourne and gave invaluable voluntary help. A Glynde resident put her large car and chauffeur at the disposal of the nursery.

On 3rd September at 11 a.m. the staff gathered in the front hall to hear on the radio the declaration of war – in Mr. Bing's words – "a piece of history being made."

At this stage, I shall include some of the notes made by Monica Edwards – "Preceding 3rd September, there were those two days of intense activity; I remember the round of palliasse filling with the straw from the farms and, later, as the babies arrived in bus-loads with little equipment, the long slog of fitting together the five piece, heavy iron cots that had been dismantled in haste – with very mixed results!

The immediate need for black-out screens for all windows gave rise to a background of hammering as estate carpenters dealt with this problem – not yet aware that both they and the 'boys' who helped so willingly, would soon change their skills to using guns and flying aeroplanes. Arthur Howell remembers being sent up to Glyndebourne to 'blue' every light bulb.

Countless messages to help in the early organisation of staff and volunteers to do with the accommodation and meals; journeys and meetings re fire-fighting, were relayed from the main office by a few of the young people who already knew the geography of Glyndebourne fairly well. Both boys and girls helped with feeding and care of the babies, as the nurseries lacked their full complement staff, while some remained in London to pack equipment and to receive still more babies for evacuation.

With the 3rd of September announcement, no one knew what it would mean or what would happen. Out of doors, in the warm sunshine that morning, I caught a glimpse of Mrs. Bing, in her soft grey dress, hovering moth-like round the curtained cots set out under the trees, she rocked them gently as she moved among them and watched over the tiniest of the babies, thus releasing a nurse for continuously demanding round of feeds. There were twice daily nappy changes for 300 visiting babies – and Glyndebourne residents came to the rescue here, with many people immediately volunteering their services.

Also – and sadly, reflecting the bewilderment and fear of some mothers, or single fathers – there were a few babies who had been 'left' in hope and faith on nursery doorsteps, labelled or not, but each in desperate need of care and safety. Two of us, in the late twilight of that evening, went from cot to cot searching the tiny marked wristlets for the word 'unknown.' "

19

I will come back to Monica Edward's writing's soon, but here I think it would be apt to add some more lines by M.Fowler:

'The members of the Glyndebourne and L.C.C. staffs and other volunteers, worked happily together and each will have their own memories, both light hearted and grim; skating on the frozen ponds in the hard winter of 1940, the long unwelcome period of night duty – both in the nursery and outside firewatching – making jam for Glynde Church Harvest Festival or collecting sack loads of conkers for the war effort (though I was never clear what Macleans did with the conkers – toothpaste or ammunition?), supplementing the rations by combing the hedgerows for rose-hips, blackberries or elderberries; preserving of fruit and salting of beans; the weekly visit to the village post office to pay in the regular National Savings, augmented by periodic marathon efforts in response to special appeals for 'war weapons' of 'wings for victory' weeks (in connection with one of these, a very classy auction sale was held under the skilled hammer of Leslie Turner before he left the Estate Office for the R.A.F.). Fire drills and evening cycle rides in the country lanes in summer; stopping for a refreshing shandy in the village pub; country dancing and periodic grand dance in winter when the Canadians were stationed on our doorstep – the army and the young nursery staff were not an easily controllable combination.

The preparations for Christmas were very special and, eventually, the long awaited day arrived and included the opening of stockings, singing of carols, tea parties and Christmas trees and, at last, with the children finally asleep, the staff sitting down to a splendid Christmas dinner – followed by traditional party games.'

Lastly, from Monica Edward's – 'My fondest memories are of when the spacious lawns were hayfields and a joy to the children, and how they played and wandered in the surrounding meadows, white sun hats visible above the buttercups – also of endless happy afternoons in the coppice woodland among the flowers and trees throughout the year, their games of 'house' and 'family,' their scolding voices and their laughter and their funny confidences. And then, for us, if we so wanted, the late informal evenings of listening with Ruddi Bing to opera recorded at Glyndebourne in other years – what a privilege it was!'

Not far from Glyndebourne, at the village of Fletching in Sussex, Michael Butcher was just eight and a half years of age when evacuees arrived there in the early September of 1939. He had lived there, with his parents, from birth. His father had served at Gallipoli in World War I and would soon be playing an important role in the local Home

Guard. Michael says – "On the day the evacuees arrived, in Fletching's case – in coaches from the East End of London. A central reception area was set up in the reading room, which my grandmother was caretaker of, so she was very much in the forefront of the organising alongside other volunteers from the village – including members of the W.V.S. For the Fletching families that did take in evacuees, the choice of who they got was made for them and they were allocated according to what space they had – so it was very much 'pot luck!'

Many of the children had never ventured further than the neighbourhood that they had been born in and, consequently, many things in the country came as quite a shock to them. For instance – discovering that milk came out of cows and wasn't just 'something' that was bottled! Quite a few children refused to drink it on discovering its true source.

Quite a number of the evacuees had arrived in family groups – in other words a mother with children or just one child – but, within moments of arriving, many of the mothers expressed their shock at finding that there were no 'fish and chip' or 'eel and pie' shops in Fletching, and quite a few of them refused to stay and went back on the same coaches. Things were quiet in London at that stage in any case – it was the beginning of the 'phoney war' and it would be another year before the blitz would make the evacuation of large numbers of children much more urgent. At that time however, several of the mothers said that they would sooner face the bombs rather than go without the necessities of a lifestyle that they had been born into and which had been passed down through countless generations.

Our particular evacuees, a mother and her small child, found the countryside much too quiet for them and, after three days, they decided to return to London. After a couple of weeks or so there were only a 'handful' of children left from the several coachloads that had first arrived. Apparently the same had happened in some other areas as well and, as far as those places, as well as Fletching were concerned, it was a 'non event' and, although quite some effort was put into the planning, there hadn't been too much thought of how the enormous change in lifestyle might affect those who had had to leave the sanctity of their homes – in order to stay alive!'

One person who helped with evacuations and who had joined the W.V.S. shortly after its originations in 1938 was Marjory Allen (now Marjory Manton); she had joined just after Lady Reading's first appeal for volunteers. Marjory and her husband, Bill, a trainee manager for

Marks and Spencer's, lived at Streatham before the outbreak of war and one of her first duties, after joining, had been issuing gas masks at Streatham Baths. Eventually, Bill had been moved to the Hastings branch of M&S and Marjory had joined him in Hastings, and was still an active member of the W.V.S. – she was there to help when evacuees from the East End of London started arriving in Hastings. On their arrival at various addresses, it was discovered, by some of the people they went to live with, that quite a few of the children had inadequate amounts of clothing – including underclothes, and they went to their own expense to buy more clothes for them.

Bill told Marjory, that at his branch of M&S, on the Saturday that they had arrived, they had kept the shop open until after 7.30 p.m.; so that they could fulfill all the needs of the children and, after that, it had taken them until nearly midnight to cash up – they had taken so much money that they needed a police escort to take it to be deposited at the bank!

These evacuees didn't stay long however – it was soon discovered that Hastings would be in the front line, should there be an invasion – so, after going back home for a while, they were eventually evacuated to safer areas.

Another evacuee to be sent to the coast, to start off with, was Elsie Taylor. She lived at Gillingham at the outbreak of war – which, being a garrison town and next door to Chatham Dockyard, would be a prime target in the event of there being air raids. Elsie, like many others from the Medway Towns, was soon caught up in the 'hurly burly' of evacuation. Although I have written this book as chronologically as possible, I shall put in here some of the experiences Elsie has written down for me – even though they go up to 1941, when, aged 14, she returned home to – "Earn a living!" – Elsie writes:

'I was twelve years of age when the war started and came from a large family – mother, father, five boys and three girls. Later on, three of the boys and my father were serving in the forces. Where we lived at that time, in Forge Lane, in Gillingham, many of our neighbours and friends were quick to join the A.R.P. and, a little later, the Home Guard, which were known as The Local Defence Volunteers (L.D.V.) to start with – which most of us interpreted to mean – 'Look, Duck and Vanish!'

On the 1st September 1939, all children to be evacuated met at various schools, bringing their gas masks and suitcases, containing their belongings, with them. We had labels, with our identities written on

22

them, pinned to our coats. My younger brother aged ten, sister aged seven and I, were sent to Herne Bay, on the Kent coast. We found the train journey there exciting – coming from a large family, outings to the seaside had been few and far between. The war meant little to us then – we didn't understand. When we reached Herne Bay station we were walked, crocodile fashion, by the teachers who came with us, to the pier. Some ladies of the W.V.S. helped them. At the pier we were given carrier bags with food in them – to take with us to where we were going to stay. Later on, there was a concert held for us at the pier, to cheer us up, and I remember I went on stage and sang 'South of the Border' and, apart from the applause, received a bar of chocolate for my efforts!

There were twenty of us in our group of children – fifteen boys and five girls; we were billeted at a boarding house run by two spinsters and their aged mother. We all did our share of work in the house and all got along very well together. Our 'schooling' carried on, and was held in various halls – even at the pavilion on the pier. However, with little or no enemy activity throughout the cold winter of 1939/40, we wanted to return home and, eventually, in February, my elder brother arrived and took us back home on the train.

By June, after Dunkirk and with the fall of France, everything started to look very bad and, once again, there were evacuations – this time we were sent to Glamorgan, in South Wales.

By this time, we were more aware of what was going on – especially after the news about the troops coming back from Dunkirk, and all the German advances into Belgium and France. We knew that we might be invaded at any time and it was very frightening.

At the beginning of our journey to Wales, at Gillingham station, the porters were all very patriotic and were singing 'Keep the Home Fires Burning.' The volunteer ladies, who were there to help, joined in with them – so did some of us; I remember that I did, with tears in my eyes, and I wasn't alone in that respect! I didn't know it then, of course, but my future husband's father – Walter Denne, was the station inspector at Gillingham station at that time. On the journey to Wales, because I was thirteen years of age by this time, I was given charge of some very tearful children – some as young as five, and others ranging up to eight years of age.

When we arrived in South Glamorgan, we were taken to a school for a medical; I was most embarrassed – having to strip to the waist in front of all the boys and girls and held my vest against me until the last minute.

From there we went by car to the small mining village of Abertysswg. In spite of the misty rain, I immediately fell in love with the mountains and, when we arrived at the school in the village it seemed that everyone who lived there had turned out to welcome us. We were gradually partnered off to families – my sister, Dorothy, and I, were taken by car to the house of a young couple who had a four-year-old boy.

My first impressions of the village were of 'blackness' – the rainwater ran black in the gutters and I remember seeing the tearstained black face of a small boy. The pit was at the end of the village and all the miners walked to and fro in their coal dust blackened clothes; also, black beetles seemed to be everywhere.

However, we were lucky with the family who had taken us in, who we called by their Christian names, and we were well cared for. My brother, Victor, had been sent to a farm in another village, and didn't fare so well as some of us – having to rise at 5 a.m. for work, cleaning out and feeding the pigs and cattle before going to school. When this was discovered by my parents, they had him transferred to our village, where he enjoyed a better and less exacting way of life.

The times that remain in my mind, the most clearly among many happy memories though, are the adventures into the countryside. Entertainment was limited – no cinema in the village, of course, but we were never bored. We walked miles, picked wimberries from the mountainside, swam in the reservoir and, sometimes, gathered sheep's wool that had become entwined on hedges and bushes as they had grazed close to them on the mountains. This wool was then sent to the wool mills and, after this, the wool would be dyed. I remember being told by the teacher to knit khaki socks for my father, who was in the Territorial Army – he had also been in the Royal Marines in the First World War but was now in charge of a searchlight in the Medway Towns. I also remember that I was told to knit small squares, which were to be sewn over holes in the socks, and he later told me that they caused great mirth when on 'display' in the N.C.O.'s mess.

A couple of months or so after our arrival at Abertysswg, more evacuees arrived; this time from Bethnal Green, in London. This was something of a 'culture' shock for everyone there. The girls wore make-up and trousers – in that area, unheard of in those days! The boys were a rough bunch, who knew all the swear words – and used them! They didn't stay long, however, and went home, within weeks, saying, "we'd rather face the bombs than suffer the quietness, the 'busybodies' and twice a day chapel!"

24

"The winter of 1940/1941 was very bad, and there was no central heating in the house; nonetheless, we kept nice and warm and cosy because of the free coal that the miners got. I shall always remember the roaring fires in the hearth, but also remember having to collect water from the nearby spring carrying it in jugs and pans – the pipes were all frozen up. Summing it all up, I can only say that they are happy memories – treasured in fact!"

Going back to the beginning of September 1939, but going further north in the United Kingdom – at cities such as Manchester and Liverpool and other such vulnerable areas, evacuations had also been going on. Georgina Merrick had been one of the ones who had listened to the earlier appeals to – 'Join your local ARP' – and had spent quite some time before that well remembered September going from her job as a trainee manager with Marks and Spencer's to help run the control room of the ARP at Fleetwood in Lancashire. Much of her duty was done at night time, and this had entailed alerting the fire brigades and ambulances when there were emergencies – it was all good practice for the real thing. However, things began to get a lot more hectic when the evacuations started, and a job that Georgina, with a few other volunteers, found themselves doing, to start with, was finding enough black material for the windows of a large building just outside Fleetwood which had been one of the Sunshine Homes for disabled children – "I remember there seemed to be countless windows." Georgina told me. "This building was to accommodate a large number of evacuees from the big cities. They succeeded in getting enough material and then set to and effectively blacked out all the windows – it was quite a job, something I shall always remember."

Still up north, but this time on the east coast, at Hull, Harry Tate who had joined the Hull City Police in 1937 also played a part in the evacuations. Harry says – "Friday September 1st, 1939, the day was dull and overcast when I reported for duty at Crowle Street Police Station at 6 a.m.

On that day the force had gone on to a war footing with all leave cancelled and 12-hour shifts instituted. All men carried steel helmets and service respirators. It was the day that evacuation plans for school children were to start. In many instances entire schools and staff moved out of Hull into supposedly safe areas of the country – just where they were going was unknown to all but a few, and I wasn't one of them.

My duty that morning was to go to Williamson Street School, to make sure the children, teachers and some parents, going as helpers, got away safely and with the minimum confusion.

The children looked pathetic and bewildered, as well they might, not understanding why they should have to leave their homes, parents and school, for some unknown place, to be cared for by some unknown people.

Finally, the children were sorted out into groups and boarded on waiting coaches and just after 9 a.m. there were tearful scenes as the coaches drove away leaving parents without their children and having to return to empty homes. I never did find out just where those children went to."

These have been accounts of just a few of the evacuations and, in including these particular ones, I hope this has given a reasonably broad view of what it was like to be evacuated at a time of not knowing what the next day might bring – at a time of danger. For many it was a bitter experience; for some it was terrifying, but, for many, it had been an enjoyable and eye opening adventure in early life. However, for nearly all the evacuees, there had been the awful wrench of leaving home and parents behind – never knowing when they might see them again.

Chapter Three

Dunkirk.

The day after war was declared, advance parties of the British Expeditionary Force were sent across the channel to help the French and, eventually, Belgian forces to keep 'The Hun' from the door – both 1 and 2 Corps were in France by October 1939.

At home, in Brighton, after the initial panic, everything had quietened down and we carried on with our lives almost as we always had done – with the exceptions, of course, that we carried our gas masks wherever we went, and that the blackout had to be strictly kept to, whatever the circumstances. However, there was still a lot of work going on in people's gardens, in the building or re-enforcing of air raid shelters. These shelters, although including quite a few constructions of the householders' own designs, were mainly Anderson shelters, which had first been issued to people with gardens, near to the time of the Munich crisis. Generally, though everything was very quiet – we were at the beginning of what the Americans had dubbed – 'The Phoney War' – or, by many who were expecting, even hoping, to see more action – 'The Bore War!"

On 30th September, 1939, a day short of four weeks from the sounding of that well remembered first siren, our daily paper said – 'After a month of anxiety, false alarms and uncertainty, Britain is settling down for a wartime winter. The government had expected 100,000 casualties during the first few weeks of the war. Hospitals had been cleared, mortuaries stacked up with piles of cardboard coffins and lime-pits dug to cope with the dead. Every home had a hand operated stirrup pump and long handled shovel to deal with incendiary bombs. Memories of the Spanish Civil War and Guernica were still fresh.

But the Blitzkrieg did not happen – instead; Britain is being bombarded by regulations and petty officialdom. Public information leaflet, number one, urges everyone to carry a luggage label with his or her name and address. A national register is being completed and identity cards will be issued by the end of next month.

As they stumble home through blacked-out streets, avoiding vehicles with dimmed out headlights, Britons are fast becoming used to air raid wardens shouts of – "PUT THAT LIGHT OUT!" Giant posters have appeared, urging the populace to Save, Dig, Work, Buy War Bonds, Not Travel, Not Waste – Nor Spread Rumours – All For Victory!

The blackout is total, with the shops long since sold out of blackout material. Householders are urged to paint the edges of their windows black – even the slightest chink of light can lead to heavy fines. Road deaths have doubled, forcing the government to ease vehicle lighting restrictions – headlamps had to be covered with cardboard with two inch wide holes, and allow only one headlight to be lit. Commuters glow an eerie blue in dimmed railway compartments, while unlit buses cause chaos to drivers and passengers alike.'

The one bit of information that this article tells of, that I have no recollection of and nor has anyone else I have spoken to, was the supposed issuing of a stirrup pump and long handled shovel to every household – we certainly didn't get these! However, the bit about hospitals being cleared, reminds me of a piece that I have also included in my book 'The Tree Climbers' – about wartime Brighton. A group of us children were sitting together in a 'camp' we had built near the top of one of the big fir trees in the gardens in Sussex Square. I remember one of our group, Janine, saying – "You see that house where those men are taking furniture into – well in a few days time that's going to be what they call a workhouse."

"What's a workhouse?" Another member of our group, Peter, asked.

I answered before Janine could – "My father said it's a place where old men with no money and no homes go to. He told my sister and me that they would be there for as long as the war lasted, and that we should be polite to them if they spoke to us!"

"Where've they come from?" Peter asked.

"From Brighton General Hospital, near the race hill, it's needed as extra hospital space – at least, I think that's it." I said.

In fact, a section of this hospital had been used as a workhouse for some time – it was mentioned in W.H. Davies – 'Autobiography of a Super Tramp.' – now, all available space in hospitals was being prepared for any eventualities and, thus, the 'evacuation' of these old men from the workhouse to live in a luxurious house, in extremely pleasant surroundings, and – much to their delight! This was something that didn't go down too well with some of the residents of the square – but I'm glad to say, that my parents and their friends weren't amongst those! In fact, they went out of their way to help and befriend some of these unfortunate men, as did the local ladies of the W.V.S. – several of whom, lived in the square and nearby crescents. Quite a few of these old men had served in the First World War and, we sometimes, saw them proudly wearing their medals on the lapels of the thick, 'dark tweedy' jackets they had been issued with.

To help out in the hospitals at this critical time, a call had gone out for more young ladies to join the Voluntary Aid Detachment (V.A.D.) of the Red Cross. 'General' Henri Dunant had founded the Red Cross in 1859, after the extremely bloody battle of Solferino. This was when patriots, under the leadership of Garibaldi, had sought to free northern Italy from the Austrians. After the battle, Henri had walked among the wounded and dead and, from the terrible sights he saw, he decided that there should be a neutral organisation to help all those wounded in time of war. Since then this essential and dedicated organisation has gone from strength to strength and the name, Red Cross, has become synonymous with medical aid and nursing – in particular, in time of war.

At the beginning of World War II, there had been no shortage of volunteers to join the Red Cross – serving as V.A.D's in particular and, on reaching the age of nineteen, joining the forces in this capacity. One of these volunteers was Ursula Reed (now, Hall-Thompson), whose father was the Commander of the Small Arms Garrison at Hythe, near Folkestone. Ursula had joined at the same time as Frances Deeds, the sister of Lord Deeds – they had immediately become good friends. They were two of the first from any of the voluntary organisations, to come, face to face, with the enemy. They had been allocated to work at Shorncliffe Hospital, in Folkestone, and spent most of their time there working in the operating theatre. Shortly after starting in this job Ursula had had to attend to some Germans who had – "Apparently arrived in this country by parachute; they were wounded, not seriously, by shotgun pellets, and it was my job to extract these. The hospital was under heavy army guard at the time, and they were soon 'whisked away' – after they had had the pellets removed by myself, Frances and some of the other V.A.D's."

On trying to find out more about how these Germans came to be there, I have been given several different theories but nothing 'concrete,' and how they came to be there was obviously hushed up! As far as the pellets are concerned, one can only assume that they parachuted onto farmland and received a swift and, by no means uncertain welcome, from a farmer's shotgun!

"Shortly after this incident," Ursula also told me, "a Royal Navy ship was blown up in the channel and many sailors were brought in to the hospital suffering from the most terrible burns – sadly, many of them died."

Before long, things would start to get even busier for Ursula and Frances – Dunkirk was 'just around the corner' and many of the more seriously wounded would come into Shorncliffe Hospital – but more of that later.

Although this was still the quiet period before things really started 'hotting up,' there were still air raids taking place from time to time, but, as yet, nothing of any serious nature near to us.

I believe that this would be an opportune place to tell of what was going on across the Channel at this time. By the spring of 1940, the British Expeditionary Force in France and Belgium had increased to nine divisions; this meant that a large part of our army was now across the Channel – considerably weakening our own defences, should we be invaded. On May 10th 1940, what up to then had been a relatively peaceful time for the B.E.F. suddenly changed to all out war when the German Blitzkrieg began. General Rommel's tanks had crossed the southern end of the Belgian frontier – heading for the river Meuse at Dinant. At the same time, the forces under the command of General Guderian, were told that their eventual aim was the Channel. It was at this time that the British Army, now realizing that the German armament was far superior to their outdated weapons, started to fall into some disarray and, before long, the order would be every man for himself on the retreat to the beaches at Dunkirk. However, even before this, there had been quite a lot of confusion in what exactly was going on, both with the troops over there as well as in the press reports in the British newspapers.

Jim Peall, a corporal in the Royal East Kent Regiment (The Buffs) had arrived in France on April 19th. He told me – "I would like to make it quite clear here that the whole time I was in France, I never knew where I was, where I was going or what I was doing – hardly anybody did, the top brass wanted it that way!"

Back at home, by the beginning of May, the letters my father had been receiving from friends in the B.E.F. had ceased, and he wondered what was going on that the papers weren't telling about. His friends at the hospital had also stopped receiving mail from associates in the B.E.F. and were equally mystified.

It was my parent's custom, as it was by just about the whole of the country, at this critical time, to listen to the nine o'clock news in the evenings; even we children started listening in eagerly now, if allowed by our parents to stay up that late, not so much for hearing the news, but to hear if Bruce Belfrage was reading it – he, his wife and son, Julian, had recently moved into the top flat at number thirteen, and Julian had joined our set of friends. My father quickly struck up a friendship with this well known newsreader, and often tried to glean from him – "what was going on behind the scenes." This was mainly without much success, because, even those at the BBC weren't by any means in possession of much more knowledge of the state of things on the continent than the rest of the public. He did say though, that he thought that things were considerably worse than was being reported.

In the Daily Mirror, on May 21st, an article was headed – 'The French Drive Nazis Back.' In actual fact, the French were preparing a counter offensive on Arras for the 23rd of May, but the British had gone ahead and launched their own attack at the same time as the Mirror readers were digesting what the paper said the French had already done; in other words the counter attack by the British was on the 21st of May – making the Mirror report incorrect, yet, in a way, prophetic!

It wasn't only the Daily Mirror who were printing contrasting reports, as I have said, all the papers were, by now, under heavy censorship and the public hadn't got a clue about how serious the whole situation was. General Von Rundstedt was later to say that the Arras counter attack was the only allied offensive that inspired any fear in him in May 1940 and certainly the Elan of the Panzer Force, had been badly shaken. However, with the German advances continuing, all the time pushing the BEF backwards towards the Channel, and cutting off other retreat routes, the only option left was to head for Dunkirk, and try to get back across the Channel from there.

Before all this, back on the home shores, Mr. Chamberlain had resigned and Winston Churchill had quickly been elevated from First Lord of the Admiralty to Prime Minister. "At last, the right man in the top job!" My father echoed what most of the country were saying.

Shortly after this, with the distinct fear that England might be invaded, Mr. Anthony Eden, the new Minister for war, in a reshuffled government who had already broadcast to the nation on 14th May, asking for volunteers for what would eventually become the Home Guard, now sent a telegram to General Gort, the Commander in Chief of the British Expeditionary Force, saying that – "If all the information he was in possession of was true, as far as the plight of the BEF was

31

concerned – the only course open to you may be to fight your way back to the west where all the beaches and ports east of Gravelines will be used for embarkation!"

On 26th May 1940, Mr. Churchill contacted Vice Admiral Ramsay at Dover and ordered that Operation Dynamo – the evacuation from Dunkirk – be put into effect forthwith!

Just before this, on Empire Day, with the outlook everywhere looking extremely grim, King George VI, in a broadcast to the nation, had called for Sunday 26th May to be a day of national prayer – little knowing that this would also be the day that the evacuations from France would begin. "Make no mistake, it is no mere territorial conquest that the enemies are seeking" – he said in that broadcast – "it is the overthrow, complete and final, of this Empire and of everything for which it stands and, after that, the conquest of the world!"

About that Sunday morning, Mr. Churchill, in his memoirs, recalled the 'pent up passion' of the people attending the service at Westminster Abbey. At home, mother and father attended the service at St. Marks Church, nearby to Sussex Square. Father didn't usually attend, but mother was a regular churchgoer; she later told us that the church was packed and I remember that Jill and I both noticed that father was unusually quiet and mother, white faced, drawn and preoccupied. Later on, I heard father saying to a friend of his that he wondered whether 'all' the children would be sent away from the town in the event of an invasion, because Brighton would be one of many towns, in the south east, that would probably be in the front line of the fighting when the invasion came. I remember, he said this as though it 'would' happen! He also talked about what a difference it would make to get all or most of the troops of the BEF back home – "Then we'd stand a good fighting chance!"

Also, on the 26th May, after a desperate and brave defence, the port of Calais had fallen. In the preceding days to this, many casualties had been sent home from this port – helped by members of the Red Cross as well as those serving in the Royal Army Medical Corps. At Shorncliffe Hospital, Ursula Hall-Thompson found things were steadily getting busier and the wounded troops had now started 'flooding' into the hospital, necessitating her and other Red Cross colleagues to spend long hours in the operating theatre, which was in constant use.

Back on the 20th May, at Dover, Vice Admiral Ramsay had called for a special meeting to decide what procedure would be taken in the event of the situation on the Continent worsening – making it necessary for a wholesale evacuation of the troops from across the Channel. The 'main' planning for Operation Dynamo took place then – just six days before being brought into effect.

At three o'clock in the afternoon of the 26th May, Ramsay, in the light of information received from the French coast, had taken matters into his own hands and started to send ships to Dunkirk; by before midnight that night the first troops from the port of Dunkirk were disembarking at Dover, but there were big problems to be faced – not only were there magnetic minefields to contemplate, but also, at Dunkirk, the harbour was under constant bombardment and ships were being sunk. Ramsay knew that before long, if the port became blocked by wrecks and the quayside severely damaged, the rescue of the BEF would have to continue from the beaches – something that no one had really contemplated before this, or, if they had, dismissed it as an impossible task, as the waters close inshore to the beaches were too shallow for the larger boats.

The ships that were available to Ramsay, at this time, apart from the destroyers, were mainly made up of cross Channel steam packets (some of which had been converted to serve as minesweepers), coasters, barges and tugs. Ramsay now realised that smaller craft would soon be needed to ferry the troops from the shallow waters inshore to the larger ships further out to sea.

Back on the 14th May, the same day that Anthony Eden had broadcast his appeal for people to join the Local Defence Volunteers, the BBC has also made the following announcement:

'The Admiralty have made an order requesting all owners of self propelled pleasure craft, between 30 ft and 100 ft in length, to send all particulars to the Admiralty within 14 days from today, if they have not already been offered or requisitioned.'

Because of this, the idea of using private yachts or similar boats kept for the pursuit of pleasure, as naval auxiliaries was already reasonably well established. With the coming of Dunkirk, there came an absolute order to pick up the usable boats. The navy once more reverted to press-ganging – the difference being that this time it was for the boats not the men.

Many people were asked to help in this operation and this was when Tough's boatyard, at Teddington, came to be called on to play a major part in getting some of the boats that could eventually help in the evacuations. Early in the morning of the 27th May 1940, Mr. H.C. Riggs, of the small craft section of the Ministry of Shipping had phoned

33

Douglas Tough and asked him if he would be willing to act as agent in collecting small craft along the Thames; his responsibility was to be the Thames Valley – excluding the estuary. He was also asked to look out for the most suitable volunteers to take them down river to such places as Southend and Sheerness – or even further.

Eventually, one hundred craft were assembled at the Ferry Road Yard, at Teddington, where Tough's employees worked hard to prepare them for the sea crossing, and Douglas compiled a list of all the boat owners or others, such as watermen or people just interested in 'mucking about in boats,' who he thought capable and responsible enough to take the boats down river. On approaching volunteers for this task – no one refused!

I have already written about Dunkirk in my book 'Escape From Catastrophe 1940 Dunkirk' but it is necessary to include just a few of those stories again here; I hope the reader will forgive me for this, but they include some of the adventures of the people who volunteered their services at a critical time – at a time of danger, and with no thoughts for their own safety.

One of the boats that Douglas organised to go down river on 27th May, was *Tigris I*, a former First World War submarine chaser which had been converted by Tough Brothers as a Thames passenger boat – mainly for summer pleasure cruises, carrying up to 350 passengers at a time.

Harry Hastings, the publican of the Gloucester Arms at Kingston and owner of Tigris I, after Douglas Tough had approached him, asked his sons, Harry and Warren, both lightermen on the Thames, whether they would take the boat down river to wherever the Admiralty told them to – possibly as far as Southend or even Sheerness. They had agreed, and after they'd signed on an extra hand, fellow lighterman Bill Clark, offering him a day's pay and the fare back home, they set off at seven o'clock on the morning of 27th May 1940, on what would be a far more adventurous journey than they had been told to expect.

Towards the end of his life, Bill Clark, the extra crewman, told the lady who was nursing him, the story of *Tigris I* and its journeys rescuing troops at Dunkirk and the beaches at La Panne. I include some of Bill Clark's story, as he told it to her:

'I met Harry and Warren at seven o'clock sharp on Monday morning 27th May at Kingston Gas Co. Wharf. I stepped aboard and everything seemed okay. A bit later we were on passage to Southend where Harry had asked me to help get them to – they didn't know the waters that far down the river. At that time, all we knew was that she was wanted by the Admiralty, and we thought that this was for evacuating kids out of London. I remember it was a bit chilly that morning on the river – there was a bit of mist about. Just before we got to Teddington Lock, Harry brought me a cup of tea and told me that we had to go to Westminster Pier to see a navy bloke there for fresh orders. I said "okay, but I'm not being messed about by any navy blokes; I told my wife that I'd be home this evening – probably between ten and eleven o'clock, if all went well."

On the way down river, we washed the decks down and cleaned the brass, eventually arriving at Westminster Pier at 09.50 – not bad going from Kingston! We went alongside the pier, where we called out – "Pier ahoy." A bloke came out, he was wearing a uniform – plenty of gold braid on his sleeves and scrambled egg on his hat.

"What do you want?" he said. "We've got no berths here for you!"

I said – "*Tigris I* reporting for orders sir." Giving him all the old bull. By then, half the navy had shown up, officers and ratings. I thought we were going to be put under arrest. The scrambled egg bloke said – "Proceed at once to Gravesend Pier and report." So, once again we were on our way down river. We got to Gravesend Pier at about 1 p.m. I stepped onto the pier, where a P.O. came up to me and said – "What do you want here?" I told him that I didn't know and that we'd come there for orders. He took me to see the chief officer there, who, after he had filled in some papers with our details, said, "You'll want rations for three days for you and your crew."

I said, "Three days? – I'm hoping to be back home by tonight!"

He said, "You'll still need stores for three days, and whether you or your mates remain as crew or not, the boat will still need stores!"

I went back to the others and told them about the stores. Harry said, "Good, make sure you get plenty – anything left, glad of it!"

We talked about all this for a while and I remember I said, "There must be something big going on, do you remember seeing all those ships' and lifeboats when we came by The Royal Albert Docks? A lock full of them – must have been over a hundred boats!"

After this I went off to the chandlers, where I knew the owner. His shop was about half a mile from the pier. "What are you doing down here Bill!" He Said. "There's definitely something big on isn't there – I've been rushed off my feet all morning!" I told him what bit I knew, then gave him my list for the stores we wanted – I'd put everything on I could think of – eggs, bacon, cheese, meat, bread, candles, fags, matches, tobacco, cigarette papers . . . the lot! I had to borrow a trolley to take it all back to the boat.

By the time I got aboard, all the boats' stores had arrived as well; petrol, paraffin, ropes etc. We were ready to sail for Southend once more – the time by now was 3.40 p.m., it was low water, and we had lost two hours at Gravesend Pier.

We were under way ten minutes later, and then, punching against the young flood, we had to find what slack we could. The small ships were coming up on the tide now, but it wouldn't be long before we'd see the 'big boys' – bound for Tilbury and the Royals – best to keep out of their way! No good going from one side of the river to the other to find slack, so we kept down the south shore on the port helm until we got to Coryton. We passed one of my firm's tugs, the '*Floesco*' off Coryton, running light for Brentford. He was well late on tide. We gave each other a shout as we passed. They shouted, "Where are you bound?" I shouted back. "I don't know."

We made Southend Pier at about eight o'clock that evening; it was chock-a-block with boats of all kinds. We went around inside the pier to find a berth – not a soul about to tell us anything, so we moored up to another craft. After this we got ourselves ready for the shore, a nice pint of beer and the train home. We were just stepping ashore when a naval officer shows up with a big megaphone in his hand and shouted – "All boats proceed to Sheerness." There was no use arguing, we had to go! By this time there was activity on all the other boats – they must have turned up when we arrived. We were the last in, so we were the first to go.

We got over the water to Sheerness okay – two or three faster boats past us on the way. When we got there we couldn't go in right away, they had to find berths for us. After about half an hour though, we were berthed up. I said to the berthing master, a young P.O. – "Any chance of getting a pint in your canteen before we go home mate?" He took us to the canteen there – I ordered pints for all of us. A bit later, after we'd had a few pints, we had to go and see the captain. These naval establishments ashore are named after ships, and Sheerness was *H.M.S. Wildfire*. The captain stood up, introduced himself and we shook hands. He said, "We want volunteers to take your boat to France!"

I said, "What, that 'old cow' out there? She's as rotten as a pear! She's an old M.L. from the last war – no! Not bloody likely, not me." The captain said that was okay and that he only wanted volunteers to evacuate the British Force from Dunkirk. "Dunkirk!" I said, "Why

36

didn't you say so before – yes, I'll go." Harry and Warren immediately said they'd go as well.

After this the captain told us we'd have to sign papers for twenty-eight days service in the Royal Navy. He asked, "Who's the owner of the boat?" Harry told him his father was, and after a bit of wrangling about what the navy would have to pay us, and also after allocating most of this to our wives, the matter was settled – although I did argue that I wouldn't be paid less than the others – "Over my dead body!" I said. But this was soon cleared up as well. We then got permission to use his phone to contact our wives, telling them we'd be away for a while, but didn't know how long. After this the P.O. took us to a big warehouse, and gave us some blankets, telling us to bed down there for the night – we were in the navy now! It was freezing cold lying on that floor and I didn't get much sleep. I remember thinking about getting those men back from France. The old *Tigris I* carried about 350 passengers – I thought that we'd probably put up to 400 on board her. I didn't fancy coming back across the Channel like that.

Early the next morning I strolled down the quay to have a look at the old boat, and found some people aboard her – they were dockworkers and shipwrights. I asked them what they were doing and was told that they had to put brown paper on all the saloon windows and paint all the brass work black or grey.

Later on, after waking the others, we went for breakfast. I noticed there were people everywhere – like flies! Hundreds of blokes flying about with all sorts of gear. When we got back on board we sat there watching them for a while. While we were talking and watching all that was going on, the captain, with a lieutenant (wavy navy) and two ratings came on board; they had small valises, respirators, macs folded over their arms and food for three days. The captain told us that these three were coming aboard as the rest of the crew, the lieutenant in charge. Knowing we'd be picking up men from the beaches, we had to take on more stores for them as well. We also took on board a couple of wooden ladders – each about eighteen feet long. "What are these for – they're no bloody good, they'll float out from the side of the boat!" He didn't like my telling him this, but all he said was – "You'll have to weight them with something." We then went ashore again for the extra stores, and also gave in our gas masks – we were then given navy respirators and tin hats.

Later, after our new crew had been changed for another lieutenant with two ratings, for some reason, we set sail for Dover. Outside, in the river, was a Fish Cutter armed with a couple of machine guns. She had three red lights up her mast in a triangle; we were told to follow her, but if we lost her, we were told to make our own way – and mind the minefields! We were soon under way and took up our position under the stern of our escort. We arrived off Dover at 16.00 hours on Tuesday 28th May – the weather was a bit blowy, the sea a bit choppy. We went down to the cabin for some grub and some shut-eye.

Just after ten o'clock that night we were called out and told to up the anchor and follow the escort. By the time we got underway – all strung out, about six boats wide, *Tigris I* was in the head rank outside the starboard quarter of the Fish Cutter. We noticed that there were two destroyers accompanying us, one on each side of the boats – we were just one of many on the way to Dunkirk.

I had just finished my trick at the wheel, I'd been there for about a couple of hours when Harry came up and took over. I lent him my overcoat; I was the only one of us to bring one along. I went below and had about an hour's doze – I couldn't sleep properly, I was too much on edge, I went back on deck. Our two destroyers had vanished – disappeared in the night! I had a good look round and could see far ahead of us, to port and starboard, five big red glows – Dunkirk! The petrol pumps were on fire; I called all the others on deck. It was just starting to get daylight, we could see the volumes of thick black smoke in the distance – the sea was very calm. Some of us went below and had a bit of breakfast – the last for a long time, but we weren't to know that.

We were at Dunkirk and about to turn to starboard into the harbour, when bearing down on us was a hospital ship, all out for Blighty. Harry was at the wheel, belting ahead, I said, "Where are you going mate?" He said, "Across her head." I said, "You ain't you know – she'll cut us in half! Stop the boat and let her go, I bet he's given her a double ring and stopping for no one." We stopped. The hospital ship went across our head at about twenty knots and the wash from the ship broke all over us. One big wave broke over the focsle head and washed *Tigris I* down from forward to aft – we were drenched from top to toe.

Soon, coming towards us at full tilt, was an M.T.B., flying an Admirals pennant. Whether he was a full Admiral. Half Admiral or what, I don't know. The lieutenant was on deck, and I had taken the wheel off Harry – a bloke on the M.T.B. with a megaphone shouted out, "Proceed to La Panne."

As we were approaching La Panne, destroyers were coming towards us loaded with troops; you couldn't see any top hamper of the destroyers for men – they were everywhere they could get! Some were fully dressed, some were half dressed – they all waved to us. There was so much to see and hear – away to starboard, hundreds – no thousands of men; some lined up in companies, there were columns and groups down to the waters edge. There were others, in the background, lying on the sand – some in the sand dunes. I had never seen such a gathering of people in all my life – not even at big football matches.

Ahead of us, a lot of noise was going on; it was the machine gunfire from the navy ships – the Germans were over the top of us, dropping bombs. A small ship was coming towards us, she was about four hundred tons, an old French tramp ship by the look of her. She was going all out – the bombs dropping all around her. "She's had it!" I shouted out. "No she ain't! – She's coming through the bomb splashes." The splashes were as high as her wheelhouse. She came out of them like coming out of a fog – we gave her a big cheer, she had got away with it! I called out – "God Harry boy, what have we let ourselves in for?" – Harry said, "I don't know mate! Coming out of Civvy Street into this lot – it makes you wonder if you're awake!" More bombs dropped near us, and the explosions rocked the boat. Machine guns were hard at it and A.A. guns were going off from the navy ships.

A fast navy launch came out to meet us. An officer gave us our orders for the day and wished us luck – we wished him the same. We had been told to go to some beaches about a mile further along and ferry as many troops as we could from there to some destroyers that were about a mile and a half off shore. The sea was like a millpond, not a ripple on it, and the sky as blue as blue could be – no wind whatever. We made for the shore; I believe we were the first boat on that part of the beach. It's worth noting here that we still had our signboards up on *Tigris I*, saying – 'This way to the ladies toilet' – 'Gents Toilet' – 'Watney's Pale Ale' – 'Guinness for strength' – 'Players' – 'Wills Woodbines' ... all these adverts were still hanging about our boat.

We put our wooden ladders overside, one on each forequarter. We slowed down and then touched sand about 250 yards from the waters edge. The lieutenant started to give us orders as to what to do and how to do it. I said, "Aye, aye, sir, leave it to us, we'll make a good job of it!" I can't get it into my head I'm not in Civvy Street any more, I'm not used to taking orders like this!

On the sands the troops give us a great big cheer. There are a couple of navy P.O.'s walking up and down near the waters edge, they have

39

revolvers in their hands. I found out later on that they were there to shoot anyone who broke the ranks, but no one did at any time while I was working on the beaches. We gave the okay to the P.O. to start the men to come aboard. They had to wade the 250 yards out to us – even then the water still only came up to their waists; although in some cases if a man was very short or stepped into a pothole, he'd get wet all over. Some swam out to us, but the ladders were floating out flat from the sides of the boat, like I thought they would. They had to position a man either side of them to keep them stable. I reached over the safety chains and helped the first man aboard. "Thanks mate," He said. "We've been waiting three days and nights for you – and where's the Air Force we've been hearing so much about!" I said. "They're about somewhere mate – and doing a good job according to the wireless!" I told him to go below and make himself as comfortable as possible, then carried on helping others aboard. One of them said, "Aren't you taking us to Blighty?" I said, "No mate we're only a ferry boat."

Some of the others coming aboard, were using the rubbing bands on the outside of the hull as a ladder. Some made it okay – some fell back into the sea. These rubbing bands were about two feet apart and not thick enough to get a proper toehold. To climb aboard with a full pack and rifle called for a lot of strength. After a while I started to throw the rifle into the sea. They didn't like that and a lot of swearing and shouting started. I said, "*** the rifles! Let's have you blokes on board – and quick!" Some took the bolts out and put them in their pockets, others threw the lot away, I was to learn later what a serious thing it was to leave a rifle unguarded – never mind throwing it away!

By now we had over two hundred men aboard, I said to Harry, "You had better go astern about forty feet, Harry boy, or we won't get off the bottom." After that we got about another two hundred and fifty aboard, and we were well and truly loaded. I shouted out to the P.O. "That's the lot mate – be back for some more." We could see the men on the shore were upset as we drew away, I expect they thought their turn would never come.

On the way out to our destroyer, we had to dodge lots of little boats – all loaded and going out to the destroyers, or empty on their journeys back to the beaches. It took about fifteen minutes to get to our ship. On the way, I went down to the saloon to see how things were. Men were everywhere – in the basket chairs, on the tables, lying on the floors – just everywhere! They asked all sorts of questions, including, "Where're the R.A.F." and "Where are we going?" Some of them started to give me packets of cigarettes – twenty, forty, sixty at a time. They had loads of them, and bottles of scent; I put them all in a cupboard and locked it up. By the time we were close to the destroyer – we waited our turn to go alongside her – she already looked overloaded, there were troops everywhere.'

During the rest of that week, Bill, Harry and Warren, made countless journey's ferrying troops from the beaches out to the destroyers and other larger ships, but whilst doing this they were also trying to avoid being machine gunned or bombed – the Luftwaffe were also extremely busy in doing their utmost to stop the evacuations. Bill continues, 'By this time, we were all very tired, our eyes red, we could hardly keep them open. We decided to have a look around the boat to see what she was like, and didn't like what we saw – she is in a sad and sorry state, and we noticed that some of the windows were blown in, with glass all over the place. We cleaned this up as best as possible, then returned on the deck. We noticed that the boat was rolling from side to side, because the fore part of her was on the bottom. The safety chains were off amidships so that the troops could get aboard easier. Harry was lurching to and fro with the motion of the boat, his hands in his pockets; all of a sudden she gave a big roll – Harry walked backwards and was overboard, flat on his back. We all laughed, then pulled him back on board – spitting and spluttering and cursing us for laughing at him. "Serves you right, mate!" I said. "I've told you before about having your hands in your pockets, but never mind – at least you've had your feet on French soil, which is more than we've done!"

By this time, things were looking bad for *Tigris I*, she had taken an amazing battering and was now 'coming apart at the seams.' She certainly wouldn't get back across the Channel – not until she'd had a lot done to her, in any case. A patrol boat soon came over to us and we were told to abandon ship. A bit later we got a lift back to Blighty on the last boat we had helped load up with troops – a Tilbury mud hopper.'

Although I shall mention about lifeboats of the R.N.L.I. in association with other incidents in the book, this would be the opportune place to tell of the parts played by some of these boats in particular, in the Dunkirk evacuations:

Harry Philcox, of the Shoreham Lifeboat – *The Rosa Wood and Phyllis Lunn* – was sitting in the cinema when flashed on the screen came the words – "Would Mr. Philcox report to the lifeboat station immediately." He got there by 9.45 p.m. and by 10 p.m., he and the crew, coxed by Lenny Baker, were in the water and under orders to proceed straight to Dover; this was on the evening of the 29th May. The Shoreham Lifeboat was just one of eighteen lifeboats that were called upon that day; another one of these was the Hastings Lifeboat *The Cyril and Lilian Bishop*, coxed by George Moon. On arriving at Dover, there was quite a bit of waiting about – in other words waiting for orders from the navy. It wasn't until 3 o'clock that afternoon that a launch arrived at where the crews had congregated; the commander on board this craft called for all the coxswains to gather around him. He told them that they wouldn't be required to take their lifeboats across – the navy was going to crew the boats. This order, as one can imagine, was received with very mixed feelings and caused much controversy. Harry and several of the crewmen, including those from Shoreham and Hastings went into the naval offices at Dover, asking why they couldn't crew their own boats, and were told that they were to be towed over under cover of darkness, and being towed over – several boats (all together) – would make it more difficult to be detected by the German Asdic.

That night, Harry and the other crewmen returned to their homes, but the next day, 31st May, many of them returned to Dover to see if they could help in any way; the word was that they were still looking for men to man some of the boats – Harry was one of those who were accepted. It turned out that they were shorthanded for an assortment of boats that were ready to go across to use them to ferry troops from the shore to the destroyers. They spent quite some time doing this – all the time under fire from the enemy. When it was all over they returned to Dover in their 'little ship' – crammed full of troops. Eventually, when all the lifeboats were back at Dover, they simply waited where they were until their crews arrived to collect them and take them back to their respective homes. Harry was joined by coxswain, Lenny Baker, and other crewmembers and duly took the *Rosa Wood and Phyllis Lunn* back to Shoreham.

There is still controversy to this day about the navy taking over many of the R.N.L.I. boats, but two of the boats that went over with their own crews were the Margate Lifeboat, the *Lord Southborough* and the Ramsgate boat the *Prudential*.

The first engineer of the *Lord Southborough* wrote the following shortly after the conclusion of Operation Dynamo:

At about 11 a.m. on the 30th May 1940, at the boathouse, I received a phone message from a Royal Navy official from Dover, requesting to speak to the coxswain. I immediately found the Coxswain, Edward

42

Parker, and he got in touch with Dover. Mr. Parker was asked if the Margate crew were prepared to man the Margate Lifeboat and proceed to Dunkirk, to assist in the evacuation of the British Expeditionary Force – he replied in the affirmative, and duly informed the crew, which included his brother and nephew. He also had a son in the navy who was helping with operations on the mole at Dunkirk.

We were provided with steel helmets, and awaited further instructions. On instruction, the boat launched at about 5.20 p.m. and put off into the Margate roads where we made fast to an Admiralty barge. A quantity of rations and cigarettes were handed to us, and at about 5.40 p.m. we proceeded in tow to Dunkirk, arriving there just before midnight. As we approached, we could smell the fires that were raging in the town and on the docks – the whole seafront was a mass of dense smoke and flame.

The craft, which was towing us unfortunately, touched the sand bank, but we succeeded in running an anchor off for the skipper. He than wished us the best of luck and we went inshore, with the engine running dead slow and a small anchor astern. We got as close as possible and saw masses of troops assembled at the waters edge. We got about eighty on board at first – they were French; we put off and got them aboard a nearby craft and then returned near to the shore. A British officer swam out to us – he came on board and told the Coxswain that he had a large number of his men further along the shore, and guided us to the spot. He instructed his men how to make their way to us – telling them it was their last chance. They soon came swarming through the water to us, up to their armpits, and practically everyone had his rifle slung across his shoulder. Some had removed their boots and trousers; they were assisted aboard. Among them were several who were badly injured, and their mates were holding them shoulder high on improvised litters. We then put off again and got them aboard another craft. We returned repeatedly to the shore for more troops – many of these were transferred to *H.M.S Icarus*. Whilst alongside, someone on the bridge shouted to us to lay off; we let go and were passing under the destroyers bow when several German aeroplanes arrived on the scene, discharging bombs and machine gunning – pandemonium reigned for a while! However we were fortunate enough to escape any damage or injury, and later on went alongside again. A large pot of stew was passed to us, and although we were busy in the work of rescuing, we managed to help ourselves to some of it now and again – fingers before forks.

At about 7 a.m. on 31st May the wind freshened, making it impossible to get to the beach again. Some troops had been drowned in their efforts to reach us through the broken water. The Coxswain reported to the destroyer the circumstances and was told to make a search along the shore for anyone who might be on rafts or wreckage. This was done and quite a number more were picked up. One small motorboat R.N., which had been doing good work along the shore, was caught in the heavy swell and rolled over and sank. Everywhere around one could see sunken craft and hear the bursting of shells from the German guns. We were told that these were only three miles outside the town. We could see dive bombing and explosions all over the place, and troops frantically trying to dig out of all sorts of small craft which had been left high and dry. Cattle were wandering along the waters edge, looking bewildered, and near to us were the charred remains of one of the popular pleasure steamers – *Crested Eagle*.

When there seemed to be little more we could do, a naval whaler was seen in a precarious condition, we got it alongside and the occupants, all of them R.N. personnel, came aboard, they were members of a beach party, seventeen of them, including two commanders – Comdr. Kerr R.N. and Comdr. Richardson R.N. We then set course for home, leaving off at about 8.30 a.m. and arriving at Margate at 3 p.m.

The Ramsgate Lifeboat, *The Prudential*, had been a gift to the R.N.L.I. from the Prudential Insurance Company. The coxswain was Howard Knight – there was a crew of eight. They had been towed over by a Dutch barge. Just before it got completely dark they could make out the flames from burning oil dumps and warehouses at Dunkirk. Reflected from the glow were the shapes of other boats, almost ghostly in appearance – these could have been anything, even German E-Boats preparing to attack them.

The coxswain in his report says – "A little later we saw that some of these were British boats on their way back home and already filled with troops. Aircraft started dropping parachute flares, they could be seen hanging about in the sky like stars or moons and, for a time, we could see the other boats much more clearly – all floating targets in what would have otherwise been the cover of a dark night.

The place was a shambles – there were wrecked boats everywhere, and the beaches were just a mass of men. We let the officer in charge here – one of the naval shore party – take the cans of drinking water we had brought with us, and then started to take the men off."

44

They used a wherry to tow the men from the very shallow water to the lifeboat, and could only take eight at a time doing this, but the trips were short ones and it didn't take too long going to and fro – in a calm sea *The Prudential* could take 160 aboard. Whilst all this was going on, so was the bombing and shelling. That night they brought off about 800 men and took them to the destroyers or other large vessels. One of these larger vessels was full of troops and ready to make for England, but had developed engine trouble, so two of the crew from the *Prudential* were put aboard her – to help with their knowledge of the currents in case she came to grief on the Goodwin Sands.

After this, with two men short, they carried on ferrying troops from shore to ships, until by Saturday June 1st they had take off a further 2,000 men – they then went back to Ramsgate.

The next morning, the *Prudential* went out again, this time helping to bring ashore some badly wounded troops from a boat in Ramsgate Harbour. Two nights later she went out again, in answer to flares, and searched until daybreak looking for boats that had broken down in the Channel. They found a small motorboat towing a rowing boat – they were hardly moving. Both of these were loaded with French troops – 68 in all. None of them had any knowledge of the sea, but they had managed to start up the engines of the motorboat and nearly make it across. They had had no food or water for twenty-two hours, and were taken on board and taken to Margate instead of Ramsgate.

Another boat, like the *Lord Southborough*, the Margate Lifeboat, which had three members of its crew from the same family, was *Sundowner*, which also became something of a family affair in the part it played at Dunkirk.

The yacht, *Sundowner*, was owned and skippered by Comdr. C.H. Lightoller R.N.R. (retd.) of *Titanic* fame. He had been second officer on the *Titanic* when she sank, and a chief witness at the enquiry after the disaster. Comdr. Lightoller was an excellent seaman and, in 1939, had been selected to secretly survey the European Coast – gaining all the information he could – similar, in a way, to the adventures written by Erskine Childers in his famous book, 'The Riddle of the Sands.' I have included the following piece from Comdr. Lightoller's personal account of the evacuation:

"My eldest son F. Roger Lightoller and I, with Seascout Gerald Ashcroft, took her out of her winter quarters at Cubits Yard Basin, Chiswick, on the river Thames, on 31st May at 11 a.m. and proceeded according to instruction to Southend."

45

The following is from *Sundowner's* log:

'1st June, Southend to Ramsgate. 3.15 a.m. hove up left in company with five others. Proceed at seven knots to allow others to keep station. Calm and clear. 9.00 a.m. arrived Ramsgate and entered harbour to obtain charts and sailing orders. Instructed to proceed to Dunkirk for further orders. 10.00 a.m. left Ramsgate by route laid down.

"In Ramsgate, I had been given a set of charts and sailing instructions – giving, as I expected, route buoys, channels etc. Half way across we avoided a floating mine by a narrow margin. Having no firearms of any description, not even a tin hat, we had to leave the latter for its destruction by someone better equipped. A few minutes later we had our first introduction to enemy aircraft, three fighters flying high. Before they could become offensive, a British destroyer, *Worcester*, I think, overhauled us and incidentally drove them off.

At 2.25 p.m. we sighted and closed with the twenty-five foot motor cruiser *Westerly*, broken down and badly on fire. As the crew of two and three naval ratings she had picked up at Dunkirk wished to abandon ship – and quickly – I went alongside and took them on board, thereby giving them the additional pleasure of once again facing the 'hell' they had just left. We made the farther way buoy at 3.00 p.m. and entered Dunkirk roads shortly after seeing the sinking of a French transport with severe loss of life. Steaming through the wreckage and other things we entered the roads.

For sometime past we had been subjected to sporadic bombing and machinegun fire, but as the *Sundowner* is exceptionally quick on her helm, by waiting until the last moment and then putting the helm over hard – my son at the helm – we easily avoided every attack, though sometimes were near lifted out of the water. It had been my intention to go right on to the beaches where my second son, Second Lieutenant R. Trevor Lightoller, had been evacuated from some forty-eight hours previously – but the survivors from *Westerley* informed me that the troops were all away from there, so I headed up for the Dunkirk piers.

By now dive-bombers seemed to be forever dropping out of the clouds of enemy aircraft overhead. Within half a mile of the pier heads a two-funneled transport had overhauled us on a converging course and was just passing us to port when two salvoes were dropped, in quick succession, right along her port side. For a few moments she was completely hidden in smoke and I certainly thought they had got her, but she reappeared out of the smoke, gaily steaming on and heading for the piers – which she entered just ahead of us. The difficulty of taking troops on board from the quay high above us was obvious, so went alongside a destroyer – *Worcester*, I think – where they were already embarking.

I got hold of her captain and told him, with a certain degree of optimism that I could take a hundred – though, the most I had ever had on board before was twenty-one! He, after consultation with the military commanding officer, said, "Go ahead, take all you can." I may say here, before leaving Cubits Yard, we had worked all night stripping her down of everything movable, mast included, that would tend to lighten her and, make for more room. Roger, as previously arranged, packed the troops in down below, and I'll say this – he packed to some purpose! On deck, I detailed one naval rating to tally the troops on board. At fifty, I called below – "How are you getting on?" Receiving the cheery reply, "Oh, plenty of room yet." At seventy five he admitted that they were getting just a little bit cramped, all equipment and arms being left on deck, so I told him to let it go at that and then come up and pack them on the deck – having passed the word for everyman to lie down and not to move. By the time we had fifty on deck I could feel her getting distinctly tender – so took no more. Actually, we had one hundred and thirty on board including the three of us on *Sundowner*, and the five we had taken off *Westerley*.

During the whole embarkation, we had quite a lot of attention from enemy planes, but derived an amazing degree of comfort from the bark of the *Worcester's* anti-aircraft guns overhead. Casting off and backing out we again entered the roads where it was continuous and unmitigated hell. The troops were just splendid and, by their own initiative, detailed lookouts ahead and astern and abeam for inquisitive planes, as my attention was pretty well occupied watching the course and passing word to Roger at the wheel. Any time an aircraft seemed inclined to try its hand on us, one of the look-outs would just call quietly, "Look out for this bloke Skipper," at the same time as pointing. One bomber that had been particularly offensive, itself came under the notice of one of our fighters and suddenly plunged vertically, hitting the sea and some 400mph, about fifty yards astern. It was a sight never to be forgotten – so were many others for that matter. Incidentally, it was the one and only time that any man on board raised his voice above a conversational tone, but, as the big black bomber hit the deck, they all raised an echoing cheer.

My youngest son, Pilot Officer H.B. Lightoller, lost on the very day that war broke out in the first raid on Wilhemshaven, flew a Blenheim and had, at different times, given me a whole lot of useful information about attack, defence and evasive tactics, at which, I learned later, he was particularly good and I attribute to him a great measure of our success on getting home."

I should like to add to Captain Lightholler's narrative that with one hundred and thirty men on board, packed like sardines, they were nearly sunk by the sheer weight before arriving safely back home.

With the rescues from the beaches now in full swing, experienced men were being called for, to man some of the boats that were still available to go to Dunkirk, but which didn't have the crews – more volunteers were needed.

Bob Hilton, who had been commissioned into the army in 1936, but later, medically discharged, had been trying to volunteer his services to man a boat since the beginning of the evacuations. He knew the Thames well and was acquainted with small craft. One of the boats that was available to be taken across was *Ryegate II* – a 40 ft motor yacht with a 10 ft beam. Bob, managed to convince whoever was in charge that he was the right man for the job. He was told that there would have to be a crew of three for the trip across, but, eventually, just two of them – himself and a man called Shaw – took the boat down river and across the Channel. When they arrived at Dunkirk they found that *Ryegate II* couldn't get right to the sands, so they tied up behind a Dutch Schuit (skoot) – the *Horst*, and commandeered a ship's lifeboat lying nearby. They then rowed to and fro from the shore to the larger boats lying off shore – one of these being a destroyer. Bob said – "We stopped for a breather and some refreshments aboard this destroyer, and all the time there was plenty of activity from the Luftwaffe – bombing and machine gunning. I remember there was a radio playing on board – 'Children's Hour' – it seemed strange to hear this with all the activity going on all around us!"

After this, they carried on ferrying troops – sometimes getting swamped and the boat turning over, but quickly put right by the troops, eager to be away from all the mayhem as quickly as possible.

At the end they were taken back across the Channel in a steamer, whilst *Ryegate II* was towed back home. Later on, Bob did manage to join up again – this time in the navy – winning the D.S.C. as Lt. Commander R.N.V.R.

One more of the little ships that I feel that I should also include again here was called '*Sylvia*' – this 45 ft boat, built by the Launch and Boat Company in Southampton, in 1913, endeared herself forever in the mind of the Harbour Master at Ramsgate – he never forgot the way *Sylvia* returned after she had picked up troops from Dunkirk. She had been machine-gunned, set on fire and, on the port side, just above the water line, was a hole which the troops had plugged with their tunics to keep the water out. He had congratulated her skipper on bringing her back to port so badly damaged and 'full to the seams' with soldiers. On talking to this man, the Harbour Master tried to dissuade him from going back across again, and had begged him to take into consideration the condition of the boat, but the man was more than determined, and said – "I have seen the sea red with blood – arms and legs and other terrible things – it's a sight I shall never forget! The Lord is with us, the sea is calm, and if she goes down – I shall go down with her!"

The following day, the Harbour Master, Lt/Comdr. H.J. Maynard, heard a lot of shouting and cheering going on – there were ships blowing their hooters and, even the troops returning on other vessels, joined in the cheering when they saw the little ship '*Sylvia*' arriving back in the harbour at Ramsgate, full of troops again. "If she had had to go another mile and the sea had been choppy she wouldn't have made it – she would have sunk! When she was moored her skipper walked out of what was left of her wheelhouse and I never saw him again." The Harbour Master said. However, he did see *Sylvia* again – many years later. *Sylvia* is also included in the epilogue.

Perhaps the youngest person who went on one of 'The Little Ships of Dunkirk' is Albert Barnes, and at that time in 1940 when he went on his adventure, he had just left school, and was fourteen and a half years of age.

Albert told me that he remembers going to and fro to the beaches, ferrying the troops to the destroyers and other larger ships. He said – "It seemed as though we were going at it non stop!" He spent most of the time as 'general dogsbody' – making cups of tea, washing up and other such tasks. He also remembers that when they got back to Dover he noticed some men on one of the ships coming in had their legs hanging over the gunwales – they looked dog tired and could even have been asleep. As they came to berth against the quayside there were screams as their legs were crushed – there was nothing anyone could do to prevent this happening, " – it was all so quick." He said.

When he did eventually get home, he told his astonished mother and other relatives where he had been – it was the first they knew of it! He was so tired that, after sitting down, he flaked out completely. They had to undress him, wash him and put him to bed; this was after having quite a job in extricating him from his boots. They also had difficulty in getting his socks off, but when they did at last manage to – they stood up like Wellington boots!

This tells of just a few of the people who volunteered to 'have a go' and bring the troops home; but, in the meantime, back at the home ports, the voluntary and other essential services now found themselves at their busiest – there was a vast job going on in receiving the wounded, dishevelled and hungry troops. Fortunately, like the people who had volunteered to go over with the little ships, there was no shortage of volunteers for these duties, which they also carried out, with extreme determination.

Chapter Four

God Bless The Ladies – An Army Returns.

In England, at the ports that were receiving this rescued army, voluntary services such as The Red Cross and W.V.S., were now doing everything they could to help the returning troops – many of them wounded, some of them nearly naked, having shed their uniforms whilst in the water, many with uniforms in tatters and all of them dog tired and ravenously hungry. The rescued men, received an enormous and most unexpected welcome wherever they were put ashore – "We were treated like returning heroes rather than a defeated army – I think the people were all the more pleased because it meant that we had come home to fight another day, to strengthen the home shores against possible invasion." One veteran said to me.

In 'Women In Green,' a book about the W.V.S. during the war years, Charles Graves has written – 'At first it seemed that nobody realised the implication of Dunkirk, and the first call on the W.V.S. was for darning needles. Nonetheless, the endurance and selfless devotion to duty of these ladies reached new heights during this period. When the chairman, Lady Reading, had been talking to the mayor of a coastal town before the outbreak of war, urging him to give his support to the W.V.S., he had said. "The W.V.S. – they'll never stick to it when the time comes – I'll bet you twenty pounds they won't stick it!"

Lady Reading was not a betting woman, but on this occasion she accepted the bet. On her next visit to the town the mayor handed over twenty pounds – "I owe it to you," he said, "as the troops returned from Dunkirk in every kind of boat, we showed them into cinemas, churches and halls. As they came in through the doors, many of them fell asleep straight away. You should have seen your women rolling them into lines, removing their equipment, their boots and socks, washing their feet as they lay there, and then taking their socks away to wash them, returning them later! I went round and watched them, and I thought how much the men's feet had bled; but then I looked again and saw that it was not stale brown blood, but fresh red blood that came from the women's hands."

Centre organisers in ports and important railway stations were asked to organise canteens, which opened at short notice and functioned as long as they were needed. The usual stores of the station buffets had to be supplemented with quantities of tea, coffee, milk, bread, sugar and many other foodstuffs, such as cakes, biscuits, sausage rolls and meat pies. As night came, the W.V.S. workers tried to sleep, when they could – on hard chair and floors.

With boats arriving all the time, there was a never ending stream of men passing through the canteens; they continuously answered greetings with a nod or a dazed smile, but they drank the mugs of tea that were thrust into their hands, and then headed for the waiting trains and fell asleep. Great jugs of tea and coffee were carried down to the boats to serve the crews or the wounded men, waiting to be taken away on stretchers.'

At Margate things had also been all of a bustle. Early in the morning of the 27th May, the local police and emergency services were briefed to be on the highest alert, as – "something had gone wrong over the other side." Many of the people who were involved at that time said that they had no idea of the events that were about to unfold. The ridiculous security decision not to tell them about the B.E.F. in France, meant that they thought they were probably getting ready for the invasion, which had been a very real threat for some time. To make matters worse, and increase their fears, the Margatonians were dismayed to see the army pulling out of their defence positions around the town to proceed to a new defence line further in land.

The jetty, scene of so many outings and events over the years, was mined with demolition charges to deny its use to the Germans if they arrived, and two sappers stayed behind to blow the charges if required. In the afternoon of the 27th May, personnel of the Royal Navy arrived and took over control of the harbour and jetty, making their headquarters in the Droit House, nearby. There was still no hint of what was going on or what was going to occur over the next few days, and Margate was ill equipped to deal with any kind of emergency anyway. There were no emergency stores of food, blankets or clothing in the town.

Dorothy Parker has vivid memories of that time. Along with the late Nora Doughty, she had been a founder member of the Margate Ambulance Corps when it was formed in the mid 1930's. She recalls how, on 28th May, she and her colleagues were told to "get down to the jetty." When they asked why, no explanation was forthcoming –

just a repeat of a blunt order. When they arrived there, the reason quickly became apparent, when, in the afternoon sunshine, vessels crowded with khaki clad cargoes of men from the B.E.F. started to arrive at the famous old jetty. They were day-trippers of a different kind, but just as pleased to see Margate as their peacetime counterparts had been. One cockney soldier was heard to say – "I've enjoyed many happy outings in Margate – but this is the best of them all."

The first vessel to arrive was the *Sandown*, which brought 201 men; this was followed by the *Gracie Fields*, which brought a further 281. During the following week, over 100 vessels brought to the safety of Margate 46,772, which was one seventh of the total numbers evacuated from France.

The emergency services and towns folk all worked ceaselessly to care for the wounded – and there were many of those landed at Margate. They saw to the needs of the exhausted troops, many of who had lost clothing during their ordeal. The town and the surrounding area were scoured for food and drink to supply the needs of the men, and the townsfolk gladly gave from the meagre stocks in their larders. Appeals for clothing and blankets met with an overwhelming response, with over 2,000 shirts, hundreds of coats and blankets, and plenty of pairs of trousers, even underwear, appearing from the half empty town. The great problem though, during those first few days, was finding footwear – lots of boots had been left in France, but once again the town turned up trumps, with hundreds of pairs being found. Eventually the army got its act together and supplies of boots began to appear from the quartermasters store at Dover Garrison – some uniforms as well.

Parties of volunteers from the town ranged all over East Kent to secure what supplies could be found – those in Margate soon having been exhausted. The job of feeding the troops went on unabated, and it was estimated that 100,000 cups of tea were served to the troops as they passed through the town on their way to the trains that whisked them away, and they all got something to eat!

East Kent buses were laid on to ferry the troops to the railway station, but first they faced a long tramp down the jetty to the shore. Obviously, there was no time to be lost in getting some of the more seriously wounded to the hospitals, and the brave decision was taken to drive the ambulance of the Margate Ambulance Corps up the jetty, in order to speed their treatment up. The jetty had a deck of two-inch planks, and it's a wonder that the ambulance didn't drop through it into the sea. Some of those present at the time said that the jetty was creaking and groaning as the ambulance went on its way, but it stayed intact – another small miracle of Dunkirk!

Thousands of stretcher cases were treated at first aid stations set up at Dreamland and The Winter Gardens, while The Royal Sea Bathing Hospital dealt with 500 and Margate Hospital 230 of the more seriously wounded. Many of the cases dealt with at the hospitals were spinal injuries, caused by compression when vessels were hit by bombs and blown out from under their feet.

Finally, every effort was made to ensure that all the troops were given either a postcard or a telegram form to notify their families that they were safely back home – and this included the French.

All the troops were given postcards to write home, including the French; but with the French troops, things were much more difficult. They could still write home, but with the strict censorship now imposed, there was a problem, and Admiral Ramsay was aware of this and asked one of his staff at Dover whether she could help.

Robert Chown has sent me this account about his grandmother Florence Fullager, who was the member of his staff that Admiral Ramsay approached to help the French soldiers to write home:

"My grandmother, Florence Fullager (Nana) of Folkestone, was trained by the Red Cross at The Royal Victoria Hospital, Folkestone. As the situations deteriorated in May 1940, she was told to report to The Royal Victoria immediately, even though she had not received her uniform yet. She was sent straight to the Buckland Hospital, Dover, and remained there as a resident in the nurses home.

My grandmother spoke fluent French, having been born to English parents living in Chantilly – she was brought up there. As the French soldiers were now arriving more frequently, she was asked personally by Admiral Ramsay to write letters to loved ones for the ones that were more seriously wounded. In spite of the fact that many of these were extremely seriously wounded and not expected to live, she wrote that they were safe and might soon be home – if they so requested. Many of these French soldiers were middle aged reservists.

One day, after being given some leave, Nana was sitting under a railway bridge waiting for a bus to go back to Folkestone. She was writing in her notebook, in a mixture of English and French. A young soldier considered she was acting suspiciously in a restricted area, and asked to see her identity card. She didn't carry it with her – she considered such things unimportant! The soldier took away her notebook and arrested her. He hailed the bus and escorted her to

Folkestone police station. Once they got there, she was instantly recognised by one of the policemen on duty – she was well known locally – her husband had been chairman of the Chamber of Commerce and also the general manager of Lewes Hyland's department store near the police station."

During this time, it had been necessary, of course, to organise trains to take the huge numbers of troops arriving at the ports, on the next step of their journeys. With hundreds of trains quickly becoming available, it was thought that chaos was bound to be the outcome in transporting them from stations, such as, Sheerness, Margate, Ramsgate, Folkestone and Newhaven – with Dover getting the lions share – but, everything went like clockwork! With thanks for this information from the York Railway Museum – the procedure that took place was as follows:

'As soon as the word 'Dynamo' was received, the divisional superintendent at Orpington held a meeting of his assistants, and sub-control offices were set up there and also at Dover Marine, Tonbridge, Ashford, Faversham, Chatham and Dartford. Inspectors were placed at the two stations at Dover, and then the stations at Folkestone, Ramsgate, Margate, Ashford, Headcorn, Paddock wood and Faversham – all stations mentioned here are in Kent. On other parts of the line there were sub-controls at Haywards Heath, Chichester and Shalford. There were two liaison officers appointed who were in constant touch with the military authorities at Dover Marine – one by day and the other by night. Empty trains were held at Queenborough on the Isle of Sheppey, Faversham, Margate and Ramsgate, and the problem of not having enough of these empty trains, and the problem of handling them, were two ever-present anxieties – especially at Dover where the numbers of men were sometimes overwhelming. Yet, in the end, empty trains from other railway systems came so thick and fast that at one time four of them were held at Willesden, since they could not be accepted at the ports!'

At the stations, members of the public were quick to join in and help in any way that they could. Some of these had heard what was going on by 'word of mouth.' Others like Winifred Thorne had as she put it, "Simply come upon this amazing scene going on right in front of my eyes!" Winifred told me, "I got a train at Gillingham to go and see my husband, who was stationed at Canterbury, and probably soon to go overseas. When we got to Faversham we had to pull into a siding so as to give another train priority of passage. This train was full of troops, I could see them quite clearly as they pulled in right beside the train I was on, on the adjoining platform. They were dishevelled, dirty and obviously very hungry – it was like a scene I had seen pictures of, of World War I. My heart went out to them. The people on the station, The W.V.S. and ordinary people like myself were giving out refreshments, so I thought that I must do something as well. I got the pork pie, sweets, biscuits and cakes I'd got specially to give to my husband, and handed all to the troops, they were so grateful, one of them even kissed me – I'll never forget it! I remember some of them asked me what the news was – they didn't know anything at all about what was going on, and asked if I had a newspaper. I hadn't, but I remembered that a man in my carriage had got quite a bundle of them, so I went back to the carriage to ask him if he could spare one or two of them. He wasn't in his seat, so thinking that he'd just gone and left them, I picked up the whole bundle, walked back over to the troops and handed them over. A little later, when our train continued on its journey, the man came back and loudly asked what had happened to his newspapers. I kept quiet; I could feel that I had gone red in the face – all in a good cause though!"

Later Winifred had to explain to her husband why she hadn't bought him all the things she had promised she would; this explanation was met with a few moments of stony silence – then laughter, as her husband told her that if he'd been in the same position, he would have done exactly the same thing!

Dot Weedon, who now lives at Chatham, told me – "I was in the A.R.P. (Air Raid Precaution) at the time of Dunkirk, and working at Shorts at Rochester, who made the Sunderland Flying Boats. I was a secretary. One day there was a call to the factory asking for members to report to Chatham station, to help feed all the troops on the trains going through. When I got there I saw that there were people from all walks of life – all eager to help, all keen to do what they could. I remember seeing one man cutting up loaves of bread, he got about six slices from each large loaf – they were like giant doorsteps, but much appreciated!"

Dot told me. 'The manager of the Co-op at Chatham had heard about what was going on, and with help from his staff, took all the 'immediately eatable' food, such as sausage rolls, pies, cheese, bread and all sorts of other things, to the station for the people working there to dole out – "To hell with what my bosses will say!" He said, and with that as a parting shot, he, with his staff trailing behind him, hurried off to fetch some more.'

At Headcorn Station, where there was only a staff of a stationmaster and two porters, they fed 145,000 troops. The R.A.S.C. provided the food, with forty soldiers to hand it out – but fifty or so lady volunteers helped these from the neighbourhood including some from the W.V.S. and other voluntary organisations. For nine days and nights they worked in shifts of eight hours each; but eight hours were not enough to satisfy their enthusiasm, and one of them stayed on continuously for twenty-four hours. Their headquarters were in a large barn in a nearby field – this was where the food was made ready and then carried across some fields, then across the railway line and then on to the 'up' platform. As far as tea and coffee was concerned, for the troops, one of the helpers said – "The whole of Kent could hardly have produced enough cups for the men to drink from, and the refreshing liquids went into the trains in tin cans. When time was up for each batch, the R.A.S.C. troops on the platform shouted out to the troops in the train – 'sling them out' – and a shower of tin cans clattered onto the platform, and these were quickly collected by the amateur and professional staff on the station, washed up and ready for the next train."

When the troop movements had begun, Phyllis Knott and some other members of the W.V.S. at Folkestone, were called out in the night to make sandwiches and prepare other refreshments. In the early morning they were told to make haste to Westenhanger Station, just by Folkestone Racecourse. She remembers arriving there on that first day to be greeted by a dawn chorus. "It was just beautiful – and everything else was so quiet, but then the first of the train arrived, and very quickly everything changed. There was one every quarter of an hour, and you should have seen the troops; they were wet, bedraggled – some with hardly any clothing, and they were all starving hungry. Amazingly, they were all quite cheerful, but I suppose that that was because they were all so glad to be back home. Some of them gave us postcards to send for them – they'd quickly scribbled on them on the journey from Folkestone Harbour to say that they were okay. It was an experience that I shall never forget."

One other person who just happened to be caught up in all the goings on at one of the stations, was Patricia King, who lived near Paddock Wood in Kent. She had arrived at Paddock Wood station to start the journey to her fiancé's parents' home at Edenbridge; he was due home on leave there later that day. She had spent months making him a multi-coloured pullover from bits and pieces of wool she had unraveled from old garments, and had only just finished making it. She noticed that there were lots of people sitting around tables on the station making sandwiches and handing out cups of tea for people to carry to troops on a train that had just arrived. Patricia told me – "Most of the troops looked scruffy and dirty – not like troops usually look. Although they seemed quite cheerful, I could tell that they had been going through some sort of hell. I felt very sorry for them, particularly one of them, who hardly had any clothing on at all, so, on the spur of the moment I handed him the pullover. I've always been glad I did this, because, in later years, when my husband and I talked about it, we always had a good laugh – he had been dreading wearing it and was more than pleased that I'd given it away."

Amongst the returning soldiers, Jim Denne, of the R.A.S.C., who would later in life marry Elsie Taylor, the evacuee from Gillingham, I have written about in Chapter Two, had come back over the Channel in what he thinks was a Swedish coal boat. For some reason this boat wasn't allowed entry into Dover Harbour, so they finished their journey tying up to Margate Pier! They were given refreshments here at the A.F.S. canteen and, later, more refreshments at Faversham station, on the journey to wherever they were going. It was at Faversham that Jim spoke to one of the station staff, telling him that his father, Walter Denne, was the Station Inspector at Gillingham, just a little further up the line, and – "could he get a message to him through the railway communications." A little later, before they left Faversham, Jim was told that his father had just gone off duty, but that the only taxi available at the station had been sent to his home to collect him. The outcome was that Jim's father, mother and brother-in-law were waiting at Gillingham station. He managed to say a brief hello and goodbye to his mother and brother-in-law, as the train slowed going through the station, enabling his father to get on board. During the few minutes it took to get to Chatham – less than a mile up the line – Walter Denne learnt as much as he could from his son about what had been going on, gave him some money and then got off the train at Chatham after, as he described it – "The shortest and most meaningful journey of my life!"

Jim and his mates finished up at the Military Headquarters at Shrivenham – where they were deloused, bathed and rekitted.

Many of the seriously wounded that had been landed at the ports, quickly found themselves being tended to in local hospitals before being sent on to hospitals specialising more specifically for the wounds they had received. At Shornecliff Hospital, Folkestone, Ursula Hall-Thompson, once again found herself in the thick of things in the

58

operating theatre, she told me – "I can't remember there being any warning that we were about to receive the badly wounded troops from Dunkirk – they just started coming in. We had a constant stream of patients who were dying or who would die if they didn't have something done for them quickly. At the height of the emergency, there were three operations taking place in the theatre at the same time. These patients were mostly for amputations – hygiene wasn't exactly given top priority when they had been hastily bandaged whilst still under fire at Dunkirk or in action before arriving there. A lot of the wounds on these men had turned gangrenous and we worked feverishly to keep them alive – on looking back on it I feel we did a good job considering the circumstances."

Shortly after Dunkirk, Ursula was sent to another emergency receiving unit at Leeds Castle in Kent, where she would find herself working in the 'dungeons.' I have also included some of Ursula's experiences there, later in the book.

Another of the wounded who had constantly received treatment from nurses and doctors, both at Dunkirk and on arriving back home, was Ernie Leggett, of A Company, Second Battalion, Royal Norfolk Regiment. Ernie told me – "Whilst on my stretcher on the dunes, I was completely helpless – a fractured lumber spine, shrapnel wounds covering my whole left leg, and gaping wounds where a large piece of shrapnel had passed through my left buttock and out through the groin. I was naked except for a blanket, and swathed in bloody bandages – I was in severe pain. Every now and again a medical officer, accompanied by a nursing sister, to be given a further injection of morphine, visited me. Time was meaningless, the incessant noise of war was never ending. I thought of my family at home and vividly saw my mother, father, brother and grandfather sitting by the fire. In reality I pictured my small church of St. Peter, Clippesby, as if I was actually there. The Cross Keys, a silver key crossing one of gold, I could see quite clearly. The keys had captivated my undivided attention as a young boy, and became an omen when I realised the Second Infantry Division sign was that of cross keys.

Above the constant noise, I could hear the calling out of the wounded and orders being shouted out, until once again the MO appeared, and that blessed oblivion which morphine can bring, took over – and I fell into an unconscious sleep."

Eventually stretcher-bearers lifted Ernie to the mole, and carried him aboard the hospital ship, *St. Julian*. "My next awareness was that I was still alive and smelling fresh sea air – no noise, except for the crying of the seagulls," Ernie told me. "There was a Salvation Army nurse there, handing me a cup of tea – she lit a cigarette for me – 'You are back home – this is Newhaven.' she told me."

Ernie was operated on at The Sussex County Hospital in Brighton – this is quite near to where we lived, and I often passed by here on my walks to and from school and remember seeing men in hospital blue uniforms, who were long term patients there from the services.

Ernie remained there for a year before being discharged – miraculously still able to walk. He says, "I thank God for my life and feel everlasting gratitude for all those who cared and watched over me during my hours of distress." I have put Ernie in the epilogue.

Also, in Brighton, with the troops now flooding back into the country, my mother and my Aunt Daphne, who was now staying in the balcony flat at number thirteen, were closely listening out for news of two uncles of mine; my mother's brother, Jimmy, who was a member of the B.E.F., in the Tank Corps, who we hadn't heard from since early May, and Daphne's husband, Nat Vaughan Oliver, who was a Lieutenant on board one of the destroyers helping in the rescues. But it wouldn't be until the evacuations were over that they would hear that they were both all right.

After Dunkirk, it had become noticeable that people's attitudes seemed to have changed. My father found himself having lengthy conversations with people, who, in pre-war days, he had only been on 'nodding terms' with – now, new friendships blossomed, with many people finding a special quality of life by 'all being in the same boat together.'

In a way, you could say that although 'Dunkirk' had been a defeat, it had prepared us for the dark clouds that were now looming ever closer to the home shores and which would soon lead to The Battle of Britain being fought out in the clear blue skies over the south east of England.

Chapter Five

The Island Alone – The Battle Of Britain.

On October 8th 1939, in a letter to Sir Samuel Hoare, Winston Churchill, on the subject of civil defence, had said – "Why do we not form a home guard of half a million men over forty (if they like to volunteer) and put all our elder stars at the head and in the structure of these new formations. Let these five hundred thousand men come along and push the young and active out of all their home billets. If uniforms are lacking, a brassard would suffice, and I am assured there are plenty of rifles in any case."

Before this though, in July 1939, the war minister, Leslie Hore-Belisha, had said – "We cannot really consider putting against a first class enemy a formation armed with obsolete weapons, which we do not consider suitable for modern warfare – except, perhaps, as a last resort!" It seems rather surprising that Hore-Belisha could say this when, a few months later, the British Expeditionary Force – a front line fighting force of regulars, territorials and conscripts – when eventually going into battle, found themselves using outdated equipment and weapons that were no match for the far superior German arms and armaments.

From the onset of World War II, until just before Dunkirk, there were quite a few who would like to have seen a properly organised defence force, made up of volunteers, to supplement the armed forces and operating in all areas; certainly in the most vulnerable areas – those places most likely to be invaded. However, there seemed to be more complacency rather than enthusiasm amongst the general public for forming such an organisation – that is until things started to look really desperate across the Channel, in May 1940. After Mr. Chamberlain had resigned and Winston Churchill had been chosen as Prime Minister, Mr. Anthony Eden, the newly appointed Secretary of State for War, broadcast to the nation on 14th May, 1940, asking for volunteers to form the 'Local Defence Volunteers' – LVD – he said:

"I want to speak to you to-night about the form of warfare which the Germans have been employing so extensively against Holland and

61

Belgium – namely, the dropping of troops by parachute behind the main defensive lines. Let me say at once that the danger to us from this particular menace, although it undoubtedly exists, should not be exaggerated. We have made preparations to meet it already.

Let me describe to you the system under which these parachute raids are carried out. The troops arrive by aeroplane – but let it be remembered that any such aeroplane seeking to penetrate here would have to do so in the teeth of the Anti-Aircraft defences of this country. If such penetration is effected, the parachutists are then dropped, it may be by day, it may be by night. These troops are specially armed, equipped, and some of them have undergone specialist training. Their function is to seize important points, such as aerodromes, power stations, villages, railway junctions and telephone exchanges, either for the purpose of destroying them at once, or holding them until the arrival of reinforcements. The purpose of the parachute attack is to disorganise and confuse, as a preparation for the landing of troops by aircraft.

The success of such an attack depends on speed. Consequently, the measures to defeat such an attack must be prompt and rapid. It is upon this basis that our plans have to be laid. You will not expect me to tell you, or the enemy, what our plans are, but we are confident that they will be effective. However, in order to leave nothing to chance and to supplement, from sources as yet untapped, the means of defence already arranged, we are going to ask you to help us, in a manner, which I know will be welcome to thousands of you. Since the war began, the Government has received countless enquiries from all over the Kingdom from men of all ages who are for one reason or another not at present engaged in military service, and who wish to do something for the defence of the country.

Now is your opportunity. We want large numbers of such men in Great Britain who are British subjects, between the ages of 17 and 65, to come forward now and offer their services in order to make assurance doubly sure. The name of the new force, which is now to be raised, will be the 'Local Defence Volunteers.' This name, Local Defence Volunteers, describes its duties in three words. It must be understood that this is, so to speak, a spare-time job, so there will be no need for any volunteer to abandon his present occupation.

Part-time members of existing civil defence organisations should ask their officers' advice before registering under the scheme. Men who will ultimately become due for calling up under the National Service (Armed Forces) Act may join temporarily, and will be released to join the army when they are required to serve. Now a word for those who propose to volunteer. When on duty you will form part of the Armed Forces, and your period of service will be for the duration of the war. You will not be paid, but you will receive uniform and will be armed. You will be entrusted with certain vital duties, for which reasonable fitness and knowledge of firearms are necessary. These duties will not require you to live away from your homes. In order to volunteer, what you have to do is to give in your name at your local police station; and then, as and when we want you, we will let you know.

This appeal is directed chiefly to those who live in small towns, villages, and less densely inhabited suburban areas. I must warn you that, for certain military reasons, there will be some localities where the numbers required will be small, and others where your services will not be required at all. Here then is the opportunity for which so many of you have been waiting. Your loyal help, added to the arrangements which already exist, will make and keep our country safe."

After his broadcast, the complacency to join such a force quickly changed to overwhelming enthusiasm and police stations all over the country were inundated with people of all ages eager to become part of this new venture.

At home, my father already knew that he was too disabled to join this – "exciting, time filling and necessary new force" – as he described it to my mother. He felt very disappointed, but nonetheless, offered to help in any way he could. Many friends of his had been quick to join, and he offered to help them should they need any advice.

In Kent, The Chief Constable had sent a message to all police stations in the county with instructions to ask all volunteers four basic questions, before enrolling. They were:

(A) Are you familiar with firearms?
(B) What is your occupation?
(C) What military experience do you have?
(D) Are you prepared to serve away from home?

Similar questions were asked of would be volunteers in all the counties.

Would be members were told, that after joining, the police would no longer take any part in the organisation – they had enough to do in any case and, of course, would be organising the air raid wardens as well as doing their own duties, which by this time had increased considerably.

With a third of a million troops back on the home shores, after Dunkirk, our defences now looked decidedly more healthy than they had done on the 26th of May, but, by now, everyone wondered how soon it would be before Hitler struck out across the Channel – how long before we were invaded. It was a grim time – it was a frightening time.

In Brighton, now a restricted zone, all movements in and out of the town were restricted, as were all towns similarly situated around the southeast. You couldn't move away from the town if you wanted to, this was to prevent there being a 'mass exodus' – similar to what had happened in France and Belgium.

After the fall of France, with the country on the alert for invasion, and the Local Defence Volunteers, now, rightly, taking themselves extremely seriously, and with great enthusiasm, the only things they were short of were the weapons to fight with, and uniforms. At first, it was a common sight to see platoons of men armed with a variety of makeshift weapons that ranged from broom handles and cricket bats, to pitchforks and scythes and in some cases swords or, for the well armed, shotguns.

However, things would soon change and, after Mr. Churchill had stepped in once again, the volunteers were issued with uniforms and rifles – but ammunition, to start with, was scarce.

In its infancy, the Local Defence Volunteers had no real administration; it was a matter of individual companies or platoons sorting themselves out, but on the 24th of June 1940, the County Territorial Associations took over the administration, and these were also made responsible for the issuing of clothing and equipment in each county. It was also at about this time that Mr. Churchill finally had his way about his naming of these volunteers and, thus, the Local Defence Volunteers became known as 'The Home Guard.' Later on they would be called – 'Civil Defence' – but nonetheless, nearly everyone still called them the 'Home Guard.'

By mid July, with the Luftwaffe now targeting the R.A.F. airfields and with all sorts of aerial activity going on, the Home Guard became extremely vigilant – especially at nights. I remember being told, quite some time ago, by an ex member of the Eynsford (Kent) Home Guard, who had joined up immediately after Mr. Eden's broadcast, that it was very scary at nights, he said – "When the German bombers started coming over in force, we all kept a sharp lookout for parachutists, which we expected to see at any moment – it's difficult to describe, but

I know that I imagined, more than once, that I had seen something! Don't forget that out in the country one minute it might be nice and silent – with only the occasional hoot of an owl or bark of a fox – and then the next, the peace would be shattered with the sound of aircraft going overhead and you strained your eyes trying to watch out for anything. Sometimes, after the aircraft had gone and everything was quiet again, I would imagine I could see something moving from behind a distant hedge – a parachutist perhaps – but the light played tricks, especially when there was variable cloud passing over, and it was a relief, as well as amusing, to discover that the 'something' was a cow or a small herd, that had also been disturbed by the noise of the aircraft and was simply moving about."

Ray Gallagher, who lived in Cliftonville, in Kent, as a teenager, was still too young to go into the forces but had volunteered for the LDV after Mr. Eden's speech. In a letter to me he says – "I remember the invasion alarm in 1940, quite clearly. I was on early evening duty, with another youngster, in a dugout on the clifftop between the coastguard station and Botany Bay, when the intrepid Major Wittle, our C/O, appeared in his car with a large quantity of amunition and tidings that the balloon was about to go up. This made us feel a 'little' insecure, because, apart from a Hurricane and a light cruiser, flashing signals to the coastguard, there appeared to be only us two to repel the Wehrmacht, whom we expected to materialise over the horizon at any moment – if an invasion had come, I don't think either of us were naïve enough to think we could hold off an enemy made up of crack troops, who had 'swept through Europe,' – with just our rifles and a few Molotov cocktails (bottles filled with petrol)."

At Fletching, in Sussex, Michael Butcher's father, who I have written a little about in Chapter Two, had joined the Local Defence Corps when it was first formed. Michael told me – "Each night the members of the 'Home Guard,' including my father, who had quickly been made up to corporal, took it in turns to patrol the village – especially if there had been an air raid warning. Ammunition was scarce, so in training, to make the appropriate noises, they would use thunder flashes – rather like Christmas crackers, only considerably more explosive, without being really dangerous. During the time, the Home Guard were 'operational' there were several places they met up at – including the roadman's hut on wheels and the local reading room, where my grandmother was the caretaker. There was also a local branch of the Auxiliary Fire Service, which had a trailer pump towed behind a very ancient car. Most houses kept buckets of sand in case of incendiary bombs.

In Brighton, by August, the air raids had increased and our occasional visits to the shelter of the basement now started to become more regular. However, during the warm summer days of that August and September, we often found ourselves the spectators to amazing aerial battles that suddenly materialised – literally from 'out of the blue' and the German onslaught soon became quite devastating – with the Battle of Britain being fought out furiously in the skies above the fields, villages and towns of South East England.

While we were playing in the gardens, in Sussex Square, we sometimes witnessed fierce 'dogfights' during those tense weeks. The fighters would appear and disappear with frightening speed – often leaving wispy trails of white vapour behind them, temporarily imprinted on the clear blue drawing surface of the sky. The job of sounding the siren for all these quick skirmishes, which sometimes developed into spectacular battles, was practically an impossibility, and we often found ourselves in the gardens whilst they suddenly took place without any warning. At these times, we usually sought what protection we could – in case the enemy should decide to machine gun us – behind the thickest of the fir trees in the gardens. In my book, 'The Tree Climbers' – about Brighton during the war years – I told of one of those occasions, when out playing with a friend of mine – Timmy Martinez. On this occasion a German fighter suddenly flew, very low, over the gardens, shaking us considerably; however, we felt a lot better when this enemy aircraft was quickly followed by a Spitfire – hot in pursuit and loudly cheered by a small group of people on the nearby pavement. "Did you see the pilot in that Spitfire, David?" Timmy called over to me from where he stood, behind the inadequate cover of a small bush. Still shaking slightly, I replied – "Yes" – but I wasn't sure really, I had seen the cockpit, but it had all happened so quickly that what was inside it had only been a blur.

With the Battle of Britain now being viewed by a wide audience in the South East of England, witnessing all the action had spurred many more people on to join the voluntary services – people eager to help in any way that they could. Penny Summers, who lived in Strood, near Rochester, had joined the ARP before the Battle of Britain had started, but, by August 1940, she had been transferred to the local Auxiliary Fire Brigade, and became its first woman telephonist. She watched the Battle of Britain being fought from outside the Nissen hut she worked at, at the top of Strood Hill. She told me – "When I could find the time to go outside for a breath of fresh air, I got a birds eye view from there – it was quite spectacular watching the battles, with the Spitfires and Hurricanes trying to prevent the German planes from, at first, getting to our fighter airfields, and later, London." There is more from Penny later on in the book, but perhaps the biggest battle she might have witnessed took place on August 18th 1940, when 'all hell broke loose' during a raid aimed at the North Weald and Hornchurch Airfields. Many of these raiders had come over the Medway Towns, and it is here that I feel I must also pay tribute to those men manning the ack-ack guns – particularly, on that raid, those manning the guns at Fort Borstal, near Rochester.

Alan Rose, who now lives in Sittingbourne and is the chairman of its British Legion Branch, was determined not to be pitched, untrained, and straight into battle, "– like so many lads had in the First World War." Being too young to join up, he had joined a unit of the nearest branch of the Territorial Army – 205 Heavy Anti Aircraft Battery at Chatham. Alan can't remember the exact date he joined, but he can remember all the camps he went to and all the training, of course. His most indelible memory was of the raid I have mentioned, that Penny Summers may well have witnessed on that sunny Sunday in August 1940. This is Alan's account of that raid, he says:

This was an attack, which was made by part of the force sent to bomb North Weald, and Hornchurch Fighter Airfields, which was the overall strategy adopted by the German High Command at the time, in an attempt to overwhelm the air defence of Great Britain, a pre-requisite to the invasion of the United Kingdom.

The two attacks consisted of 58 Dornier 17's of Bomber Geschader (wing) 2 to attack Hornchurch and the other made up of 51 Heinkels of Bomber Geschader 53 to attack North Weald. It is the Geschader 2 that we are concerned.

Covering the two bomber forces were 140 Messerschitt 109's and 110's as close escort. However, there were also about a hundred Messerschitt 109's on free hunt patrols over the Maidstone area in support of these attacks.

In spite of numerous and valiant attempts by our outnumbered fighters, as the bombers picked up the coast, between Deal and Dover, the Messerschmitt escort was able to keep them away and the bombers proceeded in good formation up the coast of Kent turning into the Thames Estuary, to press on to their target, Hornchurch Airfield.

67

All this time, the fights between our fighters and the Luffwaffe Free Hunt Patrols were raging all over Mid Kent and the coast, with aircraft and pilots crashing and landing by parachute as far afield as Chilham, the Thames Estuary, Canterbury and Dartford.

In spite of all that the RAF could do however, the bomber formations were able to arrive in the vicinity of Hornchurch, having passed over Whitstable and Sheerness.

I would like to add here that it is little realised that for all the talk of the miracle of RADAR, it was no good once the enemy had crossed the coast, our defences then had to rely on the good old fashioned Eyeball technique, in fact, we owe so much to the oft maligned Observer Corps. Their information, though better than nothing was often late and was therefore assumed to be inaccurate, which wasn't so. So another function of the ack-ack was to indicate to passing RAF patrols just where the enemy was.

The anti-aircraft guns situated on the Isles of Sheppey and Grain and round Sittingbourne, engaged them, causing them to open their formation slightly, but they still continued on their course.

Having arrived on the Essex coast, the bomber leader found that the cloud which had been thickening from the north west, had come south far enough to affect the south-east half of the county, and that the target area was shrouded in ground haze because of this, leading bombers could not pin point the airfield.

At this period in the war in the west, the German Air Force had been ordered not to waste its bombs on indiscriminate bombing. German reports now say that their formations turned away because of this order.

The turn away to the south-east brought the bombers on course for the Medway Towns. As the bombers could be clearly seen from the ground, it can be safely assumed that the bombers had a good view of the River Medway, which, because of its winding aspect, was a good guide to the many juicy targets, which were a bomber's dream come true.

Chatham Dockyard, Shorts Seaplane Works, Rochester Airport, a vast built up area, crammed so conveniently into one of the bends of the river, full of workshops, both large and small, all working flat out on war work – and there was, by then, nothing to stop them!

There was not a friendly fighter to be seen or heard, as the leader of the Fighter Command, Sir Hugh Dowding, had feared, the German Air Force had succeeded in saturating our air force.

The anti-aircraft guns of Chatham, so far not having been engaged, awaited the onslaught with anxious but eager anticipation as the bombers and their escorts approached over the Isle of Grain.

The sight of these bombers will remain in the minds of anybody who saw it. The black anti-craft shell bursts on either side, seemed to form a lane or avenue down which the bombers flew, almost, as it were, in review. Then they were in range of the guns of Fort Borstal, who opened up with carefully timed and aimed salvo's from their four 4.5″ guns.

The effect on the leading bombers was astounding, the three leading bombers disappeared in huge black smears of smoke, while the tail of another was torn away. Before the following bombers could react, four more shells burst amongst them and they seemed, to an eye witness, as if they appeared to trip over the remnants of the leading bombers in their haste to get away, and it would appear that at last their nerve had broken, and their one thought was to flee. The once proud and majestic formations were now a rabble, scrambling for a chance to get away from this fresh and deadly menace. It was then that the refreshed and re-ammunitioned RAF arrived, getting in the way of the guns and giving them no more opportunity to fire, and these harried the now thoroughly demoralised bombers, all the way back to the coast.

Though there were many other days in which the guns of Chatham were called upon to play their part in this 'Battle for and of Britain,' that day, the 18th of August 1940, was their day, when those gunners, part-time soldiers, boys and old soldiers of the First World War, trained in their spare time, rose to their self-imposed task and helped to defeat the most highly trained and equipped Air Force in the world, and in doing so saved their towns from destruction.

Others, if they so wish, can claim the glory, be lauded as our saviours, as no one doubts they were. But there were others in that fight. And for us, surely, it is enough to know that when our country called, we were ready.

Another of the areas affected by the raid on August 18th was the village of Shoebury and also Shoeburyness in Essex. One person, in particular, who did all she could to help the wounded and distressed people, during the raid was Alice Rawlings, a local mother of eight children, who had joined the ARP at the beginning of the war. Her daughter, Maureen Andrews, told me, that she and her twin sister Joyce often used to take meals to their mother, when she was on duty at the A.R.P. post, at the corner of Wakering Road and Blackgate Road. As an A.R.P. Warden, working full time but in shifts, during her daytime shifts she would spend her time visiting homes, testing gas masks and checking the blackout curtains. She was a well-known, well-liked and cheerful figure in her area, where her presence at the time of air raids was a great comfort to many people.

On that particular Sunday afternoon, when the Luftwaffe crews realised that their raid had failed and had jettisoned their bombs as they turned for home, Alice didn't flinch from helping as the bombs exploded all over the area. Without concern for her own safety, she had carried on helping digging people out of the rubble of bombed houses, as well as helping those who were wounded and shell shocked.

During the raid, around 200 bombs fell on the ranges and the sands nearby, with a further 30 bombs falling on the village. It was devastating, but Alice just carried on helping where she could – an inspiration and comfort to everyone she came in contact with.

Within days, Roy White a senior A.R.P. officer in Southend, was writing to Alice to say – 'It has been reported to me from more than one source that you displayed the highest sense of duty and disregard for personal safety when you rendered assistance to casualties while bombs were still falling. Such gallant action is worthy of the highest praise. The service is proud to include members who behave in this manner and I send my appreciation and gratitude.' There are a few lines about Maureen Andrews and, her mother, in the epilogue.

With all these raids going on, there were quite a few aeroplanes that were brought down into the sea – or, being shot up, could only make it as far as the Channel. There were also many incidents where pilots had had to bail out over the sea, making it essential that the coastguards and coastwatchers kept an even more vigilant watch than usual; also, the R.N.L.I., as well as many of those who manned the beach fishing boats, were in a constant state of readiness – they all knew that it was desperately important to reach these stricken men as quickly as was humanly possible, and they were successful in saving many airmen from drowning.

In his book, 'The Last Enemy,' Richard Hillary wrote about his bailing out into the sea – a few miles out from Reculver, in Kent. He was very badly burned and in considerable pain. At times the pain was so bad and with his situation seeming to be hopeless, he attempted to drown himself and put a quick end to it all. He wrote – "I had no qualms about hastening my end, and reaching up I managed to unscrew the valve of my May West. The air escaped in a rush and my head went under water. It is said by people who have all but died in the sea, that drowning is a pleasant death. I did not find it so. I swallowed a large

70

quantity of water before my head came up again, to find I could not get my face under. I was so enmeshed in my parachute that I couldn't move."

Eventually, giving up the struggle to drown himself, he laid back and floated, in an almost dreamlike state of semi consciousness. " – Then, willing arms were dragging me over the side; my parachute was taken off (and with such ease), a brandy flask was pushed between my swollen lips; a voice said, 'okay Joe – it's one of ours and still kicking;' and I was safe. It was to the Margate Lifeboat that I owed my rescue. Watchers on the coast had seen me come down and, for three hours, they had been searching for me. Owing to wrong directions, they were just giving up and turning back for land when, ironically enough, one of them saw my parachute. They were then a few miles east of Margate (off Reculver)."

Concerning Richard Hillary's rescue, this report appears in a friend of mine, Tony Walters book 'The Margate R.N.L.I. Station and its Lifeboats from 1860' – 'At 10.15 a.m. on The 3rd September 1940, the coxswain, from the coastguard station, saying a parachute was seen to go down into the sea seven miles north east of Reculver, received a telephone message. The *J.B. Proudfoot* was at once launched and proceeded to the position given. A very extensive search was made, visibility was poor at the time and at 11.15, the airman was found, three and a half miles north, north west of Reculver. He was very badly burned, most of his clothing having been burnt away, and on the point of collapse, having been in the sea or over an hour. He was at once taken aboard the lifeboat and with the help of the Hon. Secretary, made comfortable. Owing to his state, the Hon. Secretary asked them to radio a message to Margate for an ambulance and, after a journey at full speed, the lifeboat arrived at the Stone Pier at 1.00 p.m. when the airman was handed over to the doctor and officials waiting. The airman was Pilot Officer Richard Hillary, the first time great nephew of Sir William Hillary, the founder of the R.N.L.I.'

As well as Royal Air Force pilots, quite a number of German aircrew were also picked up from the sea. Mostly, these 'enemy' flyers were very grateful to be saved from going to a watery grave, but some of them were very arrogant and pro-Nazi – even just after being picked up.

The Hastings Lifeboat, *The Cyril and Lillian Bishop*, rescued at least four enemy airmen, shot down in separate incidents. However, there was considerable hostility towards these fliers, particularly if there had just been an air raid on Hastings. After being pulled out of the sea, one shivering German pilot was given a pullover by a lifeboat man – who also gave him a hefty kick after being given a Nazi salute!

The Home Guard and even farmhands, in the southeast, found this a busier time than usual, whilst gathering in the harvest. They were witnesses to many battles fought out in the skies above them, and kept a keen lookout for any parachutists or aeroplanes brought down near to where they worked, during the long summer and autumn days of the Battle of Britain.

One incident that was reported in some of the papers, including The Brighton Evening Argus, during September 1940, concerned a 'shot down' German pilot being 'arrested' by members of the Home Guard, after a particularly kind act by the British pilot who had shot him down. The article said:

'A Hurricane pilot forced down an ME109 during Saturday's battles over Kent, after he had used up his ammunition in shooting down two enemy fighters. The pilot said – "I saw a third ME109 dive past me. I followed him down to ground level and chased him southwards. He didn't rise above one hundred feet until we were well south of Maidstone, then he throttled back. I overtook him and flew alongside him, pointing downwards to the ground. He turned away, so I carried out a dummy quarter attack, breaking away very close to him. After this he landed his ME109 in a field at about 140 miles per hour. I saw the pilot get out, apparently unhurt and, as I circled around him, he put his hands above his head – so I waved to him and he waved back. Then I circled low over him and threw him a packet of twenty cigarettes I had with me. I saw him pick them up, and again he waved. Then I saw what I believed to be members of the Home Guard go into the field and take him prisoner. After that I returned to my base.'

By this stage in the war, as far as the Home Guard were concerned, although most of its members were 'willing to have a go' at encountering the enemy and putting up a good fight, it was generally felt that the best role that they could take a full and essential part in, was security. This included manning road checks and being constantly on the alert for fifth columnists or parachutists. Anthony Eden, in his recruiting speech for the LDV had said that it was likely that fifth columnists might try to paralyse the country by seizing such important places as telephone exchanges and power stations – probably just before the invasion.

Mr. Butcher of Fletching village Home Guard, had later told his family, " – Another thing that happened at this time, that not many people knew about, was that on the night of September 6th 1940, an alert had been sent out to people in command of various sections of the

Home Guard, saying that the invasion was imminent! Apparently, in the prevailing excitement of receiving this alert, a few commanders of Home Guard units had rung the church bells in their areas to call out their men, thus spreading the impression that German parachutists had actually landed." The church bells had been silenced at the beginning of the war, only to be sounded in the event of an invasion. Corporal Butcher also said, "It was a tense time for all of us that night. I remember there was a knock on our door in the middle of the night, so I got dressed and joined the others in the roadman's hut, just down the road. Everything was quiet, apart from occasional sweeps of aircraft going overhead. From time to time we really thought that this could be it, but it all quietened down by the morning. None the less, we were still on full alert, but with instructions not to talk to anyone about what was going on – this would have caused panic, something we wanted to avoid at all costs."

Mr. Butcher also told them of a relative, who was in the Home Guard, who worked on a remote farm, near the Ashdown Forest. During a dogfight, he saw a Heinkel 111 which had been damaged and was flying very low with smoke trailing from one wing – it was coming straight at him, so he raised his rifle and took a shot at it. The aeroplane eventually crashed some distance away, but he never found out how accurate his shot was – the plane was probably doomed in any case.

The long warm days of that memorable summer continued, but on September 7th the Luftwaffe eventually changed tactics and started striking against the civilian population – with London as the prime target. However, in changing their tactics, many more areas were now affected by the bombings; sometimes by the Luftwaffe pilots turning tail for home and jettisoning their bombs, wherever they were – thus lightening their loads.

The day after this change of tactics, on the night of 8/9th September 1940, one unlikely place for the Luftwaffe to bomb, was the tiny village of Colgate, in St. Leonards Forest, just outside Horsham. Five bombs dropped there that night and the heroine of this disaster, was Dorothy White, who had worked as a nanny for a well-known local family for quite a few years and had joined the Red Cross as a VAD nurse at the beginning of the war. I think that this would be an opportune time to put in some of the piece written about her in the local paper, The West Sussex County Times, after her death in 1979:

'It is hard to realise, nearly 40 years later, that the tiny village of Colgate, hidden in the St. Leonards Forest, just outside Horsham, was once the target of an enemy bombing attack which killed two nurses and produced a heroine. The heroine of that night was Miss Dorothy May White, known as 'Nanny' not only because she was the nanny for the Barnes family, but because she was well loved in the village where she could be relied upon in an emergency. For her rescue work on that terrible night of 8/9th September 1940, Nanny White was awarded the George Medal.

Dorothy May White was born in 1894 at West Lavington, Wiltshire, and spent her childhood at Bayworth near Abingdon. From her earliest years she loved babies, and loved the countryside, often recounting how she would arrive at school with cold fingers, having delivered the milk in the early morning before starting her lessons. In 1916 she became nurse to the family of Mr. and Mrs. W. G. Barnes and moved with them to Upland House School (now Cottesmore) near Colgate, where Mr. Barnes was joint headmaster, and later to Rhododendron Cottage in the village.

When war broke out in 1939 the Barnes children had grown up and Nanny White chose the Red Cross as her war work and is still remembered as a devoted and untiring member of the Horsham branch.

On that tragic night in September, 1940, five bombs dropped on the tiny village of Colgate, killing five people, all of whom were 'on duty.' Nanny White rescued from the village hall first aid post, one of her 'babies,' 20-year-old Heather Barnes, who was also a member of the Voluntary Aid Detachment, Heather Barnes died a few hours after being rescued. It was not the end of that fatal night for Nanny, because she then visited every house in the village making sure that everyone was safe.

A few days after this, my mother became involved in the aftermath of a raid in Brighton – a raid my sister and I might also have been caught up in, but for there being a change of plans that day.

On Saturday afternoons, it had been our custom, for quite some time, for my mother to take my sister, Jill, and myself to the pictures at the 'Little Odeon' in Kemptown, Brighton to see whatever was on. This was usually a double bill programme, and it was quite rare, in those days, that they were showing anything that wasn't suitable for children to go and see, either on their own or accompanied by an adult. It was nick-named 'Little Odeon' because there was another larger Odeon in Brighton as well. We always sat upstairs in the two and threepenny seats. On Saturday September 14th 1940, my mother told my sister and me that there would be no pictures that day because she was going to visit a friend who had just been discharged from hospital after an

74

operation, to convalesce at home. She said that she didn't want us to go on our own, even if she could make sure that we got in alright – her friend lived in a street not far from the cinema. We were disappointed, but there would be other Saturdays.

That afternoon, a friend and myself were the only ones in the top gardens in Sussex Square. We ambled over to the northeasterly corner of the gardens where the mulberry tree was, to see what fruit there was in the middle of it. "There's one or two in that corner over there," I pointed to where there were several branches with just a few berries on them; I was about to tell my friend that I would go first – when the explosion came; a huge terrifying noise! My friend screamed, and immediately started running for the gate on her side of the square; she had her emergency key with her. I ran for the opposite gate, which I knew I could quickly climb over; but by the time I got there Mrs. Belfrage had opened it for me; my father was waiting anxiously on the doorstep. We quickly went indoors and downstairs to the basement, where Julian and two of the other residents were already taking shelter. After a while everything went quiet and my father left me with Mrs. Belfrage and the others and returned upstairs to our flat – "to make a phone call," he said. It had sounded as if the bombs had gone off somewhere in the direction of the part of Kemptown that my mother had gone to that afternoon. A little later I returned to our flat – everything seemed quiet now – I can't remember anything at all about sirens or all clears. I found my father with my sister, who had just returned from a friend's house in the square, trying to find out, if they could, anything about where and what had been hit, and in particular about the huge first explosion. He rang several people to find out if they had seen my mother – the friend that she was visiting wasn't on the 'phone – however, all this was to no avail. Jill was near to tears, my father red faced and very anxious, and I began to fret; but, just as I was about to burst into tears, the phone went and the sudden relieved look on my fathers face spoke for itself. I managed to suppress any outbursts as my father told us that mother was alright, and that she would be home in about an hour or so – he also told us that the Odeon cinema had received a direct hit.

A little over an hour later, she arrived home, somewhat dishevelled, but otherwise all in one piece. She and a W.V.S. lady she knew had been helping a couple of boys, who had slight injuries, up to the hospital. Immediately after the bombing, she had left her friend's flat to get home as quickly as possible, but, on being told by a passerby that the Odeon had been hit, she decided to head in that direction and see if there was anything she could do; there were other people hurrying to get there as well. When she arrived there she found that the cinema had received a direct hit. To her horror, she saw that bodies were laid out on the ground just outside it – these included some dead children. There were many people there helping, including doctors, nurses, ambulance men, air raid wardens, W.V.S. ladies and members of the general public – and what had been chaotic pandemonium, was now, slowly, coming under efficient control. An air raid warden asked my mother and the W.V.S. lady to escort one child, bleeding from high up in the leg, but still able to walk, and another slightly older boy, with cuts – who although dazed – was still able to walk to the Sussex County Hospital, no more than a hundred yards away. They arrived there to find this place also coming grimly and efficiently under control, and there seemed to be injured and shocked people everywhere. It was from the hospital that she had managed to get to a 'phone to let us know she was alright. After delivering the two boys to the hospital she had returned to the scene of devastation at the Odeon, helping where she could – all the time fiercely trying not to break down and cry for the dead and wounded – at the same time as offering countless prayers of thanks that we hadn't gone to the cinema that afternoon. An hour later, on leaving this scene of devastation, where rescue work was still going on, and would do for quite some time, she then walked back home in something of a daze – hardly believing all that happened in the course of nearly two hours of nightmare! She arrived home to one very grateful family, now all fussing around her. She sipped from a strong and soothing drink, and then the tears came – readily and deeply!

That Saturday was one of the darkest days of the war in Brighton – with 55 people killed in the cinema and various streets that had been hit by a string of bombs that had fallen in a westerly line from the Odeon cinema to Rock Gardens, about half a mile away.

There was, apart from the stories of the exemplary behaviour of all who were there to help, one particularly uplifting story that quickly spread around. Three small boys, with a small amount of change in their pockets, were on their way to the cinema that afternoon, but on the way there they stopped to buy something to eat during the show. When they got to the cinema they discovered they hadn't got enough money left to get in – so they went back home! If they had got in, they would have been sitting somewhere in the front stalls – which was the part of the cinema where the worst of the casualties were!

The day after the bombing of the Odeon, was what is now recognised as Battle of Britain Day – 15th September. On that day the Germans lost over fifty aircraft and, from then on, the daytime raids lessened considerably – the Battle of Britain had been won. However, as the beautiful autumn headed towards winter, and the night bombings began in earnest, for many, this would be the most terrifying time of all, with London, particularly the east end, becoming the prime target – at the beginning of what would be called 'The Blitz!'

Chapter Six

Sirens – Blitz – 'Hopefully Shelter!'

By the autumn of 1940, although a third of a million troops had been rescued from the beaches of Dunkirk, and the Battle of Britain had been won, the threat of the home shores being invaded was still very real and, with the Luftwaffe beginning a concentrated campaign of bombing at night, the whole situation gave the public the uncomfortable feeling that anything might happen at any time. However, whilst the extreme vigilance of the population of the UK wasn't relaxed for a moment at this time, work and life in general continued as normally as possible.

In Kent, during September, the hop picking carried on as it had done for countless years beforehand, with families from the East End of London going down to the farms for their annual working holidays – a time they thoroughly looked forward to, from year to year. During the several weeks it took to get the hops off the bines and into the oasts, they lived in huts provided by the farmers. This was always an enjoyable time for them – something completely different to their normal ways of life. However, during the 'hopping' of 1940 they had the added 'distraction' of frequent aerial battles being fought out in the skies above them – sometimes witnessing aircraft being brought down, with parachutists landing in nearby fields.

Betty Collins (now Rhodes) was fourteen years of age at that time; she had been born on one of the three farms owned by her father and three uncles (the Collins Brothers) who farmed at Yalding and Marden in Kent – the heart of the hop country. Betty told me, they used to get the same pickers from the East End of London each year. Two well remembered families being the Colleys and the Marks from Canning Town in the East End, who were there, as normal, with their young families in 1940. Their husbands, if they weren't in the forces, carried on working at their jobs in London and came down and visited them at weekends. This particular year though, they were keener than ever to get away from their homes and get some respite from the bombing – which towards the end of 'hopping time' was getting horrific. Betty said, "At the end of the 1940 hopping season, quite a few of the families

78

refused to leave the huts and stayed on for several more weeks – despite the cold, dark nights. One family stayed throughout the whole of the winter, having been told by relatives and friends, just how bad things were in the area they lived in."

In the east end, particularly the dockland areas, the bombing was soon to increase to such devastating proportions that, to boost morale, the worst hit areas were sometimes visited by the King and Queen, Winston Churchill or other high up dignitaries – 'Helping to keep the peoples' spirits up!' The W.V.S. found themselves having to appeal for unwanted clothing and blankets from outside their area, in order to help those who had been bombed out and had literally 'lost everything.' They also helped in the nightmare job of re-homing many of the bombed out, as did other voluntary services, including the A.R.P. Mobile canteens, run by various organisations – in particular the WVS – were soon being driven through the rubbled streets to help refresh those digging amongst the newly bombed out places, searching for survivors but never knowing quite what they might find, in an increasingly horrific but essential job.

For many, the nights became unbearable and they desperately sought out other places to shelter at – places with at least some guarantee of safety.

One 'safe area' in particular, that was away from the worst of the bombing and which offered good protection, even if areas close to them were being bombed, were the caves at Chislehurst, in Kent. If you were to explore every nook and cranny of these caves you would have to walk several miles to do so. They were dug out a long time ago, when chalk mining went on at Chislehurst – the earliest recorded reference to this being in a Saxon charter and written between 1250 and 1274. Since then, the caves have had many uses, and the area became particularly fashionable in 1871, when the exiled Emperor Napoleon III and Princess Eugenie took up residence at nearby Camden Place and were visited by Queen Victoria. In the First World War the caves became an overflow for Woolwich Arsenal, for the storage of ammunition and explosives – made easier to get to by the close proximity of the railway. The caves were ideal to ensure minimal damage in case of an accidental explosion, and the storage was helped by a narrow gauge railway with battery driven electric locomotives, which ferried the munitions to and from the deepest recesses of the caves. From 1933 until 1939, mushroom farming was carried on here, but from September 7th 1940, when the heavy aerial onslaught on London had begun, more peoples' attention turned towards the caves for shelter, and the handful of people who had sheltered in the entrance to the caves during the earliest raids, quickly increased in number, with people arriving by train, bus, lorry, car and on foot.

At first conditions underground were of the simplest – people slept on the bare earth, in deck chairs or anything else they had managed to bring with them. The only light came from candles, torches and oil lamps. Water came from a single tap and sanitation was an oil drum or dustbin, containing a little creosote. The caves committee, made up of volunteers, worked with a will and very soon there was electric lighting, entertainment and evening classes, with strict discipline monitored by the cave captains.

With the caves now becoming a recognised place for people to spend complete nights safely, even more facilities were quickly added. The Red Cross opened a fully staffed medical centre and the W.V.S. ran a busy canteen; for spiritual uplift, there was literally 'A Cathedral of the Rocks' – complete with its own choir – the caves even had their own Scouts, Guides and Brownies.

One of the people who helped to keep the discipline, as a cave captain, was my 'eventual' father-in-law, George Barman, who, with his wife, Hilda, and young daughters, Pamela, aged six – in later years to become my wife – and Brenda, just two years of age, had now started using the caves instead of remaining in their flat at Bellingham, which was one of many areas that were receiving quite a lot of attention from the bombers. Pam told me – "I remember being told I was going to sleep in a big cave, because it was safe there from the bombs – I think I was both frightened and excited by what sounded like being some kind of a new adventure. The first time that we went there, we got onto a lorry which had seats, in two lines, in the back of it and this became our transport, to and fro to the caves, during the next year or so – the man who drove and owned the lorry was really a banana wholesaler, but there were no bananas coming into the country at this time, so this helped him to make a living at that time.

My father was always busy whilst there – helping other people and making sure that everything was alright in our section. I remember playing with some other children there, but mum kept a good lookout for me and always kept Brenda with her. Apart from this, I remember queuing up for soup at the W.V.S. canteen, and also remember when Brenda fell over and cut herself and had to be taken to the Red Cross Post, but it was nothing serious. However, I do remember that a girl got killed whilst climbing the 'cliffs' outside the caves, it was very sad.

I think that being an animal lover, the thing I remember most clearly about the caves, were the ponies that used to pull small carts for carrying the bins of waste from the toilets; whenever we could, we made quite a fuss of them – they seemed to be very well treated."

In 1942, Pamela and her family moved to a cottage on a farm at Eynsford, a lovely village in the Kent countryside – away from the worst of the bombing. Nonetheless, even there, the Luftwaffe didn't exactly ignore them and, during one bad spell of enemy activity, Hilda and the girls went to stay with relatives in Lancashire. During this time, Pam's father remained on the farm, but when they were all back together again, it wasn't long before the two girls had to give up their bedroom and sleep with their parents – their own room being commandeered by two Land Girls – but more of that later in the book.

A few days after the bombing of the Odeon, in Brighton, there had been another bad raid; this time the Edward Street area had been badly hit – about a mile away from us in Sussex Square. In this raid eleven people had been killed – including a family of five. A friend of my mother's, who had just joined the W.V.S., helped out here together with another member, as well as people from the general public, who just volunteered their help alongside the A.R.P., police, nurses and ambulance staff. The W.V.S. found themselves very much involved in finding shelter for those made homeless in this raid – who, for the time being, found themselves alongside others who had been made homeless after the Odeon raid, the previous Saturday – all of these bomb damage victims were sheltered temporarily in local public halls.

One of the volunteers who helped in trying to clear debris and rescue victims after this latest bombing was Mr. G.P. (Bundy) Burstow, a master at nearby Brighton College Junior School, who had also joined the Auxiliary Fire Brigade, during the war years, and who would later on be one of the masters to try to get some sense in my head, on the various subjects that he taught. He later told some of us that they had carried on searching for victims well into the night after the raid, which had occurred in the middle of the evening of September 18th.

During these desperate times, there were quite a few people who went 'beyond the call of duty' and who were duly recognised for their bravery. One particular lady, who found it her natural duty to help others, especially sick children, was Grace Rattenbury, who had joined the W.V.S. just after it had been founded, and who had found herself suddenly caught up in one of the most devastating raids on London's dockland; she even found herself helping firemen injured in the line of duty – "On that never to be forgotten day."

It was the day that the Luftwaffe had changed tactics; the W.V.S. had received an urgent request for blankets for the bombed out and wounded in the Bermondsey and Rotherhithe areas. Although it was her Saturday off, she agreed to go – leaving off at just after 5 p.m. in the W.V.S. van she often drove through the bombed streets of the East End. On arrival at Bermondsey, Grace found the dockland areas were ablaze, and she immediately joined in with others to help wherever she could. First she had been sent to a block of flats which was nearly completely cut off by flames. In a desperate fight against time and with bombs still falling on the area, she helped evacuate those that lived there – including many children. With the light fading and with no time to stop to even consider her own safety, she carried on working furiously – eventually staying in the area all night, driving through burning streets and helping wherever she could. Through that frightening night, with the bombs seemingly raining down incessantly, Grace still didn't stop to take a break – "It was impossible to, the devastation was beyond belief, and you just had to carry on." She was later to tell a colleague.

During that 'night to remember,' she not only kept bringing out families from the bombed buildings and taking them to safer areas, where they were given shelter – but also helped firemen and policemen who had been injured whilst fighting the flames.

Charles Graves, in his book, 'Women in Green' wrote about her, saying – 'it was probably the first time that a woman had ever been tested under such appalling conditions. She was not a person of great physical strength, and the strain must have been very severe. The van, on her return to base, was full of steel helmets, blood soaked bandages, a fireman's axe, and other marks of a very heavy night's work.' For her bravery, Grace was to receive the George Medal.

With the change of tactics by the Luftwaffe, and with the air raids becoming ever more frequent – particularly, at this time, in the south east – there were quite a few more stories of people who, in their roles as volunteers, had gone 'beyond the call of duty' in helping others.

One of these was a young lady called Rose Ede, who lived in the village of Wadhurst in East Sussex. One night, a string of four HE bombs had landed on the village, with a farmhouse receiving a direct hit. The adults in the house were instantly killed, but three children remained trapped in the debris. Mr. & Mrs. Ede and their daughter, Rose, still a teenager, were the first on the scene and, hearing the cries of the children, they quickly succeeded in rescuing two of them – but a baby remained trapped under the wreckage of an upstairs room. By this time other volunteers had arrived on the scene, but, as Rose Ede was the smallest of all those present, she quickly volunteered to crawl under the beams of the house – which, now being totally unstable, could have crushed her at any moment. She worked furiously for over half an hour in trying to get to the child through the debris. Eventually, she managed to reach the baby – which she then began moving, inch by inch, to safety, all the time trying to comfort him as she did so. All this time she'd been working in almost complete darkness, the only glint of light coming from a hole in the bombed roof. The rescue wasn't made any easier by the rain, which was pouring through the hole – and all the more frightening because she could still hear the sounds of what she thought were enemy planes, overhead. For her gallant night's work, Rose Ede was awarded the George Medal.

Another lady who showed little concern for her own safety, during an air raid over Sherborne in Dorset, was Maude Steele, who was the supervising telephonist at the telephone exchange there at that time. During what was described as 'a horrific raid,' she managed to make sure that vital communications were kept open. She too was awarded the George Medal – receiving it from His Majesty King George VI at Buckingham Palace on 27th May 1941. Her citation, which was also printed in the London Gazette is as follows:

'A heavy air bombardment caused many casualties and extensive damage. Miss Steele was in charge of the telephone exchange at the time and showed distinct courage and devotion to duty, at the risk of personal danger, by refusing to leave the exchange, although bombs were falling all around the building. By her action, and that of the temporary telephonist, who remained with her and whom she inspired by her courageous attitude, police, fire and air raid precaution services were kept in constant touch with their respective headquarters, and other resources were maintained until the majority of the local lines were put out of action and the exchange became untenable. Even so, when a heavy bomb exploded within the post office precincts, Miss Steele proceeded from the refuge room to the exchange, hoping she might still be of service. She was magnificent in the face of real danger, and by her courageous action contributed in no small measure to the effective and efficient working of the Air Raid Precautions and other services. She remained in the exchange until the position became absolutely impossible, and even then she was reluctant to leave in case she could be of further assistance.'

During the time that all these air raids were going on, with the fire brigades, A.R.P., Red Cross and, of course, the hard pressed Women's Voluntary Service, all working flat out in the blitzed areas, there was also, still, the very real fear of the home shores being invaded at any time.

So, around the coastline of the UK, the coastguards and coastwatchers were also staying more than usually vigilant at this time. One particular group of volunteers, who suddenly found themselves very much involved in a major incident, were the Roker Volunteer Life Brigade at Sunderland – an organisation that had been involved in countless rescue operations, dating back to the end of the 18th century.

On the 17th October 1940, The Roker Volunteer Life Brigade was to set a world record for the number of people rescued by breeches buoy in an amazing rescue operation, just off from the village of Whitburn, near Sunderland – a record that still stands. I have received two reports about this incident; the first from Captain Fred Roberts of The Sunderland Volunteer Life Brigade and the second one from Mary Stephenson on behalf of her husband, Arthur Stephenson, who at that time was 19 years old and working in the local limestone quarries, before volunteering to join the Royal Navy a few months later.

Captain Roberts report, in conjunction with Steve Landells of The South Shields Volunteer Life Brigade, says:

'In October 1940, the new battleship 'H.M.S. King George V' was nearing completion at Vickers-Armstrong yard at Walker – she was to leave the river and sail to Scapa Flow, so a flotilla of six destroyers were sent, along with cruisers, to escort her. Counter measures against German acoustic and magnetic sea mines had not yet been perfected, so the six destroyers made a fast run down the course, which the battleship was to follow. The idea being that their disturbance would explode any of the new mines, while their speed would carry them clear of any explosion – the destroyers 'H.M.S. Electra', 'Brilliant' and the F Class 'Fame' (H 78) and the new tribal class 'Ashanti' (G 51), 'Maori' & 'Sikh' made the run, not knowing why they were doing it, nor the ship which they were supposed to escort, all in the interest of tight wartime security. Unfortunately, a navigation buoy off the Tyne had been moved and the Admiralty charts had not been amended to suit, so, at 4.00 a.m. in murky drizzle, the lead ship, 'Fame,' ran ashore at Whitburn at almost full speed. '*Ashanti*', right astern of her, managed to reverse her engines before striking '*Fame*' a glancing blow at 7 knots, ending up ashore alongside her. The shock ruptured oil fuel pipes in both ships' engine rooms and '*Fame*' caught fire. The next ship in line, '*Maori*', also went ashore, but managed to get off again with just the loss of her asdic dome. The other ships managed to stop in time. The defence post onshore, thinking that the invasion had started, raised the alarm, but the morning light found the two ships high and dry – Roker V.L.B. arrived on scene at 5.00 a.m. and national fire service crews from South Shields were put on board by means of V.L.B's breeches buoy, pumps and equipment being manhandled over the rocks to tackle the fire on '*Ashanti*'. The rising tide showed both ships to be well aground and the swell caused bottom damage to both ships, releasing large quantities of fuel oil into the sea. Equipment and stores were jettisoned but the ships would not refloat. By 9.30 p.m. it was clear that the ships were not going to get off and one of them started to heel over, so, assisted by about 200 soldiers, Roker V.L.B. started to take off the crew from '*Ashanti*'. South Shields V.L.B.'s equipment had also been brought along by some of their team and it was set up to '*Fame*'. The two teams brought 272 men ashore – Sunderland 186 and South Shields 86 – in a period of about five hours; the teams being on duty for 32 hours all told – this was with the ever present danger of German air raids on the ships. This rescue, never publicised because of wartime censorship, was, and still is a world record for the number of people rescued by breeches buoy in a single wreck service. It took two weeks to refloat the two destroyers, still under intense security, but both were eventually repaired and returned to service. "*King George V*" meanwhile made her trip to Scapa Flow almost unescorted.'

In his letter to me, written on his behalf by his wife, Mary, Arthur Stephenson, who witnessed these rescue operations, says – 'I remember well the night of October 17th 1940, when the destroyers, '*Fame*' and '*Ashanti*', ran aground at Whitburn. It was a dark, misty night, the weight of autumn seemed to hang in the air and, in the blackout of war, no light pierced the gloom of this village by the sea – making it a night to seek your bed early and hope for a better day tomorrow.

No one dreamed that a small piece of wartime history was steaming towards us at full speed ahead, in the shape of six destroyers heading for the river Tyne, in order to escort the new battleship '*King George V*' to Scapa Flow. Owing to a vital navigational buoy being moved and the lacking of chart corrections, Whitburn villagers were awakened by such noise and confusion ensuing from the sea, as to believe that the long expected invasion was imminent!

Families were gathered together by women, whose husbands were at work in the mine, young babies were placed in prams, sleepy children, family pets and aged parents clustered together as food and necessities for possible evacuation were collected ready to await instructions as to their immediate circumstances. All this was punctuated by shouts and running feet as uniformed men headed towards the cliff tops and the unknown. Daylight, however, brought the knowledge that invasion was not the cause of their distress, but the fact that two destroyers had run aground beside the rifle range in a bay, known locally as 'The Coal Hole.'

By this time the Roker Volunteer Life Saving Brigade were on hand to give assistance. Helped by the Shields V.L.S.B. and 200 military men from around the area, the rescue began.

Unable to fire a rocket on account of oil spillage, communication was established from the destroyer and secured by Captain B. Robinson and Brigadesman W. Burton, wading into the sea and securing a line between ship and shore – then began the task of taking men off the 'Fame' which was on fire and put aboard A.F.S. firefighters. An attempt was made at 3 p.m. to refloat the vessels on the rising tide, which unfortunately failed. Another failed attempt was made at 9.30.

During daylight hours there was always the chance of air raids that were commonplace in the area at that time, for our security Bren Guns were set in place, and a rest hut was also put at the V.L.S.B's disposal.

At 2 a.m. the order was given to abandon ship as the sea was worsening and one of the vessels was in danger of heeling over. The V.L.S.B. was instrumental in the rescue of 272 men, 186 by the Roker V.L.S.B. and 86 by the South Shields V.L.S.B. – it is my belief that this record still stands.

Most of the crews of the 'Ashanti' & 'Fame' were accommodated in and around Whitburn while work went on day and night to repair the vessels enough to be refloated a fortnight later and taken into the local rivers where they were refitted and almost rebuilt.

Was it good luck that made it possible for these much needed vessels to be able to run again or was it good workmanship, courage in adversity, or loyalty? The enemy had a fortnight to target these destroyers and Whitburn lived in fear of an air raid. Remember the old wartime slogan of 'Careless talk costs lives,' I like to think that the villagers were aware of this as it is only now that this and many other instances are being told.

With the air raids continuing and even becoming more consistent and widespread, communications between the A.R.P. posts in the towns and cities became very important and one person who showed considerable foresight during the early days of the war, was Councillor Gillman, of West Ham, in the soon to be hard hit east end of London. He reasoned that in the event of there being air raids, normal communications might break down, and he proposed that a way of keeping them going would be to use cyclists. He had proposed his ideas to West Ham A.R.P. controller, Mr. M.C. Bennett, who also happened to be the Mayor at that time – Mr. Bennett had then put out the following request in the search for volunteers:

'It has been proposed by Councillor Gillman that in our present state of war, inasmuch as our chief concern in West Ham is the protection of our citizens, he should organise a Volunteer Corps of Cyclist Messengers. Their job will be one of the most difficult and dangerous in the Borough; in short, it will be to take messages through the streets during an air raid, however fierce, whenever required.

Councillor Gillman wants to make it very clear, that he only wants "daredevils," who are prepared to give all and ask for nothing in return, and Councillor Gillman went on to say that volunteers would have to provide their own bicycles and that although protective equipment would be provided, there would be no compensation for damaged bikes. He said – "It should be emphasized that we must be able to absolutely rely on those who volunteer to be there on their appointed duty time, as the lives of our people, and perhaps their own relatives, depends on such cyclists being at their posts – age for volunteers must not be less than seventeen years."

When the bombing started, 'Gillman's Daredevils,' as they quickly became known as, soon became very successful and very much relied upon. They did enormous service in the east end, keeping communications going, during the most terrifying air raids. Many other areas soon started using the same system – it was an excellent way of keeping A.R.P. Posts and other vital services in touch with each other during raids.

However, the minimum age of seventeen wasn't always kept to; there were plenty of younger people eager to join in in this 'exciting project' – even Boy Scouts in some places.

In the midlands, in the West Bromwich area, Charity Bick was decidedly underage for such a job – but she carried out her duties so bravely on one particular occasion, it earned her The George Medal.

Although only fourteen years of age, she had gone with her father, William Bick, to enroll in her local group of Messenger Cyclists. On getting there they discovered that the minimum age, for this area, was sixteen, so Charity lied about her age and, with her father also lying and backing her up, she was readily accepted – she looked sixteen, in any case!

On the night of a big raid in November 1940, Charity found herself the sole link between the wardens' post in Sam's Lane and the Control Centre, at the Town Hall a mile away.

During this raid, incendiary bombs had been dropped so as to guide the heavy bombers where to aim at, and it was thought that untrained civilians might help in putting these out. Charity and her father saw incendiaries landing on the roofs of nearby houses and, with stirrup pumps, put them out. One incendiary went through the roof of a pawnbroker's shop – they had to climb on top of a small false roof space to get at it – it was tricky, but Charity's father handed her a bucket of water and she managed to put the fire out. However, as she returned to the window she had got out of the roof gave way and she landed in a bedroom below – hitting her back on the bedrail of the large bed. Throughout the rest of that night, she tried not to show that she was in considerable pain from this – in case she was sent home!

By this time, with most of the telephone lines down, Charity was sent, by bicycle, to and fro to the control centre with messages – cycling through fires that seemed to be everywhere and with the bombs still raining down. She often fell flat in the gutter when a bomb exploded close to her – and then carried on again.

In the citation for her George Medal, she was called an A.R.P. Despatch Rider – unofficially, she was the youngest person to be awarded this medal!

(a) Evacuees at Glyndebourne – 'Lovely Summer.'

(b) Evacuees at Glyndebourne – 'Busy In The Winter.'

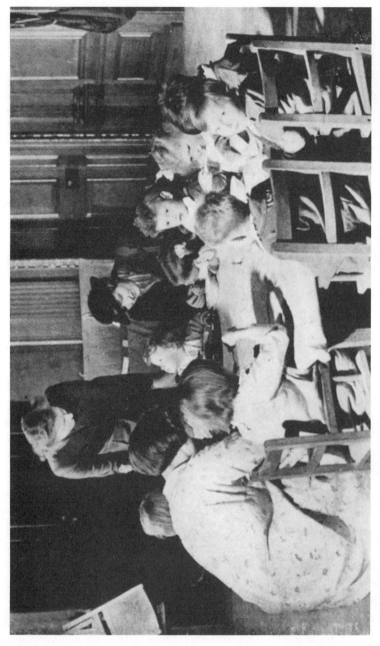

W.V.S receiving nurseries, through which many children were evacuated from London to war nurseries in the country.

Auxiliary Fire brigade on the River Medway at Rochester – 'Call Out Drill.'

Reinforce the West Door at Rochester Cathedral
'Before The Air Raids.'

The Tug 'Challenge', who helped towing at Dunkirk and then also helped with the Maunsell Towers for defences on the Thames Estuary. Later helped to tow Mulberry Harbours at D-Day.

(a) *'Sundowner'* – Back from 60th Anniversary at Dunkirk – 2000.

(b) *'Sun XII'* – Albert Barnes sent on this tug to Dunkirk – as a cabin boy!

(a) Dorothy Parker – one of the founder members of Margate Ambulance Corps and helped when the troops came back from Dunkirk.

(b) Dot Weeden – A.R.P.

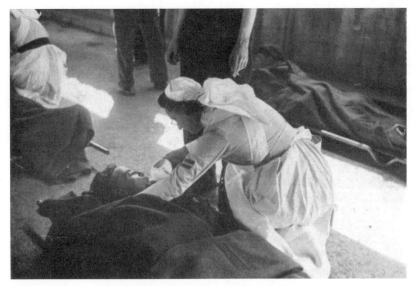

(a) Red Cross Nurses help the wounded men on Stretchers on the quays at a Kent coast – after Dunkirk.

(b) Service with a smile at Headcorn Station, Kent.
The trains go through the country to army camps – After Dunkirk.

(a) Bombed Odeon Kemptown, Brighton, September 14th – 1940.

(b) Thomas Butcher, in Home Guard uniform outside his home in
Fletching, Sussex.

(a) Dorothy White, George Medal, Red Cross at Horsham.
('Nanny White' second from left in back row).

(b) Miss P.G. Greason – a National Fire Service Despatch Rider,
handing a message to local commander G.H. Robinson, at Chatham.

Chapter Seven

'Moonlight Sonata' In The Midlands – The Story Of Coventry.

Amongst those who were planning the forthcoming raids by the Luftwaffe, it must have been someone with a warped sense of humour who thought up the codename 'Moonlight Sonata,' for the bombings of the industrial midlands, including Birmingham and Coventry – planned to commence sometime near to the middle of November.

The Luftwaffe were ordered to 'give a huge blow' to the industrial midlands – in particular to the city of Coventry. This city, renowned since the 1840's for its engineering and finely crafted metal products, had already had its 'baptism of fire' in a raid on October 10th.

During this raid, Betty Quinn, of The St. Johns Ambulance Brigade had also won a George Medal for her bravery. She was serving at an ARP post when a shower of incendiary bombs fell in her district. Without waiting for assistance she ran outside to see what she could do to help. At the time, A.A. Batteries were putting up a heavy barrage and shrapnel was falling all around. When bombs began falling, Betty soon found herself in the thick of things, and was quick to help a man who was injured by one of the bombs, to get to a public shelter. Soon, a report came in about a direct hit on an Anderson shelter. On hearing this, Betty, knowing exactly where it was, ran all the way there and commenced digging in the crater with a spade. She remained there digging – with other people eventually joining her – until seven people had been got out of the debris, in which they had been trapped. She then attended to their injuries, and stayed with them until an ambulance had taken them all away – all the time, with shells bursting overhead. She then returned to her post and carried on with her duties, which mainly consisted of helping distressed people.

The most devastating raid on Coventry – indeed one of the most devastating raids of the war – came on 14th November 1940.

Although there had been predictions that the midlands would probably be badly hit that night, because of probable clear skies making it ideal for the bombers, Coventry, unlike London, had received no 'prior warning' until the raid was upon them.

99

Just before the raid, The Motor Cycle Despatch Riders of the 12th City Battalion of The Home Guard had arrived at their headquarters, Grove House, on the Tamworth Road. A full moon was beaming ominously down as the riders stood in groups outside the guardroom, smoking cigarettes or munching sandwiches. Presently, Vernon Muslin, the officer in charge, emerged from the guardroom saying, "We had better get ready men – I've just had a 'phone call from the RAF plotting room at Keresley Grange and there's a big bomber force heading this way – it could be either Coventry or Birmingham, but they don't know which."

Vernon went inside, leaving his men engaged in animated talk on the probable outcome. Ten minutes later, the sinister wail of the air raid sirens commenced and a sudden silence fell as conversation was cut short, all ears straining for the sound of approaching aircraft as the last dying moan of the sirens was replaced by the eerie, muted throbbing of engines. Suddenly, all hell broke loose as the anti aircraft guns opened up, followed by the distant thump of bursting shells.

An urgent call from Col. Pugh, the Home Guard zone commander, requested four dispatch riders to go the Spon End Water Works, the zone headquarters, on standby. Hurriedly stubbing out their cigarettes, the four riders jumped on their motorbikes and roared off down the Tamworth Road. As the raid developed, a red glow could be seen over the city, and the phone calls, in quick succession, asked for riders to be sent to key points in the city.

The conditions were perfect for the bombers to do their worst – the moon was full and extremely bright.

The first bombs to fall, badly affected the city's supply routes and life was suddenly brought to a standstill. Public services, such as electricity, gas, telephones, even water supplies were put out of action – it was absolute pandemonium. "A bloody nightmare!" One Coventry man told me.

The late Albert Fearn, a member of a civilian rescue party, had also had his 'baptism of fire' in raids on the city. Albert, a bricklayer was particularly strong – one of his feats of strength was to lift 1 cwt. bag of cement above his head – with one hand! Their team had been put on twelve-hour shifts – they were quite often sent out on rescue work to nearby villages and towns, even as far as Birmingham.

The rescue party that Albert was in, had been given a big eight cylinder American car – with 'De Soto' written on the bonnet. There were seats for eight, a tow bar and a big purpose built trailer hitched onto the back – with the word 'RESCUE' painted in red on either side of it.

On November 14th, with the population more or less resigned to the fact that the weather conditions would probably guarantee a raid that night, Albert noticed that there was already quite an exodus of people making for the open country and hopeful safety. He said, " – some walked, a lot cycled and a few left in cars – I remember remarking to a mate that, at this rate, and if there was a raid, we'd have no customers left to rescue!"

This is Albert's own description of that night, which first appeared in a Coventry Evening Telegraph special publication, and which his son, George, has given me permission to include in this book.

"It was a cold, sharp night. The purple alert came by 'phone just before six thirty in the evening. Raiders had crossed the coast. The red alert followed soon, then the wail of the sirens.

I stood watching the fascinating spectacle of German planes ringing the air with brilliant flares, hanging almost motionless in the cloudless sky and then shooting down the balloons, which fell to earth in balls of fire. It didn't seem like war, more like a scene from a gigantic stage show. Soon the bombs and incendiaries began to fall.

Almost immediately our 'phone rang. Proceed immediately to Brympton Road, about 200 to 300 yards away, so we went on foot to do what we could at the site where three houses had been demolished. We worked to recover five bodies before returning to our depot to answer the next call. It was to some underground shelters on Gosford Green, between Humber Road and the railway line, which had suffered a direct hit. Ironically, on this night of all nights, our vehicle was unable to start so we took to our bikes.

What a strange sight we must have looked; six cyclists, helmets on, carrying crowbars, shovels, ropes and torches, riding along completely deserted roads in the brilliant glare from the hundreds of fire bombs which littered the grass verges and roads. The magnesium burned with a curious brightness as we dodged among it. A man up a ladder in Stoke Park called for us to help put out a fire on his roof, but we yelled that we couldn't help.

On reaching the shelters, a warden took us to where a man was buried up to his chest in wet clay. Getting behind him and locking my arms under his arms and, using my leg strength, I sucked him clear, leaving his Wellingtons behind. He was moaning and had head injuries, which he must have sustained when he hit some props. I asked a First Aid man to attend to him but was upset when the man pronounced him dead without checking him over. In the heat of the moment I tore him off a strip, but when the First Aider checked again, he was indeed, dead. I heard later the man had been rolled in a blanket and left for four days and nights under a bench in an undamaged part of the shelter as no vehicle could get near owing to the roads being blocked with rubble and impassable with bomb craters. There was also a boy missing and known to be in the shelter – we searched off and on for weeks, right into December, even having the water pumped out, but he was never found – He could still be down there for all I know.

On returning to the depot from the shelters on Gosford Green our next call out was to the bottom of Momus Boulevard, on the corner of Bromleigh Drive, where a bomb had dropped. By then, it was getting very difficult even to cycle round the town, as the bikes were continually getting tangled up in the wires which were lying everywhere. The bomb had hit a bungalow. We found a hole in a wooden fence where a man had been blown straight through. We found him on the lawn at the other side choking in his own blood; I turned him face down – we couldn't help him any other way – I never heard anything else about him.

The bombs were still falling all around, making a most terrible noise, but the guns were beginning to fall silent.

Our phones at the depot were out of order and police messengers were bringing in news. My own feeling, at the time, was that sending a boy of 15 or 16 years of age into the carnage from Central Control, under the Council House, with a message or information, was an unnecessary risk of a young life, even though the lads themselves were quite willing to accept these, to me, quite suicidal journeys. I know for certain of one lad who was killed – and, by a weird coincidence, his name was Messenger!

Our next job was for a warden, who came to ask our assistance in freeing a young couple trapped in a house in Bolingbroke Road, off Humber Road. A young woman and man were sitting in front of the fire when the house next door was hit. It was now about 5.30 a.m., and they had been there for several hours. The dividing wall between the two houses had fallen over onto them and the old metal fireplace crushed the girl's legs against an enamel sheet. Using three crowbars, which actually bent as we applied pressure, I managed to lock my fingers round the girl's ankle and slowly drag her free. As the enamel sheet was fairly smooth, this was accomplished without doing any more injury to the girl. We left her in the house opposite – along with the man, who had been easier to release but had sustained more injuries and died later from them. We did not know their names – we should have found them out for our records but never did.

It was now broad daylight, or it would have been, but for the pall of smoke which hung over the whole of the City and outlying districts. I believe the all-clear sounded between 6.30 and 7 a.m. and by now the whole of Coventry was in chaos. I had been on duty for some 30 hours and tried to get a message to my wife that I was still safe. I was walking up from the Gaumont Cinema towards the Council House, which was still standing among the devastation. I got quite disoriented as I stood among the debris and smoke trying to get my bearings. A butcher spoke to me, asking my opinion as to opening his shop for business. He must have been the supreme optimist – as the shop next door was burning merrily and the flames were already licking round the blinds of his shop!

It was strange how the Council House escaped serious damage, being so close to the Cathedral. Even now you can see the shrapnel and bomb markings on the stone.

At the top of Hertford Street, I met my brother-in-law Edwin Briggs, who is now a St. John's Superintendent, and was on duty at the time. He promised to let my wife Olive know what was happening. Unfortunately, what I didn't know was that he was kept on duty for another 12 hours, while my wife frantically toured around the city on a borrowed bicycle trying to contact our rescue party to find out if I was safe.

Our help was needed everywhere. A long narrow street opposite Robbins' Motor Showrooms in Cox Street, ran up to the Cathedral wall. We joined a party who were working on a bombed house right beside the Cathedral wall – a municipal car park stands there now. We uncovered two children – both dead – their mother and father were both there, being restrained by a policeman from rushing back. I held up the removal of the little bodies while trying to get the parents removed from the scene. They were hoping against hope – I felt furious at the whole thing – the feelings inside me have never been forgotten!"

For his actions during this and other raids, Albert Fearn was awarded the George Medal, and received this from His Majesty King George VI on May 27th 1941.

During that night, the fire brigade had been stretched to well beyond anything they had been trained for, but had reacted magnificently, and although there must be many individual stories of extreme gallantry here, many of these will never be told, as 36 firemen lost their lives that night.

However, through the help of one of the present day serving firemen, Danny Moynihan, who is station officer at the city's Radford Road fire station, I have been able to include the following extracts from a report submitted by the chief fire officer of that time (Mr. W.H. Cartwright, M.I.Fire. E.).

'FOLLOWING THE ENEMY AIR ATTACK ON THE CITY ON 14th/15th NOVEMBER 1940'

'The yellow message was received at 7.05 p.m., the purple at 7.08 p.m. and the red warning at 7.10 p.m. Action commenced quickly in brilliant moonlight, and the first fire was reported at 7.24 p.m. Throughout the night there was no perceptible lull in the attack, and the white message was received at 6.16 a.m. on the 15th November.

Within the first five minutes a gas main was fired in the central part of the city, providing a beacon for early raiders. Fifty-six calls were recorded in the first half-hour, and many of the fires called for three and five pumps as first attendance, and few were single pump jobs.

Previous experience of large scale raids had been that fires, in the early stages, were confined to one or two districts, due to what would appear to have been the result of a straight run across the City. The tactics employed on this occasion must have differed in-as-much as in the first half hour there were fires in six widely separated districts, fortunately, the local organisation was based on six zones with which the outbreaks roughly coincided, and, therefore, it was possible to bring pumps into operation quickly at all the early fires.

First stage (in and out of the district) of the Regional Scheme was operated at 7.40 p.m. – sixteen minutes after the first call. At this time all the fires were being controlled, but at 7.59 p.m. it was felt that the attack was developing on a large scale and Second Stage (in and out) was operated. By now seventy on calls had been received and all the local pumps were in action, and First Stage assistance was only just beginning to arrive. Thirty pumps from Stage Three and two turntable ladders were requested at 8.02 p.m., as it was then apparent that the raid was unusually heavy.

The intensity of the bombardment increased and all the reports indicated that the attack was of an unprecedented nature for a provincial town. Incendiary bombs, explosive incendiaries, oil bombs, high explosives of all calibers, parachute mines and flares were all being used. This "all-type" bombardment continued throughout the night, whereas in previous raids incendiaries had been used only in the early stages followed by high explosives. Many large factories, stores and serious risks were involved, and initial calls for assistance indicated that most of the fires had secured a good hold on the first instance. Outside aid was arriving, but, owing to the swiftness of developments, not quickly enough to provide the maximum first attendance of pumps required at most outbreaks. To add to the difficulty of the operation, fires were started in the roof of the Headquarters Fire Station, after the second of which it became necessary to abandon the control room. Water from these fires caused the switchboard to become 'live,' and by 8 p.m. all the lines were out of order. The main lighting failed and the emergency lighting was badly affected.

Reports of water shortage from the town supply began to come in, and at 9.10 p.m. three heavy relaying units were requested with the remainder of Third Stage assistance. Telephone communications had now become difficult and indistinct. Static water supplies were already in use and, as the towns supply position worsened, long relay lines were introduced. The prepared dams in the River Sherbourne were used at each of ten points, and at no time did this supply fail, as fortunately, there was a very good flow in the river that night. Swimming and ornamental pools, which had been earmarked, were brought into full operation, as well as factory reservoirs. In some cases these latter had only been installed after much persuasion. The pre-arranged relaying schemes were operating satisfactorily, although blocked streets and debris necessitated diversions, and subsequent collapsing buildings called for new lines by different routes. Supplies from the canal were also utilised until it was hit by high explosives at a point at which a storm water culvert passed underneath – the sudden complete loss of water in this important section of the canal, near the centre of the City, was not explained until daylight.

At 8.47 p.m. the remainder of the telephones (except a private line to the Control Centre) were out of order for outgoing calls, and only two operated spasmodically for incoming calls. When incoming calls were received from reliable sources on these lines, the opportunity was taken to relay outgoing calls elsewhere. In this connection a line was kept open for a time to the Leamington Fire Brigade, and many calls were transmitted by that route.

At 11.15 p.m. forty more pumps were asked for, also the assistance of professional officers to replace one killed and two injured from our own Brigade.

By now the position was critical, but, having regard to the assistance on the way, did not appear to be beyond our control. Thereafter we had many difficulties with which to contend. Outside assistance was held up by road blockages at considerable distances from the Central Fire Station, and had to be marshalled and diverted. This presented almost insuperable difficulties. All available messengers and spare men were engaged in piloting and guiding out-of-town crews, but new road blockages were so frequent that traversable routes could only be found by actual trial. Even so, it was impossible for the great majority of crews to report to our stations. In the circumstances, of course, guides were instructed to take them straight to fires. In addition, many out-of-town crews found fires and got to work on their own initiative. The messenger system was used to the full extent, but it will be realised that we had a tremendous task attempting to pilot every assisting crew or convoy via innumerable diversions. The whole time there was a feeling of uncertainty regarding the safe arrival of messengers – not until each had returned to report could any satisfaction be felt.

The fires in the centre of the City eventually combined to make a single incident, and owing to the congested nature of the property, there was no alternative but to concentrate on preventing the spread of fire. In spite of attacks upon pump crews working on static supplies – which probably reflected in the moonlight and fire glare – and repeated destruction of relay lines, the spread of fire was checked with a large measure of success.

The early loss of the services of three Regular officers and several Regular men soon began to make itself felt, and meant a tremendous strain on those left. The directions of operations called for strategy and resource for which there were few previous standards to act as guidance. Fatigued and under continual bombardment, everyone worked without relief or refreshment. Times out of number fires were extinguished and buildings practically saved only for the buildings to be, partly or wholly, destroyed by fire or high explosives due to renewed attacks under the eyes of the crews making up equipment.

The number of fires recorded up to the breakdown of communications was 204 – in addition during this time, many fires were not reported, some of these being dealt with by the Police, Wardens and other services and civilians. The numerous fires, which occurred after the breakdown of the telephones, were not recorded, of course, but must have numbered several hundreds.'

Concerning the burning of the Cathedral; after the sirens had wailed the alarm, and the fire watchers and air raid wardens had quickly scurried to their posts up and down the city, the provost of Coventry Cathedral, the Very Reverend Richard Howard, lifted his tin hat from its peg and put it on as he dashed to the Cathedral – for there was no time to be lost! As he entered the dark, echoing building, a shadowy figure joined him. The dim light from the provost's hand torch showed him that it was Jock Forbes, a skilled stone mason, one of the Cathedral guard for fire watching.

"Full moon tonight Jock," the provost remarked.

"Aye, it's a raiders' moon right enough, Provost," Jock Forbes agreed. "When it's full up, it'll be like a spotlight on the city. I'm afraid we'll have trouble with the roof again tonight, sir."

"Yes, I fear it too," the Provost agreed, staring up above him, though his eye could not penetrate the gloom.

They were joined by two more watchers, Mr. W.H. Eaton and Mr. White, both younger men. These four men formed the Cathedral guard for the night – away in the starry skies the droning began.

"It looks as if we shan't have long to wait," Mr. Eaton said grimly as they took up their posts.

The Provost was worried about the roof of the Cathedral. It had been built five hundred years ago and, though it was a fine piece of workmanship, it had been made in such a way that modern fire bombs could lodge in it in unreachable places. The ceiling inside the Cathedral was flat, of beautiful oak panels that rested on huge beams that spanned the church. Above this inner ceiling, with a space of about eighteen inches between them, was an outer wooden roof supported on cross beams. The whole of it was covered in sheets of lead with their edges wrapped to each other round thin rollers of wood.

If a fire bomb managed to crash through the lead roof and come to rest on the inner ceiling, it was almost impossible to get at in that narrow space. First, the lead had to be stripped back with crowbars to give the watchers room to work the stirrup pump on the flames. By the time this was done, the roof could be well alight. The fire watchers already had experience of this in a raid a month earlier when a fire bomb had lodged in the space between roof and ceiling and started a fierce blaze which the stirrup pump could not reach. The fire brigade had arrived just in time and managed to put it out, but not before a certain amount of damage had been done.

The firewatchers made their way to the roof of the nave, the central portion of the Cathedral. The flat roof sparkled with frost in the moonlight.

"Ye'll need to watch your footing Mr. Howard," Jock Forbes warned the Provost. "These roofs will be slippery."

The drone of the aircraft grew louder, throbbing, throbbing through the sky.

"There sounds like a lot of them tonight," Mr. Eaton remarked.

The horrible beat of the enemy planes was almost overhead. A little to the north there was a sudden crash and almost at once flames leaped up into the darkness. Another crash, to the south this time, and another huge fire started. There was the heavier rumble of high explosive close at hand. Yet another fire sprang up, this time closer to the Cathedral.

"That looks like Owen Owens's store," someone remarked.

"They sound to be right overhead. It's time we took cover," the Provost decided. "We'd better step into the shelter of the spiral staircase." This was the place where they usually took cover during the worst of the raids. From the top of the spiral stone staircase that ran down from the roof of the nave of the north aisle, they could keep watch over a large part of the roof.

The whistle and crash of the falling bombs came closer and closer. Soon the horizon to the northwest was ringed with a semi-circle if light.

"This is no ordinary tip and run raid, with a few bombers. This is going to be a bigger thing," Mr. Forbes declared grimly.

It was all too plain that he was right. Soon there was a circle of fires around the centre of the city. Two of the watchers went to take up a position where they could see the roof of the south aisle.

Within the centre of the city an inferno reigned – there was the constant crash of high explosives; the roar and rumble of the buildings collapsing; clouds of dust blotting out the stars; appalling flames suddenly leaping up as the fire bombs fell and exploded; the hiss of water from many hoses; the shouts of the air raid wardens and firemen; the clatter of the ambulances; the clang of the fire engines. Within the Cathedral all was dark, silent and waiting – the watchers held their breath.

Then there was a sudden, fiendish whistle of falling bombs. Three firebombs struck the Cathedral at once. One fell on the roof near the east end – another plunged right through the roof and ceiling and fell among the pews at the head of the nave, and the third lodged in the roof of the south aisle, just above the organ. Instantly, the firewatchers sprang into action.

One of the younger men smothered with sand the bomb which had fallen on the chancel roof and, shovelling it up quickly, flung it over the battlemented wall into the Cathedral garden below, while another of the guards dashed to tackle the one which had fallen through the roof to

108

the floor of the nave. The bomb there was a large one and just beginning to blaze away among the oaken pews. Desperately, the fire watcher flung several buckets of sand over it before he could manage to extinguish it, shovel it into a scoop, and dash outside the Cathedral with it.

While all this was going on, the older fire watchers were tackling the bomb which had lodged between the roof and the ceiling. Both of them were trying feverishly to rip the leaden sheets off the roof with crowbars. Above them was the never ceasing drone of enemy aircraft and the whine of falling bombs. Below them, in the cleft just above the organ, the bomb was blazing furiously on the oak ceiling. Once the ceiling gave way, the bomb would fall into the organ itself and there would be little hope of tackling it there. Heaving and hacking at the lead roof, so that they sweated heavily, even in the frosty air, the two men managed to make a hole big enough to pour in sand, but already the roof was blazing beyond the reach of the sand.

"We must get the fire brigade at once," the Provost decided, and passed word to the police to direct the fire brigade to the Cathedral.

"Aye, we'll get one right away, as soon as possible," the police officer promised and once again began to telephone the fire brigade headquarters. The two fire watchers dashed to the roof to help with the spreading fire when they had dealt with their own bombs.

"This one will take all of us," Mr. Forbes panted, as he worked the stirrup pump.

The four men worked feverishly, directing the jet of water to the fire, pumping frantically up and down, dashing up and down the ladders to bring buckets of water from the tap in the Smith's Chapel. The tap could just fill one bucket as fast as it could be used by the stirrup pump, so the guards had barely time to draw breath as they snatched up a bucket in turn from under the tap and placed another under it to be filling while they raced up to the roof with the full one.

Suddenly, there was a loud burst of high explosive as one of the men was going down the ladder to fetch water – the blast struck him and knocked him down. He fell to the bottom of the ladder and knocked his head against the masonry – the other heard the sound of his fall and came running to help him – "Are you all right, man?" Jock called out from the top of the ladder as he saw a rather dazed figure rising to his feet again.

"Yes. I'm all right. The leather on my steel helmet took the shock." In another moment, the man was racing along with his bucket again.

All this time, the men had been working the stirrup pump and hacking back the lead sheets to let them get at the widely spreading flames. At last the fire was smothered out in the spray of stirrup pumps, but not before a large area of the roof had been burnt.

"Well, thank goodness that's out, but it took all four of us!" Mr. Forbes gasped, dashing his arms across his brow to wipe away the perspiration. "If we get more than one at a time between the roof and the ceiling, it'll be more than we can manage without more help."

Hardly had he spoken, when another shower of firebombs fell and struck the roof of the Cappers' Chapel on the south side and passed through the lead and inside the ceiling and fell in a cascade of burning pieces. As the fireguards were already on the south side, they got to work at once with stirrup pumps and sand. Through the clerestory windows one of them caught a glimpse of leaping flames on the roof of the north aisle.

"There's another bomb on the Smith's Chapel!" He exclaimed.

"I'll see to it," one of the younger men cried. "It's not gone right through the lead yet."

Only one of them could be spared to deal with this new menace, for the rest were busy tackling the bombs inside the roof of the Cappers' Chapel. Water was running short, but they managed to extinguish the blaze. In a few minutes the one who had gone to the Smith's Chapel returned.

"Luckily, the bomb had burst into fragments and the pieces hadn't gone through the roof," he explained. "I managed to put them out all right."

The fire guards were now panting for breath, perspiring profusely and almost exhausted. Beyond the Cathedral, the crash and roar of bombs was deafening and, from a hundred points in the city, flames soared upwards. Overhead, the drone of enemy planes went on and on. Hardly had the fire guard turned from one extinguished fire than there was another terrific rattle, as a further shower of fire bombs fell, four of them striking the roof of the Children's Chapel at the east end. They burst through the lead sheeting and lodged on the oaken beams, exploding into flames, and soon the roof was a raging fire. The four men dashed round the building towards it – through the holes they poured sand and water, but the fire grew fiercer as it spread.

"We've nearly used all the sand," one of the men gasped as he humped a sandbag up the ladder. "Only one or two more bags left now."

"We'll have to rely on water then," another man said, working the stirrup pump feverishly up and down. "If only the fire brigade would come."

"The fire's gaining on us!" Jock Forbes exclaimed in despair as he redoubled his efforts to smother it out with a jet of water.

"The spiral staircase is filled with smoke. We'll have to use the outside ladders now," one of the younger ones reported, coughing as he staggered up with a bucket. This meant a longer, more difficult journey to get water. The flames began to gain even a stronger hold. Though they still fought hard, the strength of the fireguards was becoming weaker with exhaustion in the face of the great heat from the flames. Four men could no longer keep those spreading fires in check. The ceiling was well ablaze.

Thick smoke drifted down into the Cathedral, to the Smith's Chapel where the water tap was. One of the younger men, undaunted, went in to fill his bucket again, but came out choking and groping for the entrance. Overcome by the smoke, he had to be assisted by one of the others. It was impossible to enter the Smith's Chapel again, so now the faithful fire watchers could get no more water to fill their buckets. There was nothing they could do now to extinguish the blazing roof, but hope and pray the fire brigade would reach them in time to save the rest of the Cathedral.

Worn out as they were, they still set about saving what treasures they could from the east end of the Cathedral, the cross and candlesticks, the silver plate and chalice and anything else they could manage to carry out before the fire should spread to the roof at the end of the church. Streaming with perspiration, they worked till the smoke and fumes drove them back. Then they went to the south porch to wait for the fire brigade to come.'

In his book 'The Gentlemen at War,' Roy Ingleton says – 'At the police station, the first warning that the Cathedral was in danger came in the form of a shout from the battlements which was relayed to the police station. The station sergeant, Walter Groom, described the incident:

' – Special Constable Marshall came in. "Sergeant," he says, "the Cathedral's on fire" – I was at the desk so I made my air raid message pad out, picked up the direct line to the fire station which was one of the old 'candlestick and snuffer' telephones – the fire station answered straight away."

"Yes, police?"

"Fire at the Cathedral."

"Right," and down went the phone. Off went Marshall – I told him. "It's been reported, let them know." A quarter of an hour later he was back again. "Sergeant, can you say when they're going to send the fire brigade up to the Cathedral? The fire's spreading to the roof." So I rang the fire station again and spoke to the officer in charge there. "All our appliances are out." He said, and of course that meant the Cathedral was doomed.

The Cathedral authorities, realising this fact, lost no time in removing some of the most valuable and historic items from the building, including the altar cross and candlesticks, the colours of the Royal Warwickshire Regiment, the altar service books and the books of the Epistles and the Gospels, all of which were conveyed to the comparative safety of the police station where Sergeant Groom saw them arrive.

A solemn little procession came into the police station. The Reverend Howard, Provost, bearing the flag of the Warwickshire Regiment, led it and there was another flag being borne in – the Union Jack. In followed Supt. Brennan, Inspector Pendleton and one or two more with pieces of silver which they had rescued from the Cathedral. The party went through the charge office and down to the C.I.D. office in the sub-basement of the Council House. Now, I have trooped the colour on Horse Guards Parade when I was in the army, but never were colours carried more reverently than they were on that occasion – '

A few hours after the raid, F.G.H. Salisbury, the Daily Herald war correspondent, at that time, had this to say:

'Coventry has been the victim of the most concentrated, if not the worst raid since the war began.

I have just come back from the centre of the city, which now looks exactly like one of those French towns that were laid level during the last war by an intensive bombardment.

The Cathedral is in ruins, except for its tower, and over a large area surrounding it there lies the stench of burning houses.

The number of casualties cannot yet be determined, but it is certainly large. (Preliminary reports says the Ministry of Home Security, indicate that the number of casualties may number 1,000) The damage which has been inflicted on this city must run into millions of pounds.

I was told by one of the inhabitants that the noise of falling bombs was practically continuous, and then after a short time everyone was literally dazed by the noise.

112

I approached the city from Rugby, a few miles out of Coventry. I encountered the first large body of refugees walking along the roadside exactly as the Belgains and French escaped from the last German invasion. Children were being carried in their fathers' arms and pushed along in perambulators. Luggage was piled high on the perambulators. There were suitcases and bundles on people's shoulders; little families trudged along hand in hand with rugs, blankets, and in fact anything they could have salved from their ruined homes. There were so many motorcars parked by the roadside, in which people would pass the night despite the intense cold. Nevertheless, those with motorcars will be luckier than those without. For despite the hospitality of surrounding towns and villages, it will have been impossible for everyone to get a bed or even a shelter. I saw several people making preparations to lie down under the leeside of buildings or against hedgerows.

Very soon after the raid began the Germans succeeded in starting their first large fire, and from then onwards they had no difficulty in sighting their targets. Fires in the centre of the city multiplied and spread rapidly despite most magnificent work by the fire brigades' auxiliary fire services and the A.R.P. – indeed, all the services which could be called out to deal with this tragedy. It was a miracle that the firemen contained the fires as they did. In one place they had to blow up a building with dynamite to check the path of the flames. Extra police and A.R.P. also rushed in. Every conceivable assistance to Coventry has been rendered by her neighbours. But nothing can minimise the appalling extent of the tragedy, which has rendered scores of thousands of people homeless and severely damaged the heart of the city.

On my way to the Cathedral, I encountered a girl of, perhaps, 12 years of age, and I asked her what was going on. The air was thick with smoke and a fire was still blazing in a house not 20 yards away.

"Oh," she said, "I'm just having a look round." I asked her where she was going to sleep that night and she replied, "Why? Here of course, we were lucky!"

"Have you got any water or gas?" I asked. "No," she said, "but we'll do some cooking on an oil stove and the water will turn up somewhere." Then she admitted with a smile that she had been very frightened last night and resumed her tour of inspection.

There was of course no work done in Coventry to-day, largely owing to the failure of the power supplies, though I understand there were some factories which manufactured their own electricity.

Nevertheless, the workmen were there ready to start again if it had been possible. This is not a mortal blow to our war production by any means, and I should not be surprised if quite soon work is resumed in Coventry to some extent.

The authorities are doing everything possible to get the homeless people and refugees out of the city into neighbouring towns and rest centres, but their main difficulty is the transport. There is nothing like enough transport for the people who wish to be moved, and the result, as I have said, is in these pathetic streams of refugees walking along the roads. Nevertheless, the spirit of the people, without any exaggeration, is magnificent – I even saw many smiles!

In every heart there is no fear, only the most passionate hatred of the enemy, and a determination to carry on at all costs.

In fact the spirit of battered Coventry was very well expressed by a Union Jack, which I observed stuck over the shattered doorway of an otherwise completely ruined building.'

Although Coventry was to have more bad raids, during one of which, in April 1941, Joyce Burton, the Matron of Coventry Hospital was awarded the O.B.E. for her bravery and reorganisation of the hospital – taking heed of the November raid – the raid of November 14th was the one that the people of Coventry will never forget.

Curiously enough it was the King who, in the immediate aftermath, did much to help Coventry. He arrived on the second day and was taken to the Mayor's Parlour, which was lit by candles stuck in beer bottles. He found the emergency committee quite dazed from what they had been through. 'I walked among the devastation. The people in the streets wondered where they were – nothing could be recognised.' He wrote afterwards in his diary, and to his mother, Queen Mary: 'The old part and centre of the town looks just like Ypres after the last war.'

His visit was of great psychological importance to people who had been shocked and cut off from communication with the country by a wrecked telephone system and a cordon stopping all traffic from entering the city. One citizen said, "We no longer felt that we were alone. If the king was there, the rest of England was behind us."

Chapter Eight

'Jim Crows' – Searching Across The Nights – At Birmingham, London, Croydon, Chatham, Margate And More – Also To The West And Wales, At Cardiff And Bristol.

Birmingham was to get a series of raids, starting just five days after the Coventry raid, in which, although schools, churches and factories were badly hit, the city's war production wasn't too badly affected.

The A.R.P. and Fire Brigades found themselves working flat out during these nights of terror, as did all the voluntary services as well. Finding alternative accommodation for those who had been bombed out, also became something of a nightmare for the hard pressed W.V.S. – who also had to try to find large amounts of clothing from wherever they could.

Hospital staffs, including Red Cross nurses, were also to find themselves working flat out. In the raids that started on 19th September, nearly 800 were killed, and many more than that injured.

By the end of the blitz it was estimated that Birmingham was the third worst hit city in the British Isles.

In the meantime, further south and with a month to go before Christmas, on Sunday 24th November, the people of Croydon were badly affected by the 'attentions' of a single raider – causing much damage and havoc in the town. C.W. Berwick-Sayers, who was the chief librarian at this time, was working in the Town Hall at the time of the raid. In his book 'Croydon and The Second World War,' he says:

'The single plane had slipped through the defences and reached Croydon before gunfire opened up on it. Its engines were heard by some of the staff in the Croydon control and south report centre and, fortunately, at this time they were a skeleton staff – it being the practice of the whole duty staff, dispersed in various parts of the town hall, to go to their posts at the sound of the siren.

On this night, the siren hadn't gone, when a 1,000 k.w. H.E. bomb, which had not have been aimed, as visibility was nil, struck the east side of the building, exactly opposite the police station, penetrated to the basement – and exploded.

The second bomb fell on the Central Croydon Liberal and Radical Workmen's Club, within a stones throw. The writer, on duty at the

115

time, at the South Report Centre, had just seated himself at his table, under a window protected by boards, which gave on to the 'moat' round the Town Hall which itself was girdered, iron roofed and sand bagged. He heard neither the plane nor the whistle which preceded the bomb, but, suddenly, everything round him seemed to dissolve and he felt that the cataract of rushing sand and water was carrying him down to abysmal depths. Almost immediately he came to rest, without any real sense of hurt, in a black darkness. His first sensation was that he was not dead – the second that he must be under masses of debris. He was able to shake head and arms free and call for help as his legs were pinned down. Almost immediately, a member of his staff, who had saved himself by diving under a heavy table, appeared and, by the light of a torch, helped to release him. It would appear that he had been on the edge of the vortex of the blast and he had been flung across the room into comparative safety, although badly injured, while masonry, girders and fractured glass and plaster had piled up on the very spot where he had been sitting – had the siren sounded before, as it did after the bomb had fallen, the room would have been fully staffed and there might have been many casualties – as it was, three women telephonists were killed and several were lying injured in the debris.

The services soon came to the rescue because the central position of the incident made it easy for them to reach the Town Hall, but the approach, we are told, was hindered somewhat by the thick fog of dust that enveloped the building. Many people showed great courage and a telephonist in the Control, Wendy Pauline Hollyer, although injured and surrounded by unstable masonry, remained at her telephone and summoned help. Dr. Oscar M. Holden, the Medical Officer of Health, worked his way under equally dangerous debris to reach the badly injured and administer morphia. Both were to receive the George Medal.

Three of the telephonists in another room at the centre were killed instantly. The other two were eventually rescued alive after being trapped for some time. One of them, pinned under tons of debris, was severely injured. It is revealed that Dr. Holden, at great personal risk, crawled under the wreckage and proceeded, under the most difficult conditions imaginable, to administer morphia to the girl. Owing to the very confined space, Dr. Holden had to crawl backwards and was in constant danger of being buried. He also attended to the injuries of other people, working at top speed in his shirt sleeves.

Miss Hollyer, who is twenty six years old, auburn haired and petite, lives with her parents at Temple Road, South Croydon. She joined the

116

A.R.P. Communications Service just before the war, leaving her former job of picture frame making. Her only comment on the award was: "I don't know what all the fuss is about, I only did my duty, as any other girl would have done." However, during the raid, when the bomb hit the report centre, she was pinned under the wreckage, but one of the telephones, thrown from a table was within her reach. While rescue workers were still trying to reach her, the telephone bell rang, and she took the call. Although she was bleeding badly from the wound in her neck, after Dr. Holden had dressed the wound and inserted stitches, she insisted on carrying on with her job until she was relieved by another telephonist.

The Croydon Advertiser, as well as mentioning the above named, also put in some words about a young boy scout who received a commendation for his bravery and quick thinking during the raid. It said, 'Eric Martin, of Croydon Grove, West Croydon, a voluntary Boy Scout messenger attached to the same centre, was blown out of the room into a corridor by the force of the explosion, but immediately volunteered, on recovering from the first shock, to do anything that was required of him.

He was sent to bring a rescue squad from the nearest depot, about a quarter of a mile away. Running in the dark he stumbled into the crater of another bomb, which had been dropped the same night. This crater was rapidly filling with water from a burst main, but he managed to scramble out. Very wet and badly bruised, he reached the depot and then guided the rescue party back to the Town Hall, taking another route to avoid the crater into which he had previously fallen.'

After Croydon and throughout the weeks running up to Christmas that year, there were many more air raids in various places around the country. In Brighton, we also had our 'share' of the night raids, and I can still remember the first time the siren went at night. Mother quickly got my sister and me out of bed and told us to put our dressing gowns on – then we hurried down to the basement, wondering what to expect, but, on this occasion, nothing happened. Later on we would get used to getting up at night and sheltering with other residents in the house. In my book, 'The Tree Climbers' I have written, 'Being woken from a nice warm bed in the middle of the night to go to the shelter of the basement, was one of the things I protested about the most. Some of the raids were particularly frightening and, despite knowing we were in the 'safest' part of the house, we nonetheless, felt very vulnerable. The harsh whistling sounds from the bombs falling close to the Square, or seemingly close, were – to say the least – terrifying! I can remember clamping my hands firmly over my ears and also tightly closing my eyes with each whistle – hopefully muffling the worst of the explosions – my stomach turning over and over until all was quiet again.

At the end of each of these raids, when the drone of the German bombers could no longer be heard and the explosions had given way to suspenseful silence, we would wait impatiently for the all clear and, when that came, make our way back upstairs to our long deserted beds and, perhaps, uneasy sleep.'

I can remember on some nights, when we were sheltering from a raid, Bruce Belfrage would come and join his wife and son, Julian, and it seemed odd that just a few hours beforehand, he had been reading out the news to the nation. Later on though, after quite a few raids when nothing had happened, or nothing had happened close to us, he decided to stay where he was in the top flat. – "Doing a bit of 'Jim Crow' work – roof spotting." He told us.

I think my father was a little jealous of Bruce about this. Before he had lost his leg, we had occupied the top flat, at number 13, where there was an entrance out onto the roof which led to a small glass observatory – the only one in Sussex Square and the only one I ever saw anywhere in Brighton, on a roof. Father, with his stump type of false leg, now found all the stairs nearly impossible to negotiate – especially if he was in a hurry. However, later on, he did join Bruce on a couple of occasions – "To see absolutely nothing apart from searchlights exploring the night sky!" He also later told us, adding – "but it was nice up there – atmospheric and very different from being 'entombed in the dungeon!'

On the subject of roof spotters, people volunteered their services all over the country for this vitally necessary duty, and I think that this would be an opportune place to include another piece by Portsmouth policeman, Arthur Almond. He says: "Who were the 'Jim Crows' of Portsmouth or for that matter, the rest of the country? To find the answer, one has to go back to the days of The Battle of Britain, when we stood alone and had been found quite unready for the magnitude of the war which Hitler was to unleash. The Maginot Line had proved about as effective as Hadrian's Wall might have been, we had witnessed the epic that was Dunkirk, our aluminum pots and pans from the kitchen were surrendered and flying protectively above us as Spitfires, and our iron railings were taken to turn into military hardware of some kind. We stood defiant and there may have been a shortage of 'metal' – but there was certainly no shortage of 'mettle.'

One morning in those dark days, I read in my daily paper that Mr. Churchill, as he was then, had announced that we were losing far too much production by those engaged on vital tasks connected with the war effort, spending unnecessary time in air raid shelters during 'alerts' when there was no immediate danger. It often happened that a lone raider, or two kept the Air Raid Warning on for long periods when engaged on reconnaissance only, and sent people scurrying for shelter when danger was only slight or nil. For example, a lone German plane crossing the coast at Selsey might put Portsmouth on the alert – so the Churchillian message came loud and clear for 'noses to the grindstone.' The newspapers that morning described the system it was proposed to adopt to keep work going during periods of the 'Red' air raid warning. It was proposed to introduce Roof Watchers, trained in aircraft recognition, to go aloft above their places of work so that they could scan the skies in the same way as the men of the Observer Corps, and then, alert their staff or other workers, by an eternal alarm system, when an attack appeared to be imminent.

When Mr. Churchill explained the idea for saving man-hours in this way, he said that these men, who were to be Roof Watchers, would be up aloft like 'Jim Crows,' alert and ready to give localised warning within the general alert warning which covered a wide area. The newsmen of the day were quick to speculate on the reason behind the great man's use of the expression – 'Jim Crow' and when their reference books told them all about the old American darkie minstrel song of some hundred years back, they wondered what Mr. Churchill had in mind. I think he merely had in mind the picture of a solitary crow up there watching as in La Fontaine's Fable. 'Le Corbeau et le Renard' or a watcher in the crow's nest. The expression did not catch on and those men who volunteered to go aloft and scan the skies for signs of the Luftwaffe's close approach, in order to keep the work ticking over, were officially called 'Roof Watchers.' Not to be confused with Fire Watchers whose job was to protect their premises against incendiary bomb attacks.

As I read the newspaper that morning, I little realised that in a day or two I was to be packed off to Hendon to learn from the Royal Air Force how to teach aircraft recognition in about a week, which included a spell on one of London's tall buildings where the Observer Corps had a post. This was a sandbagged enclosure on a flat roof and provided a good view all round. As the Battle of Britain was in full swing and the lads rushed out to do battle with the 'bandits' over the Thames Estuary, our lectures went on and I was initiated into the world of dihedral, high wing, low wing, radial and in-line engines etc.

It had fallen to my lot to be chosen by the Chief Constable of Portsmouth, the late Mr. T. Davies, to go to the Home Office Air Raid Precautions School at Falfield, Glos., to obtain an Instructors' Special Certificate, in order to train local instructors and I suppose it was because of my work in the training of Police, Firemen, Special Constables, Wardens and other Air Raid Precautions personnel, that I got the job of passing on aircraft recognition to Portsmouth's Jim Crows. I also found that I had to give lectures to volunteers in Bournemouth, Isle of Wight and Southampton. I still have the register of the Portsmouth men who went aloft for this job and the names of the firms etc. they represented. At the end of the course they had a certificate, which no doubt some of three dozen men still have, signed by me, or the Chief Constable who signed some in error.

Each week a return submitted to me showing the number of man hours saved by the Roof Watching System and the results were splendid. This was typical of the spirit which pervaded all engaged on the task of winning the war.

One of the more 'unlikely' Jim Crows in London, in the Regents Park area, was someone who was actually a serving Coldstream Guardsman. Joe Nixon's battalion had been part of the British Expeditionary Force – in a rearguard action defending a vital position on a canal, he had been wounded and eventually sent home on a hospital ship from Calais – just before it had fallen. Joe, just twenty years of age at this time, spent quite a few weeks in a hospital at Epsom, before going on to a holding battalion of the Coldstream's at Regents Park, London. He told me, "The experience brought home the full realities of war – the real horror of it all. Here was I, a soldier who had recently seen front-line warfare, and now here I was amongst these brave civilians, who had become Roof Spotters, Fire Fighters, Air Raid Wardens and so on, and they never flinched in their duties, just got on with the job despite the horrors of the bombings going on all around them; it's something that has stayed with me all my life – impossible to forget!"

At Margate, Mick Twyman, a local Historian who helped so much about Dunkirk in my last book, in particular about Dorothy Parker, who was a member of the Margate Ambulance Corps, Mick has also said to me – "On a personal note, my father, Arthur Twyman, was a member of the Margate Homeguard, as he had flat feet, the army turned him down, and his job in the building trade made his a reserved occupation, as the company he worked for – Rice and Son, a well known Margate building firm, contracted to the Government and Admiralty, so they were kept busy. He never spoke an awful lot about the war, but did divulge a couple of interesting anecdotes which may be of interest.

The first concerns a winter night in 1940, He was on a lone guard duty at the seaward end of Margate Harbour with his old Canadian Ross rifle and five rounds of ammunition, ready to repel the Germans should they arrive, when he inadvertently loosed a round off into the dark. As he said, it caused an enormous panic for a while and the rest of the platoon came galloping along to assist in tackling the invader, much to his embarrassment! The matter was taken very seriously and he was hauled up in front of Majors Jarman and Witts over the matter of 'the wasted asset of the discharged round in a time of great national shortage and peril', but got away with a stern warning!

The second concerns the two 6inch naval guns, which were installed at Fort Crescent, next to the Winter Gardens. Having worked on the construction of the gun emplacements for Rice & Son under the direction of the Royal Engineers, he and his mates were still finishing off and tidying up when the great day came for the first test firing. He said that the Royal Artillery (335 Coast Battery, 549 Regiment) had with them, an old and obviously well experienced naval gun officer who, on hearing that the RA intended to fire the guns with full charge, suggested that they might consider only using half charge in deference to all of the windows in the vicinity, the triangular Fort Green promenade being fringed on both its landward sides by very large boarding houses and hotels – many of them then in occupation by the services. It was further advised by the naval gent, that the windows be opened a little to reduce the effects of the concussion when the guns were discharged. This was duly done and occupied well over an hour, as there were lots of windows to see to. At last the great moment arrived, and all and sundry were advised 'fingers in ears now, we are going to fire the guns,' and so they did, and nearly every window in Fort Crescent and Fort Paragon was broken and fell out, amid much hilarity from those with 'fingers in ears.' As my father said, "We didn't mind, as it kept us busy for weeks, boarding and felting up broken windows, as you couldn't get glass for the love or money!"

Despite his flat feet, he was at Manston filling in bomb craters and repairing damage all through the 'Battle of Britain,' and was at Dover when it was being shelled by the Germans. He said that they were working on the crescent of houses which faced the Harbour under the cliff on which the Castle stands, busy patching up damage when, without warning, a house about six doors down, just disappeared as a shell landed on it. He said the strange thing was the lack of noise – until a policeman on a bike came along a couple if minutes later, furiously blowing a whistle and telling everybody to take cover as the Germans were shelling!

Returning to the bombings; on the 14th December, the people of Chatham experienced the horror of two parachute mines exploding near to the centre of the town. One of the people who became very much involved in the rescue work directly after the mines had exploded, was Ronald Piper of Watt Street – quite close to where the mines had come down. This is some of Mr. Piper's account of that day as told to The Chatham, Rochester and Gillingham News:

"I was in my garden when I saw a huge flash, about a hundred yards away, and I dashed out onto the road to see what had happened. A gas main was already alight and I endeavoured to put it out with my coat, but found it a hopeless task. When the mines exploded a number of people had become trapped under the wreckage – a Mr. And Mrs. Mattocks and their son Oliver, who Ron knew slightly, were caught in their cellar, where they had been sheltering and, next door three people were trapped beneath the local Co-operative shop. They were Mr.Moir, the manager, one of the assistants and the 'shop boy' – Leonard Humphrey.

Ron said, "I returned home to fetch a small hatchet which I hoped would help me in trying to free the Mattocks, but it wasn't much use. However, with another man, Lance Corporal William Styles of the R.A.S.C., we continued with the rescue work. After Mr. And Mrs. Mattocks and their son had been rescued, we hacked and picked our way through the nine inch wall into the Co-op, using our fingers and any implements we could find. But, owing to the fact that the shop was on a hill, this only brought us up out onto the ground floor of the Co-op, and we had to hack our way through debris, tins of food and other provisions – eventually reaching the three people who were trapped there and getting them out through what had been a trap door."

Mr. Piper and Cpl. Styles had worked solidly in the rescue from 6.30 p.m. to nearly 9 o'clock and, so promptly and efficiently did they affect the rescue that the police were still trying to trace the three staff members of the Co-op who had been unaccounted for. The conditions under which these rescues took place in were enough to daunt the

122

stoutest heart. It was raining heavily and the rescuers worked in the faint light of a torch, with the consistent threat of falling debris and outbreaks of fire menacing them.

Both Ronald Piper and Cpl. Styles were awarded George Medals for their bravery and dedication.

With the air raids carrying on so devastatingly in many parts of the UK, at home, in Brighton, the newspapers and radio kept us reasonably well informed about what was happening in other parts of the country – even if they didn't specifically name the actual places bombed. The report would only say if it was north, south, east or west and, if it was Brighton that they were reporting about, they would say – 'A south coast town' – thus, just giving the vicinity.

I remember father saying, "Giving us these facts, essentially gives us something near to the true picture, and I firmly believe that we need to be told. If there was to be any cover up of the grim facts, it would have deprived us of that feeling of all being in the same boat – thus encouraging everyone to work together to end the nightmare and return to peace."

During the Christmas of 1940/41 there was a lull in the air raids – almost as if it had been arranged that there should be a short break from the horrific proceedings. However, the bombings started again from the 27th December and the New Year had only just turned the corner when the news came through of another devastating air raid – this time it was South Wales that were the recipients.

The raid on Cardiff on the night of 2nd January 1941, was to become known as 'The Luftwaffe's New Year's gift to Cardiff.' It was a raid that the citizen's would never forget, and to say that a large number of people reacted by 'going beyond the call of duty,' would be an apt description of how many of the people of Cardiff reacted to the horrors of that night. Later on it was said that this was the Luftwaffe's reprisal attack for a recent raid by the R.A.F. on Bremen.

Cardiff had received its first sharp enemy attack on the night of the 3rd/4th September 1940, when ten H.E. bombs and some incendiary bombs were dropped on the city. During this raid ten people had been killed and another twelve seriously injured. After this, and until the night of 2nd January, there had been several small raids, but that was all.

The evening of January 2nd was bitterly cold – an evening to stay indoors, in the warmth. The alert was sounded at 6.30 p.m. It is thought that approximately 100 enemy aircraft reached the city, and the attack was widespread. Flares and incendiary bombs were first dropped, followed by H.E. bombs and parachute mines. 14 parachute mines, 150 H.E. bombs and approximately 5,000 incendiaries are recorded as having been dropped on the city. 8 parachute mines and 40 H.E. bombs failed to explode, and widespread evacuation was necessary – this is where valuable assistance was given by the police, helped by the air raid wardens, in the marshalling of the evacuees and patrolling the boundaries of the evacuated districts. Despite the freezing conditions and the roads being dangerous under foot, the civilian defence services carried out their duties admirably during the raid, in which 51 people were killed with 243 injured.

In an article in the South Wales Echo, the day after the raid, it said, 'Cardiff carried on as usual today, but it was a stern faced army of workers that threaded their way through streets littered with glass.

Firemen were still on duty. They had been battling with the flames throughout the night, and it was a miracle that they got so many fires under control. Some, with bandages or black with smoke, were still playing water on the smouldering debris – and one felt proud of them.

Hundreds of families were evacuated to schools and halls which had been prepared for their reception, and this morning the plans devised previously for feeding the homeless were working smoothly.'

In The Weekly Mail and Cardiff Times, on the 4th of January, an article said – 'Llandaff Cathedral, the most ancient ecclesiastically built foundation in Wales, suffered the most serious damage in a wide area. Dawn broke on a spectacle of hideous destruction.

The south roof of the nave had been completely destroyed. The famous west window was smashed to atoms and, inside the building the floor was cluttered with torn timber and ribbons of ancient flags, which had been torn from the walls. As far as it is possible to estimate, the Rossetti pictures and the Murillo Madonna are intact.

To the west of the cathedral a huge cavity was surrounded with uprooted gravestones – some of them hundreds of years old. One slab, weighing about twenty lbs., had been flung over the top of the building, through the air into a street a quarter of a mile away. Others, much heavier, were found a considerable distance from the churchyard. The organ was amongst other valuable things destroyed.'

Hubert Keyes-Evans was a ten-year-old schoolboy at this time, attending Llandaff Cathedral School, just near to the cathedral – their sports ground backed onto the graveyard. He remembers, the day after the raid, the boys were told to report to the playing field instead of their classrooms. Anything that meant missing classes pleased them –

124

especially any activity on the sports field. However, their moods became rather sombre when they were handed empty sandbag sacks and told to pick up all the debris they could find on the field – amongst which, were a large quantity of bones from the bombed graveyard; these were strewn over the entire field. After finishing this unusual, unpleasant yet necessary task, they handed the sacks in – the bones, probably to be re-interred in the sacred ground of the graveyard.

Hubert, also told me that his father, Dr. David Keyes-Evans, a G.P. in Cardiff during the war years, was kept particularly busy at that time. His main worry, during the air raids, rather than the bombs, was the shrapnel from the ack-ack guns defending the city, which caused quite a bit of damage when coming down to earth. Because of this, his car, which was so essential for making visits around the city, had a special steel covering made for protecting the bonnet.

With many unexploded bombs still to be dealt with, the men of The Royal Engineers UXB Force found themselves working furiously to make places safe to venture back to after the raid. They also had a bit of help from a civilian volunteer this time – someone who had a particular reason for volunteering. In his book, 'Cardiff, A City At War,' Dennis Morgan tells of this man, Bud Fisher, the service manager of Merrett and Stephens, who refused to part with his new five ton truck when the army tried to commandeer it. I asked Dennis if he could tell me more about this man and he was kind enough to send me a clipping of an article written by Dan O'Neill, for the South Wales Echo on June 16th 1997 – I have permission to reproduce this article here. Mr. O'Neill writes:

'The government's ban on land mines came a bit too late for Cardiff. For we had our share of 'em 50-odd years ago – deadly, devastating weapons of war, floating down to lie on the ground, primed to explode with the big question being ... when?

So with mines once more hitting the headlines, what better time to remember a gent named Leslie Clive Fisher – "Bud" – who got closer to the Luftwaffe's lethal loads than most.

It began in an odd way, with a phone call from a Captain Lippett, saying that he was about to commandeer the new five-ton truck, proud possession of Merrett and Stephen Ltd. Of Westgate Street.

Bud Fisher, the company's service manager, was worried about the way army drivers might treat his brand new truck. So he issued an ultimatum: "You can't have it unless I go with it."

"Well," said Captain Lippett, "do you know what you're letting yourself in for?"

125

Bud naturally, didn't. But because of his refusal to be parted from that cherished truck – surely prize vintage material these days – he'd be faced with repeated calls to the two-and-a-half ton unexploded mines parachuted silently into the city.

The Victorian thriller writers called bombs 'infernal machines.' – the description fitted these horrors.

They were equipped with a baffling variety of devices designed to make them almost totally unpredictable. Some would explode when a clock that operated the detonator was released, as acid ate through the thin copper wires. Then there were the magnetic components exploding when metal came close, while if attempts to defuse them were made, a light sensitive cell exposed to daylight could mean the end of the mine disposal team.

Bud Fisher filled in his Army disclaimer form and gave details of his next of kin – the reason was soon brought home to him. His first call was to the Castle grounds where a mine had landed – "It might be magnetic," he was told – "So get rid of anything metal." Off came the belt – trousers held up with a piece of rope. One problem; the breakdown truck, essential for the job, was also made of metal. The answer was to drive the truck round and round with the bomb in the centre of a 400-foot circle. Why? Because each circuit was logged and timed so that if anything went wrong – well, the next disposal team might have a better chance after profiting from the mistakes of the first.

Bud recalled years later: "It felt as though someone was pouring cold water down my back." He drove his truck up to those land mines eight times. Then came the dodgy business of shackling them and creeping cautiously to the 'landmine cemetery' – a disused quarry – with a police escort clearing the streets. Once in the quarry, experts drilled a couple of holes in the casing then pumped steam inside until the mine was harmless. Unless, of course, it was booby-trapped to mask the secrets of the mechanism!

One mine was found near the railway behind Ninian Park Road, another close to the old mortuary on Curran Road, off Penarth Road near the Bristol Hotel. When the experts arrived, a naval officer listened to one of the mines through a stethoscope. The clock was ticking. "Time to get cracking." He said, "That was the approach to the job."

One mine drifted down into a field at St. Mellons – there was no sign of it – until a soldier relaxing on a haystack felt the cold metal against his back. Another, in Llandough, exploded just after everyone had cleared out of the field – the slowest man wasn't hurt – but he was stripped of all his clothes except his shoes.

At least they could spot the Cardiff landmines from a distance – unlike the buried booby-trap of today.

For his work, Bud was awarded the King's Commendation "for brave conduct in Civil Defence," signed by Winston Churchill.'

In the social column of the South Wales Echo, under the heading – 'Blitz or no Blitz' the article said, 'Carry on Cardiff is the New Year motto' and went on to say, 'The Blitz has come to Cardiff and this proud city of dreaming white buildings faces its nightmare with fortitude. The tale of its ordeal is told, and the manner in which its men, women and children are bearing themselves, is known.'

The day after this raid, across the Bristol Channel, the city of Bristol received similar attention from the Luftwaffe. With the freezing weather continuing, the voluntary services did a superb job during a raid that was to last for over twelve hours.

The worst raid they had had up to then had come on Sunday 24th November 1940, when over 200 people had been killed, with nearly that number again injured. That raid had badly hit the water, gas and electricity supplies and, for a time, this badly affected the city. I feel that this would be an opportune place in the book to say some words about the dedication of the local newspapers throughout the country, who did everything they could to keep their readers up to date with the news, even during the worst of the bombings. Bristol was no exception; in his book 'Bristol at War,' C.M. MacInnes says, 'In spite of the censorship and controls of various kinds placed upon it, the local press served the city faithfully throughout the whole war. Bristol papers not only worked loyally with the authorities and with each other, they showed, at all times, a sober, responsible recognition of their important function. Like the rest of the community they suffered in the raids and production was often difficult. When the premises of one journal were damaged its competitors readily placed their presses at its disposal. Papers already reduced in size, now shrank still further – The Western Daily Press was reduced to one page and, on one occasion, it was printed on a hand press that had not been used for fifty years. On another occasion it was printed in Bath. Still, whatever the difficulties, the daily issues came out and the public was comforted, for so long as it received its papers, however shrunken, things could not be as bad as they seemed.

In addition to the press, information was disseminated by leaflets issued by the Civil Authority; it was passed on through a warden service to private citizens; it was spread by the ubiquitous and tireless W.V.S. as well as by local officials of the Ministry of Information.'

Although the raid on January 3rd was Bristol's longest raid, it hadn't caused the damage and casualties that the raid on November 24th 1940 when the city had received its 'coventration.'

There were two more raids on Bristol during the next two weeks – on the 9th and 16th January, but the severe cold of the first half of that January had increased the difficulties facing the Fire Brigade, Rescue Parties, Repair Gangs and the hard pressed W.V.S., who were constantly trying to feed, clothe and shelter those who had been bombed out of their homes. One W.V.S. worker, taking canteens to the over worked A.R.P. services and firemen, said, "The firemen were, of course, very busy and when they put their cups down for a while, to carry on, they froze! In fact, the tea froze, the hoses froze and we had the choice of being frozen, burned or drowned in tea!"

Great icicles that hung from the roofs and ladders obstructed the firefighters and were a menace to those below. The clothing froze on the fireman's bodies, so that they were encased in ice and any movement of any kind became difficult. If the water pressure failed for a moment, and it often failed at this time, the hosepipes were turned into solid tubes. Pumps were continually frozen and the roads were sheets of ice. The movement of vehicles was slowed up or stopped altogether – when speed was essential. For many hours after raids, men and women were pinned down under the rubble of demolished buildings often in great physical pain and with streams of icy water pouring over them.

People from all walks of life joined the rescue parties, including service men home on leave. WAPC Ella Johnson arrived at the Bridewell Police Headquarters and, on entering the main entrance hall, saw all around, sprawled all over the floor, what appeared to be a large number of bodies. On closer inspection, she discovered they were in fact seamen who had been sent in to help the fire service and were awaiting transport back to their shore establishment – after working all night they were so exhausted that they simply put their heads on their haversacks and dropped off instantly.

All the rescuers worked frantically and eventually came through on top, then, desperately tired but knowing that no-one could have done any more, they rested for a while – all of them having gone well beyond the call of duty.

One week after the attack on Bristol, on the night of Friday 10th January, the city of Portsmouth had its worst raid. In a special issue marking the 60th anniversary of that raid, The Portsmouth News said that in a raid, lasting just four hours, the face of Portsmouth was changed forever. Great landmarks disappeared, the Guildhall burned, the Harbour Station was a twisted heap of metal, and Southsea shopping parade, in Palmerston Road, was flattened. Three thousand people found their homes destroyed, 171 people lost their lives – with a further 430 injured.

Mary Verrier was a nineteen-year-old Red Cross nurse, working at St. Mary's Hospital in Portsmouth when the bombs began to fall. She remembers staff putting child patients into large linen baskets and sending them by lift down to the safety of the basement.

Mary went wherever she was needed, working on overstretched wards, at a first aid post clearing station, sometimes going out in an ambulance.

Some of the injured would be admitted to the hospital, while those with serious burns needed to be transferred to a specialist unit, near Salisbury, as the bombs fell.

Mary, of Southsea, says: "Sometimes I went with them, tending these poor people. It was a hazardous job and very frightening – but we had to do it."

On one run, the canvas roof of the ambulance caught fire. The hospital was damaged, but escaped lightly compared to the Royal Portsmouth Hospital and Southsea Eye and Ear Hospital.

I contacted Mary and asked her if she could remember more of that night and the part that she and her colleagues took during the raid. In her reply to me, she says: 'The German raiders came over the city in droves and we waited at the Red Cross First Aid Post, Casualty unit, for the influx of injured. The flares from the raiders and the red glow in the sky, as the fire raid continued, could be seen for seven miles. Our R.A.F. night fighters took off and shot down many planes, preventing them from reaching their target.

We were well trained in our huge First Aid Post, attached to St. Mary's Hospital; before hostilities we had worked with the armed forces, Home Guard and Civil Defence, for the reception of many casualties.

I was the youngest in the First Aid Post, our Commandant was a strict disciplinarian and we were a mixed team of Red Cross Nurses, Girl Nursing Reserve, Order of St. John of Jerusalem. Boy Scouts were messengers, with tin hats, marked M, and black and white armbands.

As the night of horror went on, a huge bomb fell near the hospital, so a few of us were sent to help evacuate the wards and care for the patients, and also support the trained medical and nursing staff. The wounded had to be evacuated from the bombed area; children on the children's ward, who could be moved, were put into huge linen baskets lined with pillows and blankets – those who could not be moved remained in the ward with nurse.

Bedfast patients and the badly injured, were nursed on the ward – where some of the windows had been blown out in some cases. To protect their heads we put the clean enamel washing bowls on their heads, for a laugh we put a white dressing towel under and one told the patient he looked like a refugee from the Desert Song.   .

The awful night went on – smoke, noise, fire, bombs, and the cries of the injured. People in the city formed working parties to help the brave firemen and tried to help save peoples belongings, help rescue teams. Everyone 'turned to.' Matron Guy insisted we always kept two clean aprons handy – it gives the patients confidence if you are clean and tidy – no member of staff left their post for hours. Early dawn, we were directed outside into the hospital grounds, to queue for some soup and bread. Our Assistant Matron, Miss J. Berich was 'in charge' and I said "Can we have a look at what the soup is like?" "Take it – eat it – with your bread, there will be no more food for some time!" Was her reply.

Next day some cartoonist had put up a cartoon of nurses queuing for the soup with the notice – 'Hospital Cats missing!' – and they were!

The awful night finally ended with the raiders going home – the Germans had struck when the tide was low, so the fire hoses were only sucking in the mud.

It is not until much later you see and realize the extent of the night's horror, my hospital, my friends, and my home, my City, gone forever. Still the casualties' kept coming in, we survived thanks to the supreme courage of the fire fighters. When later, on the following day, we were detailed to go for some rest, our ward sister paused for a short while for us to say a prayer of thankfulness for deliverance. Nurses Home destroyed, tired but proud, I curled up by the steam pipe near the children and dozed off, but not for too long as the ward sister came along and said, "Sleeping, you should be ashamed of yourself with all the work to be done." Ah well, that's what I joined for, to serve. What we did not know then was that we were to have two more fire bombing nights.

During the January 10th raid we had an American Naval Ship in port – nicknamed 'The Chicago Piano' for the amount of continuous gunfire sent up.

Later on, in hostilities period we were transferred to Queen Alexandra's Military Hospital under Southern Hospitals General Command.' There is more about Mary later in the book.

Finally, perhaps on a slightly lighter note, Naina Cox, who I will be telling more about in the book, when she was serving as a Red Cross nurse at the time of D-Day, was at boarding school at the time of the big raid on Portsmouth. The day before the raid, her mother had been to visit her at the school at Petersfield, and she was shocked to see her daughter looking 'painfully thin.' Apparently Naina refused to eat the 'grey looking spuds', which were a staple part of the school diet. Her mother spoke to the teachers about this and told them she was going to take her daughter out of school for a few days, " – To fatten her up a bit!"

Accordingly, Naina was at home during the raid – but slept through quite a lot of it. Both her parents were A.R.P. wardens, and she remembers her father coming in and going out on several occasions, whilst the bombing was going on – she also remembers sheltering under the bed for a while.

However, at her school at Petersfield, seventeen miles away, they could see that Portsmouth was being badly hit, with many fires illuminating the sky, and they thought about her and said special prayers for her – 'They worked,' and Naina returned to school, safe and sound and slightly fattened, a few days later – leaving Portsmouth, with many of its buildings in ruins, but with the spirit of its citizens, unbowed.

Chapter Nine

Plymouth – Devastation.

By this time, in Plymouth, there had already been numerous air raids, causing much damage with loss of life; but it was felt that the city, so important in the role it has played in the defence of this country throughout the centuries, was poorly defended and that much more should have been done to strengthen the area against these nightmare attacks. Their worst raid, so far, had come on the night of the 27th November 1940, when Devonport had also been hit.

Although the sound of the ack-ack guns of *H.M.S. Newcastle* gave some reassurance that there was, at least, some form of defence, it was soon found out that these guns never actually hit anything. Sir Colin Campbell, the town clerk at that time, said, "All that they succeeded in doing was showering the city with shrapnel!"

In their fiftieth anniversary of the war supplement, The Plymouth Evening Herald said, 'Defence measures were so minimal as to be a joke.' Further on in the same article, they went on to say, ' – Still no attempt was made to organise any sort of evacuation. The Lady Mayoress, Nancy Astor, had earlier proclaimed to the world that Plymouth would never be a prime target for Nazi bombers!'

Earlier on in the war, it had been thought that Plymouth would be a good place to evacuate children to, and one official report, made some time afterwards, said, "It was a blunder on the part of the central government that Plymouth should have been made an evacuation area. It was an even bigger blunder that after the fall of France, when the fear of the home shores being invaded became very real, that the evacuation of children 'out of Plymouth' hadn't been put into operation."

However, this book isn't so much about the politics of that time as about the everyday folk who were there during these dangerous times, and who helped, in whatever capacity, their fellow citizens during times of terror – and there were plenty of these.

After the first of the horrific night raids, quite a number of Plymouth people had started leaving the city by late afternoon, in order to try to find shelter in the villages or small towns not too far away. There were many

132

who spent these nights on the fringes of the moors, or in farm buildings – even under hedgerows – anything to get away from the main target areas.

By the March of 1941, despite all the battering Plymouth had endured, the citizens remained undaunted and, on what seemed more like a beautiful summer's day rather than early spring, they thronged the streets, to catch a glimpse of and cheer, the King and Queen, on their morale boosting visit to the city. On that visit Robert Menzies, the Australian Prime Minister, accompanied them. It was a gala day – made all the more special by the consistent sunshine. But what no one could have foreseen was that, that evening, as the Royal visitors were on their way home, Plymouth was to get the first of two horrific raids, carried out on consecutive nights – setting the city alight and causing damage beyond the worst scenario of any nightmare.

Amongst the beleaguered citizens of Plymouth, Ken Searle was an A.R.P. runner – despite the fact that he was still attending school. On the day of the King's visit, the pupils at his private school hadn't been given time off to see all the goings on, and had had to hear about it all from relatives, later on. His grandfather, Hugh Bryden, had joined the A.R.P. on 1938, and was soon made head warden, covering a wide area – later in the war he was made Divisional Warden. Ken's father, Charles Searle, had joined the Police War Reserves in 1938 – so his family was very much involved in the wartime actions in Plymouth.

Ken told me – "I used to patrol the streets with my grandfather to see the blackout was enforced – no lights showing! When a raid was in progress all doors had to be unlocked, so that any of the emergency services could get in and put fires out and rescue injured people. Sometimes we helped infirm people to the shelters – I also helped the A.F.S. push water pumps over the bomb rubble.

Sometimes I would help the bomb disposal men roll a defused bomb onto a flat backed truck. More than once a bomb went off whilst on the back of a truck – thankfully not when I was on or near it! The biggest unexploded bomb grandfather and I found was 2250 lbs."

There is more about Ken later, but I would like to add here that with people of all ages only too willing to help during the raids, it helped keep up the morale of the city, giving a feeling of inner security because of all being in the same boat together, and doing what they could for each other during those desperate times.

Another person who was unable to see the King and Queen's visit, was Ron Hellyer, who, at the age of 19, was working alternate day and night shifts, for The Ministry of Defence as a Naval Weapons

Engineering apprentice. This was as well as doing voluntary fire fighting work (unpaid) with the Auxiliary Fire Service. Ron told me that working those day and night shifts for the M.O.D. made his availability for fire fighting – "a bit sporadic," as they had priority on his time – even during air raids.

During the day shift routine, he would get back home in the early evening, immediately change into his uniform and wait any air raid warning. As it turned out, he was on day shift on the day of the King's visit. He told me – "On the day of the 20th March 1941 I arrived home following a routine day's work, and listened to my family's excitement at having seen the King and Queen that day on their visit to the city. I then changed into my firemen's uniform, but, by 8 p.m., felt confident that it was going to be a quiet night. Lulled into a false sense of relaxation, I literally jumped as the warning sounded that a raid was imminent – it was just about 8.30 p.m."

What Ron didn't know, at that moment, was that he would soon be experiencing fires that hadn't been part of the training manuals – in a night of sheer terror. He can remember that first night as something of a blurred nightmare, but it was the night after this that he remembers more clearly – a night many times worse than the one on March 20th. – I will turn to Ron again soon.

However, still concentrating on the night of the 20th, John Richards, who was to join the A.R.P. a year later, was just fourteen and a half years of age at the time of the King's visit and, in the evening he was at home in the company of his mother, an aunt and his older sister. He told me, "After the siren had gone, at about 8.30 p.m., we all went down into our cellar which had been converted into a shelter. We had a black cat, which normally wouldn't go into a shelter, but on this occasion he went without us – as if sensing what was to come.

We lived near the main railway station and, after a while, when there was a lull in the bombing, I went into the back garden to have a look around, and saw a train on fire in one of the sidings – it was completely illuminating the area. Not long afterwards there was a tremendous explosion from a bomb, which had fallen a few doors away, demolishing five houses – the debris landing in our garden and on the roof. We feared our house had collapsed.

Some of the people who were rescued from the demolished houses, were brought to our shelter by the rescue services, and stayed until it was safe for them to be moved elsewhere. Fortunately, no one was killed or injured in this incident – although one Anderson shelter was left on the edge of the bomb crater. There was also an unexploded bomb in the next road and we spent the night in our shelter – until the army had defused it.

My father was on fire watching duty at the post office in Devonport and we were worried about each other; but, in fact, Devonport had been almost untouched that night – however, you can imagine his relief, on returning home, to find that we were all alright.'

In The Western Evening Mail, on Friday 21st March 1941, an article about this raid, 'Fire – frightfulness predominated when Nazi raiders made Plymouth the target of their chief attack last night. In a blitz, which lasted about four hours, there were considerable casualties, including some killed and many injured. Two hospitals, three churches, two cinemas, commercial premises and many houses were damaged.' However, on the day that this paper came out, no one would have thought that anything could get any worse than this – but it could, and did, that night!

The night of Friday 21st March, it was a night that went way beyond the most pessimistic of scenarios thought of by whoever made up the training manuals for the Fire Brigade." Said Ron Hellyer.

Ron told me, "The training of the A.F.S. was very good – just about military, and you knew what you had to do, but on the night of the 20th no one could have foreseen anything like this and the system and discipline broke down a bit and you just carried on where you were. No one had seen anything like it before, consequently, by the time we were on duty the next night, the 21st, we thought we had now experienced the worst we could – but little did we realise that this night would be far worse – practically indescribable in fact, and certainly six times worse than the night before!"

In his own words, this is Ron's description of a night that would be impossible to forget – "As I reached for my steel helmet and hastily wrapped my belt and fireman's hatchet around my waist, the sirens were already wailing their warning that another raid was imminent. Such 'routine' was nothing unusual; I had done it many times before – with my mother always voicing her normal pleadings for me not to go. For some reason, almost as if with some premonition, that evening she was being particularly forceful and followed me down the stairs and along the short passageway of 14 Arundell Crescent, North Road, to the front door. I ushered her back inside, assuring her that I would be all right and concluded with – "get down the shelter mum!" I was 19 years old and a member of the Stonehouse Town Hall fire squad. As an auxiliary fireman, I was on my way to report in. In fact, the station itself occupied the then defunct Stonehouse Police Station, the latter still standing, even though the Town Hall itself had been badly damaged on a previous raid.

Number 14 was at the bottom of the U shaped Arundell Crescent, and, as I ran up the right hand hill to North Road, with the yellow glow of fire already lighting up an otherwise dark sky, I myself, had a feeling that this night would be different.

Still running, it was down into Cecil Street, turning right into King Street, then left into Octagon Street – on approach to the Octagon itself. Already out of breath, with the hanging hatchet making running difficult anyway, I slowed to a fast walk. By then the orange glare in the sky was increasing in intensity and the droning, pulsating sound of the attacking aircraft, causing the heart to beat even faster. It was then that I became aware of a strange swishing sound – gradually gaining in noise volume. At first I thought that it might have been a falling parachute mine (already known for their devastating destruction power), then fear overcame my breath shortage and I again started to run. If it was to be a mine, I knew I had very little time -it was going to land very near. Reaching the Octagon itself, I ran diagonally across Union Street to the angle shops joining Union Street to Martin Street and threw myself into the recessed doorway of a stamp/medal/coin collector's shop (I forget the name). Lying on the stone floor I coiled into a ball, faced inwards to the shop doorway, tilted my steel helmet to the back of my head and with just a "please God" prayer, closed my eyes tightly and, petrified, awaited the anticipated impact and explosion.

I am not sure how long I laid there, probably no more than fifteen seconds, when I became aware of a noise that I can only describe as a muffled machine gun fire coupled with a loud pressurised hissing sound – but no explosion. As I slowly opened my eyes, the reflection of fierce blue and yellow light in the glass door, pained my eyes. I scrambled to my feet and turned to look across the Octagon and the picture before me has vividly remained with me for 60 years. Dozens upon dozens of fiercely hissing incendiary bombs were scattered over the whole of the Octagon and Union Street area – several had smashed through the plate glass windows of Jays and Hampshire Furnishing stores and a number of settees were already ablaze; several were spitting fire just a couple of yards away in the gutter. My 'anticipated' land mine had been, in fact, a 'basket' of incendiary bombs. Remarkably, almost unbelievable but true, as I looked across the Octagon and part way into

Union Street, I could not see another soul. My only thought was to reach the fire station, not with a sense of loyalty to duty but to reach the security of the station itself. Whilst the ground floor served as the operations and control rooms and the upstairs housed the sleeping quarters of duty firemen, the ten stone steps to the below ground basement opened out to the previous prisoner cell blocks – constructed of granite stone blocks (the cell doors had been removed) the area proved an almost perfect air raid shelter. That, I have to admit – was my target to escape from the inferno that was developing outside.

Trying hard to compose myself, I again started to run up Martin Street, noted as I passed the Salvation Army Meeting Hall, that flames were already emerging from the top attic like window, then into Millbay Road and finally right into George Place – our fire station was a corner site. I paused for a few seconds at the bottom of the three steps in a futile attempt to suppress some of my fear. Eventually I opened the door of the control room. The station officer in charge, a comparatively young Ron Sutton, was chalking information on the incident wallboard. In accordance with drill procedure, I gave my name to the lady controller who turned to another duty attendance chalkboard and added my name with the time of my arrival. Other than that, we exchanged no words, even though I felt desperate to tell somebody about the Octagon scene. At that moment I could not come to terms with the almost casual and calm atmosphere of the control room with what was taking place outside.

By then the raid had been only about fifteen to twenty minutes in progress. I continued down the steps to the basement where a dozen or more of my colleagues, already in their oilskins, were lightheartedly chatting or smoking, even though, of course, awaiting call out – there was no sign of urgency or fear. It was only then that I realised that clearly they had been on duty for some time before the raid had started and had no idea of the intensity and extent of the developing disaster outside. In my already shocked condition – I commanded attention and started to relay my story – I had no time to finish! My last words were unheard, as with a deafening crash and vibration, the electric lights went out and the basement became saturated with choking dust. By comparison, the following thirty seconds seemed like a total silence except for the firemen clearing their throats and spitting out saliva dust – no one spoke immediately and the silence was only interrupted by a striking match – a fireman was carrying out the normal practice drill of lighting the first of the many emergency oil lamps placed strategically

137

around the cellar area. Gradually the initial shocked silence gave way to voices with one in particular saying "what the bloody hell was that!" – There really was no need to ask; we all knew that somewhere near, an HE bomb had struck. Almost immediately, Ron Sutton's shouting voice could be heard – "Calm down, calm down – Number One Crew now" the customary way that the teams were summoned for action.

Again, almost without a word being exchanged, four or five firemen moved toward and up the stone steps to receive their assignment orders. In a space of less than a minute, an even louder call for crew number two was evident, with them too moving up the stone steps. It became apparent that when crew number one had stepped out of the building – the almost panorama of fire facing them gave way to shock and panic. The whole city appeared to be ablaze, with the shrieking whistle and final explosions of the HE bombs adding to the terror. In that moment of shock, two or three of the first men had turned back into the station, with one being heard to shout, "You can't go out there – it's suicide!" Heated arguments erupted as Ron Sutton endeavoured to take control of the situation, but several men pushed past him down the basement steps to where my team and I were still sat. Two firemen were crying. They were tears of shock, not fear or cowardice.

In seconds, Ron Sutton appeared in silhouette at the basement entrance. His words to a now silent group, although somewhat emotional, were positive, thrusting, hurtful but effective. "You rotten b......d's, for the first time you've been called upon to do your job in real war conditions and you've backed out like scared rats – I'll tell you what! I need just four volunteers from any of you and I'll take out the first pump!" In a space of seconds, my own team leader, another lad of nineteen years, stood up and walked toward the station officer, who immediately again addressed the rest of us saying – "Oh I see, it takes a boy to do a man's job does it?"

That very comment was the turning point that totally changed a quite desperate situation. Firemen started to move, one or two at first, soon to be followed by others. One was heard to say, "Let's get on with it." The shock was over, calm organisation and action was underway. Pump one was away in thirty seconds, to be followed by the others. In less than five minutes we ourselves were assigned to Union Street (not the Octagon I had experienced some thirty minutes beforehand) but to a group of shops and a public house just east of the Palace Theatre. Union Street seemed to be ablaze from end to end – in the main it was a losing battle. On those March nights, the full intensity and horror of war and its effect on civilian life, was being fully experienced for the first time, even though the war was already 18 months on.

Sudden shock can play havoc with the body and mind, particularly when experiencing horrific scenes for the first time. The Stonehouse Fire Station crews had gone through such an event and had recovered. Archive records (if any) would reveal the outstanding work carried out by that small fire station and its crewmembers. Ron Sutton too has remained in my mind for 60 years. He was a real leader – he saved the day. For me personally, I did what I had to do, not even remotely with any attribute of bravery, but because I was more at ease outside with a hose in my hand than confined to the claustrophobic environment of an air raid shelter.'

In their blitz supplement in March 1991 – fifty years later, The Plymouth Evening Herald said of the night of March 21st 1941, 'The fires that devoured Plymouth, drove through the heart of the city like an all conquering army, sparing nothing. Fire ran down walls, swept over pavements, lurked around doors with windows roaring and crackling, as if fed by inexhaustible fuel.'

Although this was a sad time for everyone in the city, especially, of course, for those who had lost relatives and friends in the raids, the person that everyone must have had special feelings for was Joan Bowler (nee Riley). Her husband Ernest Bowler has sent me the following account of when he first heard of what had happened and his subsequent arrival, on compassionate leave, in war torn Plymouth. He says:

"I shall never forget that weekend; I had just been posted to Edinburgh with the Artillery. On the Sunday morning, I was sent for by the duty officer on watch in the observation building. He asked me if I had anyone in Plymouth and, after I had said "yes," he handed me a telegram from my wife Joan. It read – "Come home at once, only me left." I was to find out that my wife's whole family had been killed – nine of them – including, her mum, dad, brother Matthew and his wife Pat, with their little girl, also Pat.

On arriving in Plymouth, I was absolutely stunned to see all the chaos, all the burnt out buildings, many of them still burning – the whole thing was a nightmare."

Joan's tragic family was the worst hit in Plymouth, but there were many other Plymothians whose loved ones were killed in the blitz.

Exactly a month after this raid, after a lull, during which the people of Plymouth had started 'picking up some of the broken pieces,' the

Luftwaffe returned, and once again the city faced more nightmare attacks – this time, with Devonport getting badly hit.

Once again, all the voluntary and other services would spring into action, including Ron Hellyer, who, by this time, had had far more than any ordinary 'baptism of fire.'

He says, "With Plymouth 'still licking its wounds' from the widespread bomb and fire ravaged destruction of the March 1941 air raids, as the warning siren sounded on the evening of the 21st of April 1941, my first thought was – 'what else is there to destroy?' For me, personally, I had come through the March experience, luckily, unscathed, and had gained a great deal of the sensation of mass uncontrollable fire – with a one hundred per cent record that every building I faced on those nights, had burned to the ground! I would not be alone with that record – the orders were clear – 'ignore the lost cause and concentrate water on adjacent buildings and save what you can.'

On reporting in on the 21st April 1941, I was immediately assigned to a crew (not my own crew) who were just about to leave. As I clung to the side of the prime mover (a commandeered lorry), I shouted the question, "Where are we going?" The reply 'St. Peter's Church' caused a momentary heart 'blip' because that sight would be less than 100 yards from my own home at 14 Arundell Crescent, North Road, where I knew some 12 or 13 people (some being my own family), would be taking cover in one of the larger sized Anderson shelters – which subsequently was to save their lives.

As we turned into Eldad Hill, flames could already be seen 20 to 30 feet high, and as we entered Wyndam Square the roof of St. Peter's Church was already burning like a tinderbox. In a strong wind, spiralling clouds of red hot sparking timber fragments added to the hazard as they were eventually to fall to the ground level. We quickly found the hydrant cover, to find water seeping out onto the pavement and, on removal, to additionally find the hydrant cavity itself filled with water. A couple of the crew struggled for some seconds to locate the standpipe socket, whilst myself and another crew member started to run out the hoses. The standpipe connections were proving to be a problem, and it was decided to use a suction basket to empty the cavity water. In thirty seconds the cavity was empty, standpipe in place, hoses connected, with myself and another detailed to the nozzle end. We shouted back – 'water on' – and waited for the pressure 'kick' at the nozzle to take effect. It was a negative wait, with the voice of the crew leader shouting 'no pressure – roll up!' The orders were quite specific – in the event of a no water situation – it was an immediate return to the station.

As we set about rolling up the hoses, I became aware (amongst the noise and heat) of shouting and angry verbal argument in the area of the hydrant. As I got nearer to the source, I found our crew leader in a violent argument with what turned out to be – an air raid warden. What amazed me even more, was that, in the glow of the fire, I recognised the warden as a man who worked in the same factory as myself in the Royal Naval Armament Depot sited in the Royal William Yard. He was a welder by the name of Wilf Perry. It emerged that Wilf (an ex-soldier) normally of quiet personality, in the panic of the moment, had lost his head, and had referred to my crew leader as a 'coward' for leaving the scene. Wilf had wrongly and naively, thought that because the hydrant sump was gradually refilling (by seepage), that water was available, not realising that a full sump would give us just 2/3 seconds of water pressure and again dry up.

At that very moment, a 'stick' of HE bombs could be sensed (it was fairly easy to assess) to be heading in our direction by noise and explosion volume. As the fourth bomb dropped – Wilf Perry – the 'Air Raid Warden' – took over and shouted 'take cover.' Myself and another fireman dived into an open doorway as bomb number 5 landed and exploded near enough to feel the vibration and shock waves. Lying prone, my colleague and I actually wrapped our arms around each other as we awaited number 6. There was a thudding bang and some vibration, but no explosion. Two more explosions, Number 7 and number 8 were heard but in reduced volume. We returned to the hydrant area to continue 'packing up' and Wilf Perry was nowhere to be seen-it worried me, but within a very short time we were on our way back to the station.

In the early hours of the next morning (22nd April), as myself and others were damping down in Union Street – yet again – I was approached by a firemen pushing a bicycle (with considerable difficulty) through the debris. Answering 'yes' to his question – 'Are you Ron Hellyer?' – he added – 'Right, you're bring relieved; you have a problem at home!' By then, exhausted with the night's activities and quite soaked to the skin, I made my way through King Street, Cecil Street to North Road. As I reached the top of the U shaped Arundell Crescent and looked down in the direction of my house and neighbouring properties, there was a gap in the terraced housing with rescue teams still at work. As it was, my own house, number 14, although badly damaged, was on the right hand end of the destruction, and the rescue teams were able to inform me that the thirteen people (including my Father, Mother and two sisters) had been dug out and were unhurt, but had gone to other relatives and friends' houses.

Just two days later, at work in the Armament Depot, I was being approached by none other than Wilf Perry. My first reaction was to be pleased to see him, but when he asked if he could talk to me outside the workshop, to say the least, I felt a bit apprehensive. As it was, a mellow (even emotional) Wilf Perry apologized for his behaviour in Wyndham Square some two nights before and then followed up with the question – "Are you aware of how lucky you were!" On replying – "No," – Wilf then told me that bomb number 6 (ours) had landed just 25/30 yards from where we were standing – whilst he was arguing with us – and had failed to explode! For the group of us, but perhaps myself in particular, it had been yet another remarkable escape.

Finally, it is on record in the archive history of St. Peter's Church, that amongst the totally devastated and gutted interior, at the altar end, a single stone figure of Christ survived and remained standing – the figure continued to stand amongst the rubble for a number of years afterwards (I believe 12 years). However, on the very first day that workmen moved in to start to clear debris in preparation for re-building – the stone figure collapsed into many pieces – quite remarkable, but apparently true!" There is a little more about Ron Hellyer in the epilogue.

Another person who played an important role, in this and other raids, was Mabel Siddall, who, in the words of The Plymouth Evening Herald – 'Typified the unconquerable spirit of thousands, when Hitler's Luftwaffe rained death and destruction on Plymouth. This is Mabel's personal account of some of her memories of those often dangerous times:

'In 1938, at the age of 20, I joined the A.R.P. – later to be known as the Civil Defence. A friend and myself attended weekly meetings at The Oddfellows Hall in Devonport, where we were instructed by police sergeants and inspectors. I now realise that nobody could have thought of cities being bombed as they were, because our first serious lecture was on detecting smells of gases. After this, we did first aid courses, which were taken by members of The St. John's Ambulance. This led to our finals being adjudicated by a doctor – after which we received a certificate and a St. John's Ambulance badge, to be worn on our uniform.

At this time, I was engaged to a sailor – but in June 1940 he was captured and remained a POW until 1944.

I was working as a tailoress whilst I was doing part-time A.R.P. work, but I soon decided to give this up and went full time to an A.R.P. post in Devonport Park – although, there was another post much closer to where I lived. However, if the siren went when I was at home, I was allowed to report to the local post instead.

Exactly one month after the raid on the city centre of Plymouth, in March 1941, Devonport was blitzed. The big raid on Devonport, on 21st April, started before I was due to go on duty, so I reported to my local post – at this post, which was quite near to the dockyard and naval barracks, we were 'sitting targets.'

At about 7.30 p.m., the planes came over – dropping incendiary bombs. Some of these hit houses, setting them on fire, and I remember some others landing in straight lines along the streets – lighting up the roads; this caused terrible panic, because people wanted to put out the flames with sand bags, and we had to plead with them to go back to their shelters. There were people moving furniture out of their houses – hoping to save whatever they could from burning. Nobody seemed to realise that these incendiaries were to light up the area for the bombers who would soon follow.

At 8.30 p.m., when the bombs started falling, being a bit of a loner, I found I just couldn't stay in our shelter so I ventured outside to see what I could do – the shock of seeing Plymouth during and after the March raid had been terrible, but now, here was poor Devonport, where I was born, and the same thing was happening again! A block of flats at Morice Square, two churches and many, many houses – all so near the dockyard – bombed and burning!

I assisted bringing out and covering bodies from the flats in Morice Square; only to find two sisters, who I had been at school with – both dead, and one of them was pregnant.

Where I lived, there was an unexploded bomb, and I made sure the people there were out of their houses, and took them to 'hopeful' shelter from the bombing; which was going on all the time. Being young I didn't seem to realise I was in as much danger as anyone else, but I went back and looked at the 'hole' the unexploded bomb had made, before reporting it at the central report room. To get there I went through streets where many houses were burning – including The Royal Sailors Rest Home, which was burning fiercely, as was a large hardware store; also a bomb had thrown a bus onto the Alhambra, a few streets away. When I arrived at the report room, I found that they had transferred themselves to the outskirts of the city.

I don't know how the message arrived at the bomb disposal squad, but an officer came to see the bomb and when I went to show him where it was, he asked me how I knew; when I said I had been to have a look at it – I'll leave you to guess his reply! I do realise what a stupid idiot I was – when everyone else was safely tucked away in a shelter.'

Mabel was later awarded The British Empire Medal for bravery.

After these raids, the city had become almost unrecognisable with so many landmarks raised to the ground. Apart from many well-known streets being devastated, there were also so many churches, including St. Peter's, which had been so badly hit. As well as all these places, Aggie West's Sailor's Rest Home had gone, as had 'The Electric' and 'The Hippodrome.' The 'Alhambra' – where, a month before this, a packed and appreciative audience had been entertained by Billy Cotton and his band – had also been badly hit.

The Western Evening Mail had had to move its premises to Exeter, to carry on producing the paper, but the Evening Herald had carried on in its beleaguered buildings.

The horrific statistics for Plymouth, for the month of April, showed that over 1,500 houses had been destroyed and, of the better-known buildings destroyed, were the City Library and The Old Guildhall. Also, over 100 pubs had gone as well as at least 60 of the city's buses – so vital at that time in particular. Even more grim though was the fact that over 600 people had been killed.

Finally, Ken Searle, talking about the air raids, told me – "They were terrible days, especially when we stumbled across bits of flesh lying on the ground – parts of someone's body. At times I was physically sick. It was a deadly serious business being with the A.R.P. We all knew that we were constantly facing death and we didn't know when our number would come up.

Some of the older people wouldn't leave their homes for a street shelter during the raids; they carried on normally, even having their meals when they usually did – that is, if they still had supplies of gas and electricity!"

On the 1st of May 1940, arrangements were at last made for the evacuation of the city's children – "A bit like closing the stable door, after the horse has bolted!" Someone said, and probably what the whole population of Plymouth 'echoed.'

On the 2nd of May, Winston Churchill paid a special visit to the city – 'to see the devastation and hopefully lift the morale of the citizens' – showing typical Churchillian appreciation, he saw that life and work went on amongst the rubble.

After this, there were other raids on Plymouth during 1941 and later in the war – but nothing on the scale of the March and April raids of that year – when the spirit of the citizens had remained indomitable.

Chapter Ten

UXB's In Kent. Hull, More Devastation. And In The North – The Coastguards Take A Place.

During the spring of 1941, the biggest so far raid to affect Brighton had come on April 9th – with the raiders coming in from the sea, having crossed the Channel at very low level to dodge the radar. Some of these bombs fell very near some friends of ours, who lived at St. George's Terrace – but they had thankfully been unscathed. However, my father was later sad to learn that a local ambulance driver, whom he knew slightly and who sometimes used to talk to him, during the early years whilst fishing from the Banjo Groyne, had been killed in that raid.

Another lady, a friend of my mother's, who had joined the Red Cross at the beginning of the war, later told her that of all the raids on Brighton, this was the one she remembered the most because – during the raid, a family of four who she knew slightly, had all been killed. She hadn't found out about this until the next day, but apparently she had been helping with the wounded less than a quarter of a mile away, after the bombing.

Another lady, who had found herself in the thick of things at this time, was 'Babs' Davies, who had joined The Red Cross in 1940. She lived in Belvedere in Kent, which is beside the River Thames and close to where there were factories and docks. Also, and not too far away, there was Woolwich Arsenal – another prime target area for the Luftwaffe.

Because of this being such a 'prime target' area, there were lines of barrage balloons starting from the road next to where she lived and from there 'strung out,' all the way into London. On seeing that this area was so formidably defended, many of the enemy aircraft were tempted to quickly get rid of their loads of bombs, and turn for the journey back to Germany.

Babs, who helped out at a Red Cross post in the grounds of Erith Hospital, told me – "This first aid post was built like a large Anderson shelter – I think it was one of the only two of its kind in the country; the other one was at Plymouth, but sadly, this one received a direct hit in the bombings.

146

From the outset, jobs had included tending to the wounded, helping to 'delouse' children who were about to be evacuated and handing out clothing to the bombed out. A lot of this was very good clothing indeed – supplied by the American Red Cross. We only did these jobs if there was a lull in receiving the wounded from the bombings; other jobs, in quieter times, which weren't very often, were helping out at the hard pressed ante natal clinics and baby clinics.

When the casualties did start coming in – when the bombings increased in momentum – we were rushed off our feet, and it's amazing so many people managed to survive. We had the use of our own ordinary ambulances as well as 'Mobile Units' – ambulances fully equipped with operating tables and sterilizers, plus the beds and all medical instruments needed to do an operation on the spot – these units were the size of a coach, and were also supplied to us by the American Red Cross.

I couldn't possibly go through all the casualties we attended to, but I do particularly remember one lady who was so badly injured that the ambulance ladies had used her own front door, which had been blasted off its hinges, as a stretcher – she had so many broken bones, it was amazing she was still alive; it had involved less carrying by putting her on the door which was lying right beside her. Unfortunately, this lady, who we didn't expect to survive, had sadly lost her little girl in this raid. However, eighteen months later she was discharged from the hospital, after a lot of 'repair' work – both physical and mental – but, what joy it gave a lot of us when, hearing later on, that she had given birth to another baby daughter.

Another thing I can remember about this time, was seeing the bomb disposal men in their lorry going past near to where we were situated; they had a site for exploding the bombs or rendering them safe on the Belvedere Marshes – just near to us. They seemed to be quite a cheerful lot, always singing as they went by – probably sitting on an unexploded bomb, with a red flag hanging from behind the vehicle.

When they exploded the bombs they would stand behind a wall of sandbags they had built on the marshes – there would be an enormous 'VROOM' and up went the bomb! One day, later in the year, however, there was a different type of explosion – the noise was terrific and windows were shattered for about a mile – something had gone desperately wrong!

We attended to the injured from this unfortunate incident, when the UXB people had been trying to defuse a bomb by 'steaming' the fuse out –

rather than blow the bomb up. On this occasion they had been led by the 'affable' Earl of Suffolk – a usually very efficient man, highly respected and very much liked by the team of men he led. Unfortunately, both he and his lady secretary were killed when this bomb went off – they were brought to our post, but there was nothing we could do for them."

I have included another piece from Babs Davies during the latter part of the war, later in the book.

During the May of 1941, it was the turn of the northeast to get a bad blitzing – in particular the city of Hull.

Les Greef, was born in Hull in 1922 and by the time the war started, he was working as an apprentice for an engineering firm in the city. He also became a part-time firewatcher and, thus, witnessed the worst of the raids on Hull – including the May raids. He told me – "The heart of the city was torn out during those raids; the bombs sometimes rained down for three or more hours, without let up – it was terrifying."

Les also remembers many of the raids before the May blitz of 1941- he had one or two narrow escapes during these raids, but was lucky enough to come through unscathed. One thing that he still remembers clearly was going on cycle rides out of the city, to get away from it all for a while. During these rides he saw ack-ack batteries and search light units out in the country, which many people in the city had no idea of their being there. Also, he saw huge piles of wood in places and, on enquiring what they were there for, was told that they were 'decoy' fires, to be set alight at the start of a raid – to give the impression that this was where the flares had been dropped for the target area and, hopefully, make the heavy bombers of the Luftwaffe drop their bombs here, away from the city.

Les, who later went on to join the Home Guard, has also sent me copies of The Hull Daily Mail supplement – 'A City at War' – and I have permission to include some pieces from this long running series here. Although the supplements cover all the enemy activity over Hull, I am mainly concentrating on the May blitz.

In 'City At War' no. 4 dated January 25th 1992 under the heading – 'A CITY UNDER ATTACK,' the article goes on to say:

'The alert sounded at 11.15 p.m. on Wednesday, May 7. It was 1941 and Hull was facing its 45th raid. Within seconds of the siren wailing, families began stumbling through the night air to the shelters in their back gardens and in the streets. They clutched vacuum flasks and ration books and identity cards.

148

Staff at Hull's bomb damaged air raid Control Centre, in the Shell building on Ferensway, had been on the alert since dusk. They had been sent a 'Yellow Warning' as soon as the enemy planes had been picked up off the east coast. Then the alert had been heightened to a 'Purple Warning,' as the planes changed course for Hull. The 'Red Warning,' the signal for the sirens to start, had only been given when there was no doubt the bombers would be crossing the city.

Now came 'stand-by,' the warning to night-shift workers in Hull's wartime factories to make for the shelters – the enemy was almost overhead.

All across Hull the emergency services waited – the city, black and still from the air, was tense and expectant.

Firewatchers were on duty on the rooftops and at the street corners, 2,600 wardens were at their posts, the fire service braced themselves for a flood of calls. Ambulance crews fidgeted at their depots, hospitals cleared their casualty reception areas, gasmen stood by to cut off ruptured mains and water workers prepared to deal with shattered pipes; electricians and telephone engineers were ready to mend broken cables. Police reported to their station -the rescue and demolition experts waited in the dark.

Just after midnight came the unmistakable sound of the German bombers – almost immediately followed the ear splitting bark of the anti-aircraft batteries. The first bomb logged by control fell at 25 minutes past midnight – its fins whistling, it hurled through the dark towards the silent streets and the broad-roofed factories. It hit the ground on Cleveland Street where it gouged through the tarmac, smashed a water main and exploded in a subway – the debris and crater blocked the road. Nearby in Withernsea Street another bomb lay unexploded – Hull's first five-hour raid had begun.

Above the city, the bombers of the first wave were following a familiar pattern – they dropped a high proportion of incendiaries so the planes that followed would find the target lit like a beacon and ready to be stoked with parachute mines and high explosives.

For the wardens and police and the others still outside, it was a magnificent spectacle. The sky was criss-crossed with searchlight beams coming from the barges 'Clem' and 'Humph' – moored in the Humber. The bombers flares' hung over their targets, bathing everything in white light – the earth shook to the sound of guns and the air hummed to the beat of engines.

With the first explosions came the fires – a warden on Beverley Road reported five out of hand.

Fire engines with dimmed headlights began moving through the empty streets – the ambulance crews and first-aid posts knew they would not have long to wait.

Soon there were fires in Spring Street, Porter Street, Great Thornton Street, Linnaeus Street, Walker Street, Campbell Street and Norfolk Street – with the fires bombs came reports of people being trapped. Bombs had fallen on houses close to Anlaby Road crossing – people were missing in the wreckage. In Saner Street, Musgrave Flats had been hit and the gas mains were leaking as people lay buried in the burning rubble – within minutes of their arrival over the city, the bombers had managed to turn Hull into a galaxy of lights.

In their sandbagged headquarters, the control staff carefully monitored each incident; they relied on the reports from the wardens that came to them via four report centers. The wardens were often elderly men or women, working as best they could from their posts in empty shops or specially built brick shelters – they were the first line of the city's civil defence.

In the early hours of 8th May, it was a warden who reported people screaming in the wreckage of two homes in Middleton Street – across the city scores of similar incidents were being enacted – as the night wore on, the wardens became increasingly isolated.

By the close of the May raids, four fifths of the city's telephone network was out of action, and schoolboy runners were often their only contact with the organised services.

It soon became easy to imagine that the whole of Hull was burning – people at Goole, 30 miles away, could see the flames leaping through the sky – R.A.F. aircrew over the Danish coast flying home from their own raids could see the glow on the north-western horizon.

Like a mosaic, the shape of the raid gradually emerged – it was the heaviest Hull had suffered. It was concentrated on the city centre, the docks and the railway lines. The heaviest concentrations of bombs were falling on the shopping and commercial centre – fires had taken hold along the east side of King Edward Street.

Hammonds department store, opposite Paragon Station, was in flames, but it took an hour for Control, barely a quarter of a mile away, to be sent a report. Thornton Varley's store in Brook Street was burning, the bus station had been hit and was on fire and the library museum in Albion Street was in flames. In Jameson Street, the Co-op and the Midland Bank were burning fiercely, while the bank caretakers were trapped in the cellar.

In King Edward Street, Hull's popular Powolny's Café was disappearing in flames. Outside the centre, the fires were less spectacular – but the casualties heavier!

Stirling Villas on Stirling Street had been hit and people were trapped in the rubble. A warden in Wilberforce Street telephoned a request for the urgent rescue of people trapped by the collapse of part of De Grey Terrace. In Goulton Street, by William Wright Docks, a communal shelter received a direct hit.

On the east side of the city in Buckingham Street, the police were calling for lamps. They reported a large part of the street devastated and the gas mains leaking. The rescue squads were being hampered by the darkness – their request was delivered by a messenger on a bicycle as all the telephone cables were down.

At St. Andrew's Dock, where work had been underway to release people trapped in debris, the fires had grown out of control – all approaches to the dock were blocked and only the telephone in the police box was working.

In the centre of the city, all the trolley bus wires were out of action – in the Old Town, Holy Trinity Church stood in orange splendour, lit by fires in the surrounding streets. There were three major fires in Market Place, the High Street was alight in several places and Blackfriargate, Blanket Row, Dagger Lane and Nelson Street were all burning. East of the city centre, on James Reckitt Avenue, rescue workers were still picking through the ruins of houses hit by a string of high explosives early in the raid.

But, before light, the bombing began to slacken – by daybreak the last wave of bombers were heading across the North Sea for bases in occupied Europe; their crews searching the skies for fighters, for they knew it was they who were most vulnerable to attack.

In Hull, the 'all clear' came just after 5 a.m. The sirens held their long plaintive note and people began to emerge from their shelters. Smoke was rolling across the rubble filled streets. A wing of the Hull Royal Infirmary in Prospect Street was burning. In the city centre, steam mingled with fumes and firemen's hoses wormed their way among the burning buildings

Rescue squads were tunnelling for survivors – in Southcoats Lane, a mother was asking a policeman to send a squad to find the body of a child.

On the road to the city came a steady build-up of traffic – help from other parts of Yorkshire was arriving. Ambulances, fire engines, W.V.S. and mobile canteens, troops, rescue workers with mining experience, were all gathering at rendezvous points waiting to be guided into the bombed city.

The night had seen over 200 people killed and 165 seriously injured – the opening raid of the May blitz was over.'

The Hull Daily Mail, says that a reader of the Hull Daily Mail Supplement number 5, anonymously wrote that a junior librarian at The Central Library, who also did fire watching duties at this time, said – 'Shortly before I was conscripted into the Royal Air Force, the heaviest concentrated raids of the war took place, to be specific on the nights of 7th and 8th May 1941. I was not on duty on the night of the 7th, but as my home was relatively near to the city centre, after the bombing had stopped, I got out my bike and pedalled to the Central Library to see whether there was anything I could do. This block of elegant Georgian houses of three or four stories each, which stood in Albion Street, opposite the library was ablaze from end to end – approximately 100 yards. The sole attention that this conflagration was receiving was the hopeless efforts of two exhausted firemen with a 'trailer pump.'

The building next to the library was a heap of rubble as a consequence of having received an H.E. (high explosive) bomb, and the adjoining upper front corner of the library building was just beginning to burn. The duty firewatchers and I managed to get a hose of the kind provided in public buildings, out over the roof and directed in the general direction of the flames. The pressure of the water was pathetically low due to demand, and no doubt countless fractured mains, but the trickle available checked the spread of the fire, and an appeal to the trailer pump men brought a final squirt that doused it completely. As a precautionary measure, we removed the 'accessions register' from the library, so that a record of stock would exist should the building and its contents, still succumb in spite of our efforts. I got a mention in The Hull Daily Mail for 8th May as 'a boy member of staff' of a public library who made his job 'the removal of valuable records.' The report covered a host of bizarre events, including the burying in rubble in the course of the night not once, but twice, of an elderly couple. They escaped from a pub cellar in which they had been sheltering and returned to their own cottage home only to be buried again, and from this debris they escaped, still clutching their insurance policies!'

Hull was to suffer many further raids after this; some of them very severe – thus, keeping all the emergency services extremely busy. Ex-policeman Harry Tate, whom I wrote a little about in Chapter Two, particularly remembers a raid on the city just over a couple of months after the raid of May 7th and 8th. He says, ' – It was on July 18th and, by that time, I was in the C.I.D. Aliens and Special Branch – our office was above W. Massey's at the corner Quay Street and Alfred Gelder Street. The Guildhall was at the other side of Quay Street with an air raid siren on the roof. Every fourth night, three of us slept in the office as firewatchers and it was not unusual for me to sleep through the sirens – to be awakened by my colleagues if anything happened. On this night I was sound asleep when I was thrown out of my camp bed and awoke to hear bombs dropping and the siren fading away.

It was a stick of bombs, the first, I believe, landing in the Sykes Street area; the next on the YPI in George Street, the next on Queen's Gardens, followed by one at the rear of the Guildhall, then the Post Office and the last, I believe, something in the Old Town. The bombs on either side of the Guildhall, particularly the Post Office, shook me out of bed.

An armed policeman was always on 24-hour duty at the GPO and there was some concern about his safety, but apart from being shaken, he was little the worse.'

There was however, based in Hull, a last resort; a highly secret weapon to be used if the worst came to the worst and communications between Hull and the hinderland broke down. The ordinary man in the street was very much involved with it, for it was through his enthusiasm that it was there in the first place, ready in its city centre office for the use at any time. It was a carrier pigeon service, so closely guarded a secret that even today few people realise it existed. Harry Tate, a man closely concerned with it, told its story recently.

Harry says: – "The Police Pigeon Messenger Service was run on the authority of MI5 at Leeds. Up to the fall of France, all security and Special Branch work was done by police in the Aliens Department. After France fell, with the danger of fifth column activists, a number of arrests were made and other people placed under observation; for example, two men who were Fascists in Hull were arrested. Such people were interned on the Isle of Man.

The Aliens Department had its own work amongst the aliens, of whom there were a great many in Hull, including Germans. There were a lot who had lived here for years but had not taken out British nationality, and they all had to come in and register each week. A track was also kept on their proposed movements around the country, which they had to report in detail. So the Aliens Department got on with that

153

work and a Special Branch unit was set up in Hull for other work, with a Detective Inspector in charge of five Detective Sergeants.

Those of us in it were, Detective Inspector J.B. Kilvington, with Detective Sergeants Jackie Miller (who was a local boxer), Jimmy Cocksworth, Alfie Foster, Len Seage, and myself. If an invasion on the east coast was taking place and all communications were knocked out, as a last resort, a police pigeon service, which had been set up on the authority of MI5 could be used. It was established in the police forces of Hull, the east riding (at Beverley), the west riding (at Goole) and Leeds.

Tom Fowles, a well-known local pigeon fancier, was taken on as a police war reservist to do the work. In those days he lived in Gillshill Road. The using of carrier pigeons was then prohibited by law, but the Chief Constable of the whole of Yorkshire and Lincolnshire Protected Area, arranged for some to be kept. Tom recruited civilians who loaned the police their best pigeons.

These men included, Mr. Curtis of Somerset Street who was also a fish fryer on Hessle Road, Mr. Parker, a butcher in Hawthorn Avenue, and someone who lived down Haltemprice Street.

The four centres involved (Hull, Beverley, Goole and Leeds), sent two pigeons each to each other three times a week as a practice. The birds were ringed and had a container attached to them to get used to the equipment, and sometimes a message would be sent to see how it went. At least 12 birds were involved, maybe more. Tom also bred from them and got some quality birds. It was all set up surprisingly quickly, as it started from the fanciers' houses until we could get our own loft. The birds were taken to Leeds and Goole by rail and Beverley by car. At the same time each day, the birds were sent back, unless the weather was bad, when there would be a delay. The service started in 1941 and was continuing when I went into the R.A.F. in 1943. It ran for at least three years. We mostly liaised with Tom if there were any problems. I think the people who loaned him the pigeons knew about the service, but they kept quiet about it.

The birds were kept in a loft built in a room in the Aliens Department's office, on the corner of Quay Street near Hull Guildhall. There was a firewatching team in that building each night, consisting of two members of the Special Branch and one from the Aliens Department."

During the blitz on Hull, a bomb that – 'seemed to come from out of nowhere' – made a direct hit on a stable block. Within seconds, the hayloft

154

was blazing, with flames licking the sky in a rush of heat and crackling debris that flew like fireworks every which way. The Hull Daily Mail supplement tells the story of George Hinch, who, with some colleagues, was responsible for saving the lives of many of the horses stabled there. This is some of an account of a desperate race against time – to save the horses!:

' – During the raid, for a moment, the sixty year old railway foreman, who was on A.R.P. duty at the time, hesitated – then he heard the terrified stamping of horses, trapped in the burning building and heard them kicking frantically as embers of glowing debris rained on their backs from the floor of the loft.

Without a thought for his own safety, he rushed into the blazing furnace, closely followed by three colleagues and battled through smoke and heat to unleash 19 of the 37 horses trapped inside.

Racing against the clock, they tethered them in a safe area of the yard and went back into the flames. But the oil bomb had done its work – already their escape route was being blocked by falling debris, leaving them with just one option. As more people rushed to help, they started to lead the remaining horses out of the back of the stables into a street virtually blocked by demolished houses. Picking their way through the rubble, they struggled to calm the terrified creatures – unnerved, not only by the flames, but also by the constant explosions and whistling of falling bombs. Miraculously, they led another 14 to safety – three of the horses suffering severe burns to their back and legs – but were unable to go back for the remaining four which perished when the loft caved in on top of them.

Later, Mr. Hinch, described the scene. He said – "As we entered the stables, we found burning oil dripping through the floorboards of the loft and spraying over the horses. The horses were ablaze as we rushed out of the stables with them, and our own clothing was on fire. We put the flames out as best we could, but our troubles were by no means at an end as the blocking up of a passageway meant we had to use another route in which we had to climb over a great deal of rubble before we could get the horses to safety. Bombs were still dropping and there was also some gunfire. The horses were certainly frightened and would not face the fire – one of us had to lead each horse out, while another person had to stand behind driving it. After getting all the horses out of that first stable, we went to the second, where we rescued all but the four on which the loft had collapsed – had I stayed another two minutes, I would have been under that collapsed roof myself.

By this time, about 40 tons of straw was ablaze, but by using stirrup pumps, we managed to contain it enough to save a number of houses nearby. Then we smashed in the rest of the burning roof, to prevent the flames licking towards the second block of stables, where some of the horses had already been taken to safety.

Incidentally, all the men worked like Trojans and, all the rescued horses survived."

George Hinch was later awarded the British Empire Medal for his bravery during this raid. Also, he and his colleagues were to receive a number of awards from the R.S.P.C.A.

During the summer of 1941, in Brighton, our emergency visits to the basement, after the siren had gone, were still reasonably frequent – but not as frequent as they had been. I remember my father saying – "With any luck, we might be over the worst!" He felt that what was really needed was some good news – something to boost morale and lift our spirits, however small.

One extremely odd piece of news, which did eventually filter through, concerned Hitler's third in command – Rudolf Hess.

On Saturday May 10th 1941, a single unidentified German aeroplane was spotted by an Observer Corps lookout as it crossed the North Sea coastline. Quite soon after this, a report reached the RAF plotting room at Inverness, saying that the aircraft was an ME110. They thought that this was barely credible because no ME110 could have flown so far with any hope of getting back to Germany – however, this report was quickly followed by another one, saying that the aircraft had crashed!

A few minutes before this, Tom Hyslop, of The Renfrewshire Constabulary, was driving along the Eaglesham Road with his daughter – the time was 10.45 p.m. Suddenly there was a message on his police radio receiver which said, 'A single enemy plane has crossed the Clyde and is flying inland towards Glasgow.' The message continued, ' – It is difficult to identify, but is definitely hostile and may be in difficulties – all police are to watch, in case it lands.' He stopped the car to listen – for a while there was nothing at all; then he heard the roar of an aircraft as it passed close overhead, carried on flying for a few seconds – then crashed; probably about a mile away.

In actual fact the plane had crashed into a field without Hess in it; he had just had time to use his parachute before crashing.

David Maclean, the head ploughman at Floors Farm, a bachelor, who lived with his mother in a small whitewashed cottage on the farm, had heard the aeroplane flying close by and had pulled the blackout from a window to see if he could see anything. It was a moonlit night and, having heard the plane crash, he soon saw the white outline of a parachute. He rushed from the cottage and approached the pilot, who, after he had freed himself from the billowing parachute, started to stagger towards him – he had injured an ankle. David asked him if he was a German – "Yes," said Hess, "I am Hauptmann Alfred Horn, I want to go to Dunganel House; I have an important message for the Duke of Hamilton." At this stage he was determined not to give away his identity.

David took the parachutist to the cottage, where his mother made tea for her German visitor, but he only drank water. David then told Hess that he couldn't take him to see the Duke of Hamilton and that, in any case, the army would be there soon to collect him – he had sent one of the farm workers to a nearby searchlight unit to get help. This searchlight unit was actually a secret radar centre for the Royal Signals. It wasn't long before two members of 'The Signals' arrived at the cottage – placing the still unrecognised Hess under arrest. A little later a member of the Home Guard also arrived at the cottage in the company of a member of Special Branch. Tom Hyslop, who, with others had been out searching the fields for the parachutist, didn't arrive at the cottage until after Hess had been taken away.

It wasn't long before Hess's true identity came to light – and the rest, of course, is history!

David Maclean, the ploughman, in his 'capture' of the German 3rd in command, was soon back doing his normal job, but his name, purely by chance, would be linked to this major World War incident, on the home shores, forever! Not so much as a volunteer – but someone who just happened to be there and did what he considered to be his duty.

By June 1941, the news from overseas was still very much on the gloomy side. Crete had fallen on May 27th and, back at home, on June 2nd, clothing became another addition to the widespread selection of commodities that were already rationed.

However, on June 22nd came the rather surprising piece of news that the Germans, in what appeared to be a change of tactics, attacked Russia. This gave many people, including the historians, the military tacticians, the politicians and people like my father, who simply followed the news closely from day to day, the hope that Herr Hitler had made the same blunder as that earlier historical 'conqueror' –

Napoleon Bonaparte. He had also come unstuck in waging war against and invading Russia.

On the home shores, since the outbreak of war, the vigilance kept around the coasts of the United Kingdom for any signs of being invaded ourselves – or spies or saboteurs being secretly landed – had remained constant and, although there had been no invasion, there had, however, been incidents in which the Coastguards, Coastwatchers and others had had to play important roles.

The volunteers for the Auxiliary Coastguards and Coastwatchers were often made up from people who earned their living close to the shoreline – one of these was Arthur Coleman, who had taken over Church Farm, at Speeton, in North Yorkshire from his father, William Coleman, in May 1939 – just six months before war was declared.

His son Chris Coleman, has sent me the following account concerning his father, who joined the Auxiliary Coastguards in 1940:

'On taking over the farm my father bought a new case model D tractor for £185 and traded in our Foster portable steam engine, used for threshing. The pedigree flock of Leicester sheep, was still in the family, as it had been for many generations – it still is. It is one of the oldest flocks in the UK.

Such was the farm on 3rd September 1939, it included one tractor, horses and about 250 breeding ewes and a shortage of labour. On the arable side we grew wheat, barley, turnips and seeds – there was also some arable land temporarily under grass.

In the summer of 1940, large trenches were dug across the arable fields to stop enemy aircraft landing – this made land work very difficult. It was at this time that my father became an auxiliary coastguard.

Up to 3rd September 1939, no fewer than 12 vessels of one kind or another were wrecked on only three miles of the North East coast of Flamborough Head, between Speeton and Bempton. Ten of these wrecks are visible at low tide today (Feb. 2001). The reason for this is a seam of red chalk running the full length of the high chalk cliffs, having a ferrous content thus pulling old type compasses off course and the vessels also. As a consequence, a new Coast Guard station was built on a high hill near Speeton village in 1904 to house three full-time Coastguards (ex. R.N. married men with families) and life saving equipment, boxer rockets and the breeches buoy system, mounted on a rocket cart. This also required twenty volunteers from the village plus four horses to pull the cart. The volunteers, plus the regulars, plus

158

the cart and equipment went under the name of life saving apparatus (L.S.A.).

Sometime between the end of 1939 and mid 1940 the regular Coastguards were called back for war service. This left the Coastguard station empty, but the L.S.A. still manned by volunteers from the village. This is where my father Arthur Coleman came into the war. He had been Number One in the volunteer L.S.A. for six years, but in early 1940 was in the L.D.V. (Local Defence Volunteers – later the Home Guard). He took over Church Farm (430 arable acres) in early 1939 at the age of thirty seven, from his father. In mid 1940 he was approached by Captain Ramsbottom, who was Inspector of C.G.S. NE Division, to take charge of the Coast Guard station at Speeton and to take charge of the L.S.A.. This he did plus doing a six hour watch every day, plus running the 430 acre farm. He recruited six more Auxiliaries from the village and set four watches per day – 06-00–12-00/12-00–18-00/18-00–00-00/00-00-06-00. One man daylight watch and two men night watch – this system continued until May 1945.

The new volunteers had unusual dress, being khaki battle dress uniforms, but with Coastguard hats. They were armed with old Canadian Ross rifles and five rounds of .303 ammunition.

During the winter of 1940-41 and 1941-42 my father would sometimes do the 18.00 to midnight watch and, on numerous dark nights I took his supper to the Coastguard station. This entailed passing two sentries of the Royal Berkshires and, to a very frightened ten-eleven year old was a scary task – this had to be done before 22.00 hours because of the curfew.

Up to 1940 we had no telephone at the farmhouse, but when father was made an Auxiliary Coastguard a telephone was soon installed (free).

Supplementary to watch duties, a beach patrol was carried out at dawn every day. This necessitated walking down the cliff, through the minefield on to the beach and walking to Hunmanby Gap (3 miles) where a Coastguard from Filey was met and signed log books. This was a dangerous job as the beach was littered with butterfly bombs, antipersonnel mines, large sea mines and great heaps of timber. I accompanied father many times on these patrols and a sharp lookout for fresh mines in the sand or new tracks on the high water mark was kept. Any live mines were reported and dealt with by the Army Bomb Disposal or RN Mine Unit.

On the evening of July 9th 1941, the sea fog came down very thick. This is not unusual on this stretch of coast (hence all the wrecks).

159

About 23.30 hours I was in bed, dark had just descended, when a terrible roaring in the sky, with explosions awakened me, and a huge ball of flame went westwards past my bedroom window. Leaping out of bed to look out of the window, 'the thing' had passed suddenly there was a huge explosion in the direction of Philip Jackson's farm. My father was on his way to the Coastguard station to start his midnight six-hour watch. He stopped to chat to the sentry of the local billeted Berkshires. They then saw this huge ball of flame coming towards them out of the sky and thought it was going to crash on them. Father dived on the floor near a wall and the sentry landed on top of him. The ball of flame passed over them but crashed on Philip Jackson's house 500 yards away.

Father did not go to the crash scene, but went with haste to the Coastguard station to get to a telephone.

At daylight it emerged that the crash was a German JU88 bomber with a crew of four. It had taken part of Philip Jackson's barn roof and the starboard wing grazed the corner of the farmhouse before crashing in the field near the farmhouse, breaking up and killing the crew.

Soon, after the crash, a large fire glowing in the fog was seen half a mile away on the clifftop. The Royal Berkshires were soon on the scene and found the burning remains of another JU88 bomber. This one had been flying 350 feet above the sea, but was met with a wall of 350 ft cliff and just managed to bellyflop into a field, through a high bank and came to rest in another field. The crew got out, setting fire to the plane, and with a rubber dingy made for the sea in the dark – but fear of the cliffs overcame them and the Berkshires took them prisoner.

On the way to school the following morning I saw the four airmen in the guard house in the village. One had a white bandage round his head – I went to see both crash sites a few days later and still have a souvenir.

The reason the JU88 crashed on the cliff was quite simple – but it is a mystery why the bomber crashed in the village, which was on fire and losing height.

As my father was Auxiliary Coastguard In-charge, we got quite a bit of secret information during the war. It was soon learned that three JU88 bombers set off that night from Schiphol (Holland) and the third aircraft crashed at Staithes, a fishing village in North Yorkshire. It seems the fog and the cliffs had claimed three more victims.'

Also, continuing about this incident of the night of 9/10th July 1941, there is a good story by reporter – Bill Norman – of 'The Hull Daily Mail' in 'The City At War' (Number 4 – January 25th 1992) – including Mr. Coleman and other Auxiliary Coastguards, as well as about the Germans, in the three JU88 bombers. The incident says:

'Arthur Coleman, retired sheep farmer and ex-wartime Auxiliary Coastguard, will tell you that the cliffs behind his East Yorkshire village of Speeton, can sometimes ensnare unwary sea travellers, even those who might profess to know the area reasonably well.

This is particularly so in the night hours, when the grey walls blend more readily with the blackness and allow the unsuspecting to get very close before realising the danger. A trawler skipper who had once made such an unintended approach in the darkness and who had suddenly found the cliffs looming ahead confided in Arthur that, "... we thought the Devil had got us ..."

But they were lucky – they managed to take evasive action in time.

However fate has not always been so forgiving: one night over fifty years ago, sea travellers of a different kind had a less fortunate encounter. On the night of 9/10th July 1941, a flight of three German JU88 bombers of Kustenfliegergruppe 106 took off from their base at Schipol (Holland) with the intention of carrying out anti-shipping operations between Whitby and Holy Island. Each aircraft had a crew of four.

The lead aircraft 9M2+AL) was being flown by Hauptman H. Moeg, M2+ER by Oberleutnant E. Peisart and M2+CL by Leutnant H. Sinz. During the flight the raiders encountered mist. Peisart, anxious to maintain his bearings, dropped to near sea level and became separated from his companions. He continued flying northwards over the sea and would eventually reach his patrol line. However, as Moeg and Sinz progressed up the coast, they were unknowingly drifting west. As they passed Flamborough Head, they must have been very close to the coast, if not actually over it. They must also have been down 100 feet of altitude, for moments later the vague silhouette of a rocky wall suddenly loomed out of the mist and Moeg found himself flying straight at Speeton cliffs, some 280 kph.

What happened next is not totally clear, but he did just manage to scrape over the top before his aircraft bellied into the fields immediately beyond. Alan Stavely, then a fifteen-year-old farm worker, had heard its approach and is convinced that its engines were still driving as the aircraft gouged its way across one and a half fields before slewing through 360 degrees and grinding to a halt.

161

Sinz must have been to port of Moeg's aircraft, for he and his crew came to earth some distance further west. For reasons currently unknown, M2+Cl was on fire as it settled towards the ground over Speeton village. Local legend had it that the planes had collided – but there is currently no evidence to support this belief.

At 11.48 p.m. Arthur Coleman was in Wide Street, en-route to report for his six hour shift, which was due to start at the Coastguard station at midnight. He had stopped to chat with a soldier of the locally billeted Royal Berkshire Regiment: they were standing outside the village shop, just below the track that leads to Jackson's Millholme Farm and the Coastguard station beyond, when something attracted their attention. "All I could see was the glow of a big ball of fire coming towards us through the fog. It was so low that we thought that it was going to land on us, so we both dived to the ground. It only just passed over my head; it put the wind up me I can tell you – and then there was a terrific crash from the direction of Philip Jackson's farm." Philip Jackson was due to go on shift with Arthur that night, but as the blazing Junkers was aiming for his house, he was still in bed, and his sister was downstairs – both they and their parents were exceptionally lucky that evening, for Death missed them literally by feet.

The stricken plane took off the top of their barn and careered across the front of their home, the starboard wing clipping one corner in the process. In virtually the same instant, the Junkers struck the ground and disintegrated in the field alongside the farmhouse. There were no survivors. Philip's sister had seen the burning wreck fly past within feet of her window, but its true nature had escaped her. Believing the village was suffering an incendiary attack, she shouted to her brother to get up without delay – only when he got outside did Philip begin to grasp the significance of what had happened.

Among the smouldering debris that littered the landscape outside his house, he found a 'big bomb' just inside the field and four smaller ones that had been scattered on impact; he was to find out later that they had not been primed to explode. At the corner of the house lay the body of a crew member amid pieces of a charred parachute – a salutary reminder of war's waste.

Contrary to what might have been expected, Philip did not stay long at the scene: he was expected on duty at midnight and he knew that appropriate action was already being put into effect. He made his way to the Coastguard station, where Arthur Coleman soon joined him.

162

In the fields above the cliff, Moeg and his crew had survived their ordeal and were busily engaged in releasing their rubber dinghy. Having done so – and after their captain had set fire to his aircraft – they made their way to the cliffs with the dinghy, though no one seems quite clear as to their intention. In any case, they did not get far; Arthur had seen the glow of the burning aircraft and had alerted the army, but the Berkshires were already searching and the would be escapers were soon apprehended.

They spent some time under guard at the Speeton home of a Mrs. Hartley "...a kind old soul who would probably have made them a cup of tea..." Whether they got the tea is a matter of conjecture, but before they left, they made her a present of a silk scarf.

As they were driven away the next day, Moeg and his crew might well have had thoughts for the friends they had lost – and for Peisart, who had sought to keep his bearings and had thus become separated and safe.

What they could not possibly have known at the time was that Peisart's aircraft had crashed into the cliffs at Staithes, near Whitby, shortly after midnight. There were no survivors.

As I have said in this chapter – everything on the home shores during the early years and including 1941 – the news seemed 'very much doom and gloom' – however, we found that the bombings seemed perhaps a little lighter for a while in the Brighton area at that time – but there were still other areas where the raids continued badly, especially, of course in London.

Continuing about the bad news elsewhere around the world – later on in November the headlines that H.M.S. Ark Royal had been sunk – after being torpedoed by a U Boat – East of Gibraltar in the Mediterranean. They tried to take her in tow, but apparently the list had got so bad – and she sank in the early hours of November 14th, 1941. The bad news – together with the air raids and all the deprivations and restrictions, didn't exactly do much for moral at the time, and, with the onset of winter and Christmas not far away, everything seemed extremely bleak!

On December 7th the news that the Japanese had, without any declaration of war, attacked Pearl Harbour. This immediately meant that it was inevitable that America would enter the war against, not only Japan, but also the Germans, who with the Japanese and the Italians formed the axis power.

There would be more bad news later in December, telling of the sinking of the ships H.M.S. Prince of Wales and H.M.S. Repulse off the coast of Malaya.

However there was a general feeling of not being so alone on this island of ours and that the Japanese, in their murderous attack, had indeed awoken a 'sleeping giant' in the Americans – giving us a very strong and welcoming ally – even if there was an ocean separating us.

Chapter Eleven

The Baedeker Raids Hit At Beauty – Blitz At Canterbury, But The Cathedral Saved.

In Folkestone, during 1941, was one rather 'young man' – a little underage; but who still managed to join the Home Guard – his name is Eric Hart. Eric says – "I was born and bred in Folkestone, and was just a young teenager when war was declared in September 1939, not old enough in fact for 'call-up' into the armed services. In 1940, I witnessed the evacuation of Dunkirk, when thousands of troops arrived at Folkestone Harbour, with the vessels at times, tying up three abreast along the harbour wall. Tired and weary, the troops were transferred to capacity filled boat trains and hauled up to the main line by four steam locomotives, working flat out as they battled with the steepest gradient in southern England. The slow labouring progress allowed the townsfolk to throw offerings of food and drink to the lads as many of them gathered at the carriage windows for a welcomed sight of home, and to acknowledge the greetings of those lining the trackside. With the evacuation at an end, the harbour fell silent, and a block ship was positioned at the hatbour mouth with the seacocks open, thus settling on the bottom to deny docking facilities to the enemy. Likewise – The Royal Engineers blew up a section of the Victoria Pier to isolate its landing stage from the shore. The foreshore became something of a minefield, while the railway swingbridge at the inner harbour was traversed to an angle which prohibited the passage of both ships and rail traffic – made an even more formidable obstacle by having had concrete poured into the operating machinery. Large numbers of the town's civil population were evacuated or made their own arrangements to reach a safer haven, while others remained and were transferred from their normal peacetime occupations to work of National Importance.

In this state of emergency, the obligatory driving licences were waived, and that enabled me to drive motor vehicles (although, come to think of it – I was still underage!) I was soon driving an agricultural tractor on a farm which bordered the northern side of Hawkinge Fighter Aerodrome. That was my 'baptism of fire,' for I frequently had

165

to stop the tractor and dive under it for cover as the enemy planes dived low overhead, strafing and bombing. After one such close encounter, my morale was lifted somewhat, when one of the defending gunners emerged from behind his sandbagged gun position and offered me a spare tin helmet. However, shortly after this, I gained employment at Shorncliffe Military Camp with the D.C.R.E.'s (District Civil Royal Engineers). Here I became a carpenter's improver and learned quite a lot of what would be useful to me when working with timber in later life. Many of the properties in the district had been commandeered by the military, and we were kept busy, initially making blackout shutters for all the windows, and later on with property maintenance and bomb damage repairs. Humour crept in when we were given the task of constructing some 'dummy' Spitfires from plywood, and these were positioned around the perimeters of Hawkinge and Lympne Airfields as 'decoys' to attract enemy fire. The story went around just after, that 'Jerry' had dropped some WOODEN bombs on them! Another 'ruse' were the telegraph poles that we set-up along the coast, outward to Dungeness point, they were placed horizontally, with camouflage at one end to simulate coastal gun defences; giving the impression to enemy aerial reconnaissance that we were 'bristling' with defences – when in fact we were so vulnerable.

The H.Q. of the Folkestone Home Guard was at the Drill Hall in Shellons Street (now replaced by a supermarket), but a separate Platoon was formed at Shorncliffe from the civilian employees working there. Our Platoon Sergeant was none other than former Garrison Sergeant Major Hedges, who although retired, still retained his thunderous word of command that would send shivers up and down the spine of many a new recruit, but only now can I fully appreciate his frustration while endeavouring to 'pull everyone into shape.' Everyone was aware of the grim situation and after we were kitted-out in khaki, and issued with the formerly redundant Canadian Ross rifles of .300 calibre, we took over the defence of Sandgate Castle, a small fortress, truly in the front line, down by the shore – barely some 25 miles across the water from the enemy. On an average twice a week, we turned out for a tour of duty from 21.00 hrs until 06.00 hrs the following morning, with two hours on and two hours off on a rota system throughout. The more agile of us would be detailed for the cycle patrols, while the others would undertake static watches on top of the Castle Keep. My friend and companion on many of these night patrols was a fellow teenager – Donald Petts. With our rifles slung over our shoulders and with only

166

five rounds of ammunition in our pouches, we would head eastward along the Lower Sandgate Road, betwixt foreshore and the cliffs. The staked-out barbed wire each side of the narrow roadway and the skull and crossbones signs, which read 'Danger Mines' were a sobering, thought. Lights of any kind as well as lighted cigarettes were forbidden of course, although we did on occasion encounter two very contrasting examples. At intervals we would pause to scan the foreshore, looking seaward for any signs of movement, and it was quite a common to experience a strange phenomena described as 'phosphorescence' – a chemical reaction in sea water – best understood by looking up the word in the dictionary. However, when experiencing this, it always called for a second look – just in case!

The other light form was unmistakable, for this was a giant 'Surflight' of some 7″ in diameter, set amongst the foliage on the seaward side of the road – adjacent to a brick-in Diesel Generator. It was our duty to report there for a confirming signature from the N.C.O. and I suspect that it was a two-way ploy to ensure that the crew was alert! This very powerful searchlight would be switched on occasionally to scan the channel, and that task was performed from the Command Post on the Leas Promenade Coastal Gun Site above which boasted four 6″ Naval Guns, which incidentally came from H.M.S. Hood when the battleship was refitted before her tragic loss in the Atlantic. I recall one incident down at the searchlight one night when I ventured in front of the 'reposing' giant, when suddenly it was switched on! This accompanied by a deafening yell from the sergeant for me to move to the right and NOT look around. Frightening at the time – I have often laughed about it since with the thought that my shadow must have been emblazoned on the cliffs of Caps Grez Nez that night? On another occasion, when riding my cycle through drizzle on a very dark night, I was suddenly confronted with a large black object in my immediate path, I braked hard but with little effect because of the wet conditions, and I went over the handlebars as I collided with it! One would have thought the Military would have notified the Home Guard of the temporary obstruction in the middle of the roadway, via a mobile diesel generator, brought in, while the other one was being serviced – fortunately, my face just missed the horizontal exhaust pipe protruding at eye level, but left me with a few bruises and a buckled cycle wheel, so I had to walk the remainder of the patrol.

This meant that my colleague and I were late back at the Castle, but thankful to gain some respite from the foul weather outside, and the chance of a refreshing 'cuppa' – any food that we took with us had to stored in a metal container, for the legacy of rats that Henry Eighth left us weren't always confined to the dungeons below. The weird tales we had heard about the ghost down there on occasions seemed more plausible when stormy weather prevailed, and the tide battered the Castle wall. This was totally in contrast to the illusions created on a calm night, when the rising moon created a silvery wake across the placid water, to be greeted by the soulful 'hoot' of a nearby owl. The harsh reality of war seemed far removed, although all too often shattered by the 'wail' of the air raid sirens, closely followed by the drone of enemy bombers overhead. Just as horrendous were the cross channel duels of the giant 16″ shore batteries, each sending shells across, which weighed in at one and a quarter tonnes and caused immense damage and loss of life in the south eastern corner, known as 'Hellfire Corner'.

Memories of a more light-hearted nature spring to mind, such as the time we were manning a Lewis Gun in the confines of the castle grounds during an air raid. Unlike the accuracy of the Bren Gun, the Lewes had a wider cone of fire, and this was in evidence when a low flying Dornier bomber – with smoke already issuing from an engine, swooped low over the clifftop. Looking back, I realise that the target was out of range, but in the excitement of the moment, I opened fire, with the only 'hit' being recorded by my companion as – 'A couple of ricochets off Sandgate School Spire!' – So – I would imagine that the locals that evening must have wondered who's side we were on?

On occasions at week-ends, the Home Guard were approached by the Military with regard to taking part in their 'schemes' (Military exercises), and in one such exercise we mounted watch all night inside a foreshore concrete 'Pillbox'. After having completed a boring eight hours, staring along the coastline, we at last spotted an 'enemy' patrol approaching in the distance, and in the knowledge that a military umpire was hidden somewhere out there, we loaded our blank ammunition for the 'kill'. Imagine the scene, when from a house across the road, an elderly lady appeared in dressing gown, curlers and head scarf, bearing a loaded tea tray. We were a little premature over the victory we had envisaged, for this good Samaritan called out to us – "Coo-e-e, light refreshments!" Our position given away, we were to become prisoners, but I must say that the tea and biscuits went down a treat!

At one point in time, a small searchlight was installed on the battlements of the castle, and powered by a petrol driven generator.

This was brought into use on occasions when German E-Boats were suspected of infiltrating our waters. Difficulty in starting the motor one night resulted in the order being given that it had to be tested every night – failure to carry out the proper checks one night resulted in the searchlight inadvertently sending a beam of light out into the channel and silhouetting one of our own M.T.B.'s (Motor Torpedo Boats) – closely followed by a frantic phone call to douse the light! Typical perhaps of an episode of 'Dad's Army' you may think, but left untold are many more serious aspects and deeds of these worthy compatriots.

The word 'boredom' wasn't in our vocabulary in those days, for we were fully occupied with a strong sense of purpose, and with a community spirit far stronger than its like since. The wartime rationing of food, clothing and numerous other materials made us all more vigilant about wastage, a trait which many of the older generation still observe today in this otherwise 'throw away' society, and sadly so evident with the scattering of litter in our streets and public places. My fervent hope, is that we never witness anything like the hardship and deprivation of the dark days under discussion, although the reintroduction of some form of discipline would be in my opinion, good. Later on, in 1943 Eric joined the R.A.F.

In Brighton we had a quiet Christmas during the year of 1941 – and also the beginning of the New Year during 1942. However, the day before my father's birthday, in early February 1942, the news came through that the Japanese had landed on the Solomon Islands and also on New Guinea. This meant that if they were to make a firm foothold there and completely overtake New Guinea, Australia like Britain would have an enemy situated just across the water from them and a very real threat.

My grandparents, who were still living in Cumberland, had been offered by their oldest son, our Uncle Dennis, to go and join him and his wife in Australia in early 1939, when things were beginning to look very bad in Europe. They had declined the offer, but a year later wished they hadn't, now things were different again and they were glad they had stayed in this country – Australia, at that time, looked to be the place not to be!

During the end of May 1942, the Cathedrals at Coventry and Llandaff, in Cardiff having been bombed – it now came the turn of the city of Canterbury and, of course, the most famous of all the cathedrals.

When the people of Canterbury heard the news on the radio that there had been a heavy raid by the R.A.F. on the city of Cologne, on the night of Sat/Sun 30th and 31st May 1942, thoughts immediately sprang to many worried minds that there would be a reprisal raid and that Canterbury would probably be the target.

Many of them remembered that 'Lord Haw Haw' in one of his propaganda speeches on the wireless, had said that if Cologne – famous for its cologne in particular – was bombed, then Canterbury, with perhaps the world's most famous cathedral, would be bombed by the Luftwaffe in reprisal!

Consequently, the city started to prepare at the same time as holding their breath, keeping their fingers crossed and frequently praying that no such raid would take place – Canterbury was 'on its toes.'

In the 'Baedeker' raids, the Germans aimed at destroying British towns and cities, not for their military or armament factories – but for their sheer beauty – their historical importance and outstanding architecture – places that were not only well known and revered, but, also, unfortunately – to be lightly defended.

Exeter, another city with a famous cathedral, had had one of these raids on April 24th – and again, a more devastating raid on May 3rd when the cathedral had been hit and many of the historical buildings destroyed, including nine churches.

Now, after the R.A.F. raid on Cologne, it was feared that the reprisal would come quickly – and probably devastatingly. These fears were to be well founded – the reprisal attack on Canterbury came just one day after the Cologne raid – with a force of about twenty five bombers – which was about the number of aircraft used in many of the Baedeker raids. In that fierce attack on Canterbury, the Luftwaffe used about eighty bombers.

Before the war, in September 1938, the Chief Constable of Canterbury had suggested that the Dean and Chapter should overhaul their fire fighting equipment and put William Gardner, the gatekeeper of the Mint Yard, in charge – he was an auxiliary fireman and therefore would be ideal for this position. He formed a fire fighting squad of twelve men – including himself.

In January 1941, the Dean announced that a full nightwatch man and relief, had been appointed.

On January 24th Auxiliary fireman J. Wanstall, a member of the works staff, was appointed as fireman – joined in March by Mr. T. Shaw.

170

Between October 1941 and March 1942 there was a great deal of discussion about water available on top of the Bell Harry Tower or at belfry floor level, and the provision of extra men by the City Council with a trailer pump and the men to operate it – provided by the National Fire Service. As it was, all available work staff and many volunteer residents were helping in firewatching.

On 27th February 1942 the following scheme was adopted:

(1) A major appliance with full equipment was to be stationed at the action post and manned every night during blackout hours by 5 firemen provided by the N.F.S.

(2) Mr. T. Hoare will be employed as chief fire guard – posted on the roof with 3 other guards – A. Burden, T. Shaw and J. Wanstall.

This team of only four fireguards, made up in bravery what they lacked in quantity.

As far as the protection of the treasures in the cathedral were concerned, as it was not possible to remove everything of value, including the cathedral itself, they had to be protected where they stood. The Canterbury Archeological Society treated the tombs in the cathedral with special care. The tombs were wrapped up as much as possible. Sandbags were brought in in ever increasing quantities and these were piled around each tomb, especially those of the Bishop of Chichele and the Black Prince. These tombs being of national importance also had frameworks built around them. The Black Prince's effigy itself was to be put in the crypt in the event of war and the funeral achievements were removed and preserved elsewhere until the war ended.

The Cathedral itself could have no other protection but luck and the feeble web that loyal protectors could put around it. One of the methods suggested, and implemented, although no visible evidence remains, was that the roof of the Cathedral should be painted 'dark glass'. A rather bizarre suggestion, it was nevertheless put forward by a military expert and carried out by the Cathedral Works Staff. The reasoning behind this somewhat strange measure, was simply one of camouflage. Odd, as it may sound, who knows it might have had a hand in the Cathedral's lucky escape – although it would seem unlikely.

However, camouflage was not the only method employed to protect the vulnerable roof – it was imperative to protect it because it could easily be destroyed by incendiaries. This was sensible, because it would be the first to be affected by fire, the biggest danger. Loss of the roof would

171

not only be a disaster in itself, but would make the rest of the Cathedral more vulnerable and could destroy other parts if it were to fall on them. Therefore, the Dean and Chapter organised a carefully thought out scheme for surveying and protecting the roof.

These precautions were arguably the most important, since the main risk stemmed from fire. The Germans frequently dropped aeroplane loads of incendiaries to scatter devastatingly over Canterbury – not least of all on the Cathedral. Therefore defence against this, the most serious weapon in the attacks, was the most sensible and rewarding. Once an incendiary bomb burnt through the lead roofing, it could inexorably eat away at the wooden beams that supported the roof, leading to chain reactions of widespread destruction. The Dean and Chapter thought it would be wise to have a team of men working on the roof of the Cathedral to help prevent this. Other eventualities could be passively prepared for – but this aspect of the attacks could be positively fought.

At the beginning of the war, the Dean organised a network of extra ladders over the old roof, in addition to the few that were already there. This was in case the fireguards needed to reach fallen incendiaries in awkward places. For sheer magnitude and organisation, this measure was at least as impressive as the protection of the Crypt. The fireguards had two huts on the south east transept roof, given the grand title of 'Fire Post'. The fire equipment was kept there and this was where the fire guards even slept. In addition to the equipment they were provided with, there were also various water tanks – one at the east end of the Cathedral and one holding 10,000 gallons at the same level as the belfry floor. Diligent, patient and brave, these men were the mainstay of the Cathedral's protection from incendiaries, which were doused with water or pushed off the roof onto the grass where they could do no harm. Without their brave efforts, the Cathedral would undoubtedly have been severely damaged.

In order to examine the importance and effectiveness of each method, it is necessary to look at the events of the war. The 'tip-and-run' raids, although frightening at first, caused little damage and were soon accepted. Attacks were firstly mild, mostly incendiaries and a few HE's (High Explosives) requiring little precaution but due care and attention. Sometimes the German bombers would jettison their dangerous loads over Canterbury, to either fight or flee the Spitfires more easily during the Battle of Britain. Canterbury spent the first few years of the war receiving the odd bomb that was presumably intended for elsewhere. No one could know exactly why he finally chose Canterbury as a target since its only pride was of a religious nature and not industrial. It was probably because it was historically significant, the most vulnerable, and thus easy to attack for purposes of revenge and, it would have a most devastating effect . On various occasions, bombs were dropped on people's homes, not least of all in 1940 when the Deanery was dive-bombed, leaving Hewlett Johnson scratching his head over a large crater outside his front door! However the Germans had reserved the worst attack for the night of 1st. June 1942 – a revenge attack for the massive destruction caused by the R.A.F. on Cologne, it was the worst night of the war for those in Canterbury. The old town suffered heavy losses – miraculously, the Cathedral remained relatively unscathed.

There were several notable attacks. In the September/October raid of 1941, Chillenden's Chambers were badly hit. After the blitz of June 1942, the Germans tried to follow up the attack with several more, wearing the city and its inhabitants down – but they were by now, better prepared. Although in October 1942 a day raid occurred which caught the city unawares, since their heroic balloon barrage was undergoing repairs! However, none were as serious as the night raid on 1st June 1942.

On the night of 1st June, the sirens went off at 12.45 a.m., alerting everyone to another night of bombing, the worst yet. Firstly, the foremost aroplanes dropped 'chandelier flares all over the City, 16 in all, and they lit up the City, bathing it an eerie light. One was even seen drifting over the Cathedral. Shortly after that, a bomb shook the Precincts, and many more continued to fall with devastating results. Although the bombs were dropped everywhere, all the relevant sources say that the Cathedral was a focus for the raid. As bombers tore overhead, dive-bombing the Bell Harry Tower, they dropped hundreds of incendiaries. Over 6,000 fell over the City, but only a few took hold on the Cathedral and they were swiftly extinguished. The fire guards valiantly braved HE's and incendiaries to save the Cathedral roof from destruction, "...working within inches of death through the bombing."

Many HE's fell that night, several of which narrowly missed the Bell Harry Tower, but by far the worst was one weighing four tons that landed in the Precincts. A German bomber was seen to dive-bomb the Cathedral and it released this gargantuan explosive, seemingly aimed directly at the Cathedral. However, luckily, it landed 20yards away from the Warriors Chapel, damaging only the remaining (Victorian or plain replacement) windows. Through the night, many other HE's saw to the rest of the windows in their entirety. One bomb blast even swept up the incendiaries, tossed on the grass by the fireguards, and blasted them through the bare windows into the body of the Cathedral, to land harmlessly on earth or stone. Much was destroyed that night. An even closer miss was the one that completely obliterated the Victorian Library. Many of the buildings in the Precinct were wrecked. The Water Tower and Kent War Memorial were damaged, not to mention the Deanery, the King's School and the Forrens Gate. The Cathedral, 'ringed by fire,' had a lucky escape (the citizens fully expected it to have vanished overnight) helped by its protectors, and maybe even God. In any case, it still stood, proud, paternal and barely damaged on the morning of the 1st. June 1942.

Concerning this raid, The Kentish Gazette and Canterbury Press, in their headlines on Saturday 6th June 1942, saying about – 'BOMBERS RAID – CANTERBURY – ATTACK IN EARLY HOURS'. They also continued after saying about homes and business premises demolished, and said: 'Early on Monday morning, Canterbury was subjected to a savage attack by enemy raiders, apparently as a reprisal for the bombing of Cologne the previous night. As a result bombs or fire destroyed many well-known buildings.

Coming into the attack in three waves, the Huns released parachute flares, sixteen of which could be seen in the sky at one time, before diving low to drop HE and hundreds of incendiary bombs. Several of the raiders came so low that they could be seen in the moonlight.

Chief damage was done to shopping and business premises and to the buildings in the parallel streets. Fierce fires swept through this area and the glare could be seen for many miles – providing an awe-inspiring spectacle. Fires broke out in other parts of the town and destroyed stores, shops and houses. N.F.S. fire pumps were rushed from neighbouring towns and districts and so well did they work that the chief conflagrations were largely under control by daybreak, although premises here and there continued to burn for some hours. Property was completely gutted and frequently large masses of masonry fell with terrific crashes.

Among the buildings wiped out were two churches, a newspaper office, several large drapery, furniture and other stores, two banks, insurance offices etc. Although this was the chief area of havoc, bombs and incendiaries were dropped indiscriminately all over the city – four schools were wrecked, as were also a large garage, a nursery and scores of houses, from large residences to smaller cottage properties.

The Assistance Board operating from mobile offices has quickly helped victims of the raid. Their work has been beyond praise. The Lord Mayor's Air Raid Distress Fund has also offered help – there will be need for substantial help in the future.

The emergency feeding arrangements have been appreciated, the vans of the W.V.S. and the Queens Messengers rushed from London, having given invaluable services. The British Legion has undertaken to supply cases of men's and boy's second-hand clothing for those in immediate need.'

Finally, about that raid on Canterbury, I have quoted from her book 'A Time to Be Born' by Lois Lang-Sims, about the city and particularly about the Cathedral on the night of 1st June 1942:

"Someone, I thought must be out there with a very strong torch. The light had become so bright that everything in the room was starkly outlined by it. Three things bothered me. Why was someone defying the blackout? Why did the light get brighter? Why couldn't I hear the person who was making it? At last I got out of bed and looked at it.

What I saw then was more like general idea of fairyland than anything I had ever seen before or have since. From end to end the Precincts were aglow with a soft rose coloured radiance; the stone of the Cathedral shimmered; the leaves of the trees twinkled like pink stars as the light swayed to and fro with a gentle rocking movement as if it fell from a swinging lamp ... Flares ... we hesitated on the stairs; and suddenly, out of a complete silence, the world seem to burst. Windows crackled, door hinges broke, plaster rattled down in lumps. Against the back of a steady droning roar, the piercing scream of bombs ripped against the heavier screams of engines as the bombers dived. Explosions crackled in the sky and splintered the mind. The house was being shaken to and fro as if it were in the grips of a giants fist.

The target of the raid was the Cathedral itself. The planes were circling overhead and coming in by turns, low diving almost (we were told afterwards) to the level of Bell Harry Tower; so that, as we listened, it seemed impossible to us that the Cathedral had not been hit. But then in a momentary lull, we heard the chiming of the clock. There was something wonderful in the fact that it did not hurry or lose a chime or seem at all put out. An hour passed. Again and again the planes returned and now, to judge from the continuous roar, the whole of the Precincts seemed to be in flames; in the rollicking light I could see my mother's face, dust smothered, close to my own. The only sounds now were the roar and ripple of flames and voices and the running to and fro of feet ... I looked out.

It was still there; it had not been touched; and never before had I seen, never again would I see it was beautiful as this. In the light of the flames, the stones had turned blood red. The Cathedral was crimson-dyed against a backdrop of smoke. The Precincts were ringed with fire, several of its own houses were alight and the glare was coming from Burgate Street, Palace Street and Broad Street. The air was filled with a steady, mighty roar and against this sound was another, which was like the shaking together of many sheets of tin. Sparks, like giant fireflies, performed a measured dance on the wind from the flames; dipping, sailing and curtseying in the air, they drew before the Cathedral, a veil of jeweled openwork – I stared and stared."

I feel that this would be a special time to mention the 'Blood Transfusion Service' and have been very lucky to find two ladies who served during World War II, one of whom Mary Cooke, started the Blood Transfusion just as the war was about to begin. Margaret Hall began in 1942 – and they then worked together in Kent.

Margaret Hall says – "During the war, I chose the Red Cross in preference to the women's armed services, factories or Land Army. The Emergency Blood Transfusion Service began in the London Road, Maidstone, with just a handful of people soon after the war began and as the service developed, it covered the whole of the Kent's towns, villages and army camps, as well as many factories in the south east of London.

There are many stories that could be told, but sadly most of the people who could have told them – are no longer alive and my memory is a bit hazy now. However, I can tell you that there was eventually a full-time staff of between twenty and thirty, which included doctors, laboratory technicians, nurses (mostly Red Cross), clerical staff, drivers, a cook and her assistant and many volunteer helpers. It was an extremely busy organisation and, at the beginning of each workday, we were given a schedule, some worked locally, another group took the equipment in a large van – including the empty bottles in crates, to the location and the donors. Mary Cooke drove a small bus for the service. Some of the locations were very difficult to find, such as places like villages and small lanes and we quite often got lost in the dark – apart from no lights, there was also no signposts – as they were removed to confuse the enemy if they landed."

176

Before telling more about Margaret Hall – I would like to put some words from 'Life Blood' – the official account of the blood transfusion service – published by His Majesty's Stationary Office – 1945:

'By September 1938, most people realized that the experiences through which people of Barcelona had passed might soon be repeated in London, and in the spring of 1939 the Medical Research Council, at the request of the Ministry of Health, prepared for the worst by setting up four blood supply depots at convenient points, to cover London and the South-East. There were also local services in the provinces and in Wales, Scotland and Northern Ireland, supported by local funds and voluntary subscriptions. At the same time a special Army Transfusion Service was set up in the southwestern counties to collect blood for the armed forces in the event of war.

The expected air raids did not come when war began. But in the days before Dunkirk and the evacuation beaches, we saw the first large-scale use of the Transfusion Service. In those days blood transfusions were almost always of whole blood, the material for transfusion remained useful for only two or three weeks, and then had to be scrapped and replaced with new supplies. But experiments with plasma were being carried out both here and in America, and its use revolutionised the whole problem.

After Dunkirk there was no part of Great Britain that could be regarded as immune from air attack or invasion, so the Ministry of Health set up Regional Blood Transfusion Centres in those parts of England and Wales not served by the Medical Research Council or the army. In Scotland, the Scottish National Blood Transfusion Association had been formed under the auspices of the Department of Health for Scotland to co-ordinate the existing services. Besides these, there are the Royal Naval and Royal Air Force teams attached to certain civilian centres, which supplement for their own purposes, the large quantities of blood and plasma supplied to them by the civilian services. The Royal Navy also has its own service to which only naval personnel give blood, and Canada has sent substantial gifts of dried plasma.

All the different Transfusion Services have worked out their own organisation along lines which have seemed most suitable to local conditions and with the help of the British Red Cross Society, the Order of St. John of Jerusalem, St. Andrew's Ambulance Association, Women's Voluntary Services, Local Authorities, Trade Unions, Boy Scouts, Women's Institutes, Rotary Clubs, Church Societies and many other bodies.

177

The different Transfusion Services do not appropriate the blood they have taken and use it solely for the benefit of their own special interests. Broadly speaking, they supply all the various needs, both civilian and military, within their areas. Nor are they content with this – they will supply blood products also to the fighting forces overseas.

Blood, fluid plasma and dried plasma are sent to Overseas Forces, Home Forces, Prisoner-of-war camps, Emergency Medical Service Hospitals dealing with Service casualties and the sick, the Royal Navy, Royal Air Force and Allied Forces – anywhere and everywhere in fact, where blood is able to life save.

Nearly three million gifts of blood have been made and distributed during the war – figures, however, can give but a poor picture of the reality. We realise much more, what blood transfusion means if we consider the individual cases of just a few of those who would have died without it.'

Just one typical story of an incident during the war: ' – It is 3 a.m. on a winters night. There has been silence for half an hour. Before then for perhaps forty minutes, the familiar roar of returning bombers has filled the East Anglian air. We all know that sound nowadays – a rather tired sound compared with the full-throated eager roar of those bombers a few hours earlier as they passed over on their outward journey. Civilians turning over in bed hope that as many are coming back as went.

The last one has reached the airfield – no, not the last one, for once more the silence is broken. A limping sound. A great Halifax bomber home, its fuselage riddled, its crew exhausted and some of them dead.

The Halifax touched ground at last on a field in Norfolk. Not a perfect landing by any means; no wonder! The rear gunner is dead. The pilot with one arm shot away and a wound torn in his side, had pancaked down in a dream, a weary dream, for he has no strength left except in his indomitable will.

They rush him to the nearest medical post. The surgeon looks at him; "pretty near bloodless" he mutters. A few years ago death would have been certain. Now they fit up a blood transfusion set and drip the plasma into his body. Soon the pilot opens his eyes. Within a few months he is ready to work again . . . .'

Returning to the present – Margaret Hall and Mary Cooke told of one particular time when they were due to arrive for one of their sessions. Mary says –"When we arrived at one of our blood sessions in Ashford, sometime in 1942 – which was a normal session in a hut in the grounds of Ashford Hospital – the siren went. Apparently just one

German plane, but all the bombs, a heavy load, caused enormous damage to the town as well as other areas – including lots of factories, bombed during this particular raid. The town was in chaos and we quickly heard that there were lots of injuries. Because of this, we were unable to continue the blood donor session, but, fortunately, we were on the spot to give help to casualties in the hospital. We remember that many people were killed on that day – and an enormous number badly injured as well as those with minor injuries. The raid had hit the town at 9.30 a.m. and we helped right through the day and into the evening before we went back to our home in Maidstone. I remember one of our 'blood' ladies, Dr. Nelson, who had also returned with us to Maidstone, later on that day; she decided to go back to help at Ashford hospital – she hitch hiked back and carried on working through the night."

There is more of the Blood Transfusion Service later in the book.

Joy Turner, of the Red Cross – one of the Voluntary Aid Detachments, formed by the St. Johns Ambulance. Joy says: "I was at school at Latymer Grammer School in North London when the war broke out. I joined the Red Cross as soon as I was allowed. After working for the First Aid and Home Nursing Certificates and undergoing Antigas training, did duties at the local cinema, nursing homes and also the First Aid Post at the North Middlesex Hospital.

I shall always remember the night phosphorus bombs were dropped and several firemen from Edmonton got phosphorus burns on their hands and faces. We Red Cross people were asked to go to the casualty area at the main hospital, as we knew how to treat this gas. The firemen were very tired from long hours of duty and they were so brave when their burns burst into flames once they were dry and we scraped the phosphorus with wooden spatulas under water.

At last I felt useful! I worked my 'hours' on the wards of the North Middlesex Hospital; I'd decided to join the Navy as a mobile VAD.

My calling-up papers took me to Barrow Gurney, Bristol, five days before Christmas. It was the first time I had left home, I felt very lonely and a little miserable at Christmas. I'd had a load of vaccinations and injections and it was snowing, altogether I was feeling a bit low. I was 'specialling' a man found in a hangar in Italy who had such severe gangrene (legs, back and arms) that he had to be nursed face downwards and his dressings done four hourly. His dear little wife sat patiently beside the bed in the single cabin (ward – in navy terms) which had a disgusting smell of rotten flesh which we tried in vain to mask with disinfectants. Our patient died in the New Year.

179

In due course, I was posted to Chatham, and Margery Welsh, from my home town, was posted with me. We both felt more confident now that we knew the Naval expressions and routine, and went happily to Kent. The VAD Mess made us welcome, but I was surprised to see we were in tunnel type quarters (like an enormous Anderson shelter was my first impression). I liked the layout of the RNH Chatham, with its large lawned quarterdeck, surrounded by buildings and a chapel, which I found very peaceful. Everywhere looked well cared for and I was happy on the wards, but we were told we were only there until arrangements could be made to move us to the Southern Hospital, Dartford, which had been taken over almost completely for service personnel.

At Dartford, I worked on Block D, all RN patients, but with a civilian sister-in-charge, Sister Durrant, and some nurses in training. Sister was exceptionally nice to us VAD's and one could learn so much from her. She organised the Chief PO (patient) to encourage up-patients to help us and everyone worked hard, wanting to please her. She thought it so funny when she complimented a sailor on the excellent way he polished the ward floor. 'You mean how I bumper the deck Sister,' he said. After that she always asked the Chief PO, who at that time was a submariner called CPO Bussey, who was bumping the deck that day. A lovely lady, who made me think that perhaps I should take my training and become a state registered nurse. After a while on day duty, I then did a night duty. The food we took onto the wards with us was disgusting. The basket we collected was the type Little Red Riding Hood carried on the way to visit her grandmother, but the contents would not even please the wolf!''

I was sent for just after VE Day to report to the Naval Officer, where I was told I was to proceed on Embarkation leave as I was to go to the far east (where we were still at war)! I went to Chatham for my orders and was sent on leave with a rail warrant to return to RNH Chatham for embarkation – most of which was spent rushing around buying the tropical uniform required – white dresses, white shoes, mess kit, evening dress etc.

Back at Chatham, I was told that the draft had been delayed, and we were to work on the wards.

I found Chatham town an exciting place to be, as it was service orientated. The Surgeon Rear Admiral at RNH was a much admired man, who walked occasionally with a stick, not to assist his gait, we decided, but to shake at people who put a toe on the quarter-deck, or to indicate his disapproval of anyone improperly dressed or any of the sick berth staff who didn't salute smartly! When I met him at a wardroom drinks party, I was quite surprised at how sociable and charming he could be.

The day came when five of us were informed that our posting had come through – to Trincomalee in Ceylon. We went there sailing from Liverpool on the Orduna – but that is another story!

Chapter Twelve

Homeguards, Land Army, Ensa – But Still The Raids.

By the early summer of 1942, the war news, both here and abroad, from all quarters, was – 'still very gloomy!' By this time, the German offensive into Russia seemed to have some set backs; however, although the Red Army had fought valiantly, they had, by this time, fought themselves just about to a stand still – they were also aware that the Wehrmacht was preparing a new offensive on a concentration front, and things were to look desperate again.

In the Far East, the Japanese were still establishing new 'footholds' in the vast arena of the Pacific Ocean, and now looked even more desperate here!

Back on the home shores, although the threat of being invaded ourselves had now certainly diminished; none the less we were still as ready; as we could be for this – certainly, and a lot more so than, when we were in the dark days of Dunkirk.

Towards the Home Guards, by later in 1940, became more official on line with the regular army. Now plans for this volunteer force tried out, and certainly became more efficiently, organized than the early days.

By the spring of 1941, some of its secret members were beginning – 'to live off the land' and to be prepared for guerrilla warfare. By this time, also the Home Guard were better armed – long gone were the days of arriving 'on parade' armed with a pitch fork or ancient blunderbuss – they were now armed with 303 rifles, bren-guns, Thompson sub-machine guns and later, even more sophisticated weapons than these.

Alf Glover, became a member of the Kent Home Guard in the 14th Battalion (Kent) – "I was in the Higham Company of that Battalion – near Rochester." He said. "Although the chances of being invaded now were somewhat remote; we still guarded many 'would be' landing places – even saboteurs or spies, ideal to find quiet places to land. I remember we were sent to guard an old wooden pier on the river Thames – the place to guard was near the Hoo Peninsular, at what are known as St. Mary's Marshes. We travelled in an old 'bone shaker' of a lorry, which was on loan from a wood merchant at Higham – the owner drove it for us, and our backsides used to be pretty sore by the time we got to where we were going.

What we had to guard, all night, believe it or not, was a run down, very small wooden jetty that went out from the sea wall for about 50 feet and could have been no more than 4 feet wide – don't forget that the Thames and this place was very wide and of course tidal. We had to guard this all night – come what may. Perhaps they thought the Germans might do a full scale landing there, but I should think it was rotten, and I certainly didn't put my foot on it and try any weight on it!

I did almost all my training on the recreation ground of Higham School – our headquarters was a long Nissan hut in the grounds of the school. Our 'so called' guard room was a railway workers 'tea hut' which was very tight to sit all of us – 2 N.C.O's and 4 privates. Charles Dickens lived in Higham during his last years here and I believe that the railway, just near to us, with a long tunnel was apparently the one used in one of his ghost short stories about this tunnel, 'The Signalman.'

Just by the tunnel, on my patrol of 2 hours a time, and later in the war years, a lot of the steam trains would pass by on their way down to the coast – loaded to capacity with troops. At the entrance to Higham Tunnel there were banks on each side of it, and, had it rained, some of the chalk would fall on to the steep parts and fall onto the rails nearby, making it dark and suddenly making a hell of a noise, and this was very scary, until you tried to get used to it, but, even then – it made you jump!"

One who was very young, who shouldered the duties of A.R.P. was called Charles Sweeney – but to his friends in Hextable in Kent – he was called 'Sweeney Todd.'

During World War II, he was at the senior school of the Naval Orphanage in Hextable in Kent between 1939 – 1943. The location of the school on the south east corner of London close to Bexleyheath Ack Ack Searchlight Camp, that was positioned to provide an artillery barrage to stop enemy planes penetrating through to the City of London.

The school was managed by civilian staff on behalf of the Royal Naval and Royal Marines Children's Orphanage, and were responsible for the care and education of approximately 200 boys aged between eight and sixteen years of age and were accommodated in six houses with separate school and hospital.

During the first few months of the war, the raids by enemy planes were few and far between, and one was able during daylight raids to witness the 'Battle of Britain', but times suddenly changed when the raids switched to night times and became a common occurrence and more serious.

When the air raid siren sounded, all the school was alerted, with their gas masks in hand to be evacuated to the purpose built underground zigzag shelter in the school orchard. As a senior boy, it was my duty to help the younger boys, amongst panic and confusion, to dress and assemble before evacuating the building.

It was during a night raid in 1942, that four buildings and the hospital received direct hits from incendiary bombs and was set on fire. The Auxiliary Fire Service arrived after the all-clear had sounded and needed the boys assistance to break the windows so the water from the firemen's hoses could penetrate into the buildings and bring the fire under control. Unfortunately, the interior of the buildings were badly burned, and all that remained was the outer shell, making about 150 boys and staff homeless.

With the loss of four houses, accommodation was made in the school buildings and classrooms substituted as dormitories, sleeping on floors until suitable alternative arrangements could be made to make life more comfortable etc. School lessons had to be rearranged around the few remaining classrooms, which meant that one half of the boys attended lessons in the morning and the other half in the afternoon period, which was pleasing to the boys for the extra freedom to play games.

As the intensity of the raids increased, the schools authorities decided that the seating provided in the shelter should be replaced by bunkbeds to make the boys and staff more comfortable for the longer spells spent in the shelter during the raids. Conditions were far from hygienic with so many people crammed into a small area, but the 'spirit of adventure' prevailed amongst the boys who adapted to the situation.

It was after the loss of the schoolhouses and hospital the school authorities decided to organise patrols of the school premises during the raids to safeguard any further damage to buildings etc. The patrols would check buildings for any suspect device that was considered possibly dangerous, and take appropriate action to make the situation safe.

As staff at the school were mostly women, three senior boys, Fatty Rule, Jake Blake and myself were elected to carry out patrols and were issued with A.R.P. helmets and instructed to use a stirrup pump and buckets of sand to extinguish fires caused by exploded incendiary bombs.

At fifteen years of age, we had little awareness of the dangers and that we were exposed to, fragments of shells and bombs that were falling around us whilst patrolling the grounds, but were more scared of what lurked behind the bushes as we were patrolling the derelict house in the depth of winter.

Because of our schools closeness to Bexleyheath Ack Ack station, many of the exploding shells fired at the enemy planes fell as fragments (shrapnel) on the area of the school. After the raids the boys were very keen to find the fragments as souvenirs, without realising their destructive purpose.

Soon after I left school in early 1943, the school evacuated the premises because of the onset of the V1 and V2 rockets, to the safety of the Devon countryside. The good news is that after the war, the buildings damaged by the bombing, were restored and are now used by the Kent Education Authority for special needs children.

Hugh McCleod, was an eighteen-years-old private in the Home Guard. At this time, he was working in a reserved occupation and, with a friend of his, also a private in the Home Guard at that time. Hugh, has sent me this account of those particular and 'somewhat different times!' He tells that these were about the end of 1942/43:

'The Government asked for volunteers to be Anti-aircraft gunners attached to the regular A.A. Batteries. Being eighteen years old and thinking this sounded exciting, my friend and I volunteered.

Privates A. MacArthur and H. MacLeod, duly kitted out in uniform (Home Guard shoulder flashes. "Double-six domino" arm insignia and a cap badge of the Royal Artillery) reported to the A.A. Battery site at Toryglen Golf Course, Polmadie, on the south side of Glasgow, which was under the control of the Regular Army and were introduced to the Home Guard Commander, Captain Salverston and a Regular Army Sergeant. When we asked, "Where are the machine guns, Bofors and 3.5 Ack Ack guns?" Told us in a typical Sgt. Major style, that we were "looking at them." We thought we were in a S.G.B. Scaffolding stockyard, as there were over one hundred steel tubes pointing skywards. We were told that these were Britain's secret weapons, called Z Guns and that each fired two rockets with a $3''$ A.A. shell attached.

There were 64 of these 'guns' forming an 8×8 square, with probably 20 yards spacing between each gun, giving a barrage of $128 \times 3''$ rocket shells firing simultaneously. The rockets were loaded and fired in pairs and each co-partner gunner had to load his own rocket, which had been placed on the fused-setting rack at waist level. The Radar operator

185

would give the command of "Target" and you immediately applied your fuse-setting key to the nose of the shell.

Following this we would receive a setting for the fuse (the height at which the shell should explode), the shell would be loaded followed by the Q.E. (quadrant elevation) and the compass bearing. On the off "Stand By!" your co-partner pressed the safety button on the left side of the gun and you simultaneously placed your hand on the firing lever. On the command of "Fire!" you plunged the lever down, which sent a 12volt electric charge to the rockets which then exploded with a huge flame and headed (we hoped) for the German bombers. Your partner's button completed the circuit to your firing lever, which was a safeguard, ensuring that he was not behind the gun when it was fired, since it was impossible to see him during this manoeurve.

Each rocket/shell had a pointed rubber cap or 'condom' covering the fuse to keep it free of dirt, since it had five pin holes through which air had to pass in order to set off the gun cotton in the shell at the given fuse setting. In the excitement of their first action, some forgot to remove the cap, which resulted in the rockets going up and coming straight down onto the streets of Glasgow.

The only real casualty of this first action was when a Home Guard Sergeant, in the darkness, ran into another gunner's steel helmet and split his head open. Each leading gunner was issued with a flash-light in order to find his way to his own gun, but since it had a slotted metal visor, it didn't let much light through, hence the collision.

Twenty paces behind each gun, at a specific bearing, there was a six-foot 'grave' into which we were expected to dump any rockets that failed to go off! After twenty minutes waiting, it was considered safe to remove the unexploded rocket, and, moving back twenty paces from your known bearing direction, throw the rocket into the 'grave' (in total darkness of course)! We heard that many gunners in other batteries fell into these pits during the excitement of action and running to man their guns – but I can't recall whether it happened in our battery.

After our first action, we were informed by Radar that there had been six bombers coming towards us at six thousand feet, which of course we could not know about since it was 1 a.m. and pitch black – from memory, one bomber was shot down, and every battery in the vicinity laid claim to it!

After a few months we were ordered to remove our Royal Artillery cap badges and double six domino insignia and replace them with Glasgow's own regimental badge, the Highland Light Infantry (H.L.I.)

and a red diamond insignia with a hand holding a bow and arrow (in black) firing into the air. Apparently, the Royal Artillery Regiment objected to 'part-time soldiers' wearing their honoured badge. I don't think if German paratroopers had landed on our gun site that we would only be part shot as part-timers! Seventy five per cent of the battery was Home Guard manned, who came on duty at 8.00 p.m. through to 6.00 a.m. the following morning. The remaining twenty five per cent were regular soldiers who had to be there in case of raids outside these hours – most raids, however, were overnight.

It should be remembered that the majority of the Home Guard were fully employed during the day, mostly doing work of wartime importance. In my own case, because I was young and enthusiastic, I wanted to join the regular forces and even attended an interview with the R.A.F., but, because I was working in a reserved occupation, my boss complained to the authorities that I was more use to the war effort at work than I would be in the armed forces.'

Hugh McLeod, has told me that there was also another lesser known side to the Home Guard, which was set up by Captain Peter Fleming, the brother of Ian Fleming, curator of 'James Bond' – another person well versed in secret activities.

The idea was that, in the event of being invaded, there would be 'stay behind' parties. These groups of men were divided up into patrols of about – six, seven or eight men. They were selected from volunteers who had a thorough knowledge of the countryside of their localities – 'practically, knowing every twig and rabbit hole' – as one officer described the sort of people he was looking for. These men would do their ordinary normal days work, but, in the evenings and at nights, they trained in absolute secrecy, not telling their wives what they were actually up to – or supposedly so! Their aim to remain in underground passages and dug-outs, from which they could secretly observe what might be going on – literally, right under the enemies' noses!

These hide-outs were usually constructed by the patrols themselves, but sometimes, experts, such as miners, were brought in specially to instruct them.

Fortunately, of course, these secret army Home Guard units, never had to perform the duties they were specially trained for, such as acts of sabotage, including the mining of bridges and other strategic targets – anything to seriously hinder the advance of the enemy!

After the war, most of these underground hides were destroyed – so they couldn't be used for other clandestine and possibly illegal activities.

Another volunteer force, which was very much involved in helping to feed the country during the austere years, was the Land Army. This service had started in enrolling young ladies to work on the land as early as 1917, during the First World War.

In 1938, when things were looking decidedly ominous and it looked as though World War II was just around the corner – Lady Denman was selected as the Honorary Director of the Women's Land Army – she had started getting things organised, straight away.

One of my father's cousin's, Grace Corbett, had an arable and stock farm in Surrey; it was called 'Bunt's Place' and situated in the country between Reigate and Dorking – not far from the village of Leigh. Grace often talked about Lady Denman – whom she had met on several occasions and I remember, sketchily, her telling my parents stories about the Land Girls. Grace, had had two of them working on the farm in the earlier part of the war – but not by the time we went to stay with her in 1943, for a summers holiday and to get away from the bombings.

The girls who worked for cousin Grace had always been happy in what they were doing and, as Grace said, " – Damned hard work!"

Unfortunately this goes as far as my own knowledge of the Land Army, but I have been able to get other information on the subject.

By the time the harvest was being brought in the late summer of 1942, my wife's parents had settled into their cottage on the farm – Upper Austin Lodge, at Eynsford, in Kent. The farm was also stock and arable – and during the harvesting, as at many other times of the year, George Barman, my wife Pam's father, was at work from dawn 'till dusk – farming was of course a reserved occupation.

My wife and her sister Brenda, who were eight and four years old at that time, shared their bedroom, however, it was at this time that Pam's mother was asked to feed two Land Girls, who were to work on the farm. The idea was that they would sleep in a wooden shed in the garden of the cottage, but Pam's mother, Hilda, told the farmer – "Over my dead body they'll sleep out here! They'll have to have the girls' room and the girls will have to share our bedroom!" And that is what happened. They already had a lodger, who was another farm worker in the third bedroom, so it was a pretty full house! Pam remembers the Land Girls, Vera and Joyce, and Vera remained a friend of the family for the rest of her life. Unfortunately she died before I had any thoughts of writing this book – otherwise I could have asked for first hand accounts of those years.

However, I shall include here accounts by three ladies, from different parts of the country, who remember, with some nostalgia, those hard working, 'sometimes back breaking,' but quite enjoyable days of working on the land.

Nancy Tipples of Marden in Kent, recalls her days in the Women's Land Army – she says: "I volunteered for the Women's Land Army in September 1941 and remained in it until February 1946. For the first month, I was sent to Seale Hayne Agricultural College in Devon for initial training. There were about fifteen other new recruits from all walks of life – some of whom left after the month for various reasons, but most stayed on for good.

Eventually, after a few garden jobs, I then joined a farmer and started to work on the farm. There were about forty cows in milk and the usual followers. They grew wheat, barley, oats, kale, mangold-wurzel and turnips for the cattle. There were always two pigs in the sty for the farmhouse, guinea fowl and chicken. I worked with the carter ploughing and I would like as many pounds as the miles I walked, leading the horse in the furrow. I learnt to cut and brush a hedge with a hook, do a bit of tree cutting with an axe, milk cows, drive a horse and cart and keep the farms vegetable garden.

The thrashing gang came in the winter and we girls always had the chaff and cavings job – raking out the rubbish underneath. When our ten minutes morning break came, the bottles of cold tea were stood around the fire that we lit, not knowing better, I stood them too close and some exploded – I was not popular – but I learnt!

After all these different jobs, I had acquired a reasonable amount of experience; I met a farmer who subsequently married me. Fifty years ago! A good life, but not for the faint hearted!

May Hewitt of Loughborough, in recalling those days told me – "I decided to join the Women's Land Army early in 1942; I joined with a girl called Violet who I worked with in a wholesale warehouse. I remember that as she stood 5'11" tall and I was just 5'4", the staff at the warehouse were taking bets who would last the longest; I think I was the one they thought would give up first, but it was the other way about – Violet only lasted fourteen days. When I went home on a long week-end, I went to see my ex boss and he was surprised to hear I was still carrying my pitch fork – all the staff had a whip round for me, which was thankfully received.

We left on the train from Nottingham for Princes Risborough. I remember my shoes, breeches, skirt and jumpers were all too big.

189

Arriving at Risborough, we were sorted out to go to different hostels – I ended up at High Wycombe, in a hostel at the top of Mar Hill. We were in a dormitory in two tier wooden bunks, which were very hard, and two coke heaters heated the room in the winter.

Never will I forget that first day; we were working for the local agriculture committee and picked up for work at 7.30 a.m., we then proceeded to Ibsom Common and were told that the common had to be cleared of bracken. By lunch-time our hands were very sore – and what did we have in our packed sandwiches? SPAM! (Never cared for Spam since!) After lunch we went back to pulling bracken – I remember it was a very hot day. After this we went back to the hostel for a hot meal, the meals were quite good.

The girls came from all walks of life; we had one girl who wouldn't bath – we tried all ways to get her to, we put Lifebouy toilet soap on her dressing table, but she would come in from work, filthy dirty and just take a flannel round her face and say she had a date. I suppose the 'blackout' helped – her date wouldn't see her! We got fed up with the B.O., and one night, four of us went without our baths and put 20 inches of water in the bath (we were only allowed 5 inches each for a bath), we put her in and scrubbed her with a nail brush and found white skin underneath the dirt – she washed every day after this!

The next job I got was on the thrashing machine, it was a dirty job, clearing away the chaff was the worst. The men we were working with loved to put mice down our overalls – I found out that if you could stand it once, they didn't do it again.

My next move was to a hostel at Bingham, where most of the people were from Nottinghamshire. My first calamity was being told to ride a bike to work; going back to the hostel, down a hill, I couldn't stop the thing and, as I was coming to a main road, I fell off into a bed of nettles, just as a convoy of soldiers were coming along – some of their comments were quite funny.

From Bingham I went to a dairy farm which was across some fields, I had to fetch the cows for milking at 5.00 a.m., the chap I was working with didn't know much about farming, he had been a chauffeur for a Nottingham Councillor who had bought the farm. There was one cow called Dolly; when you fetched the cows in you had to put arms around her neck or she wouldn't move – when she did, all the others would follow! There was another called Pixie, who, if the farmers son was anywhere near the dairy, she wouldn't let you milk her, so the cowman and myself barred him from the dairy. I stayed here for eighteen months, and then I moved to Southall, where I was bottling and delivering milk, I was with a very nice family there.

Later I went to work as a tractor driver for an agriculture contractor; this work consisted of clearing some woodland, we used to blow up the trees, using dynamite! It was then sawn into logs, and we took them by tractor about six miles to a yard where they were sold as logs to eke out the coal ration – people used to queue on Saturday mornings for a bag at 2/6p.

Later on I went back home, as my husband had been demobbed from the R.A.F. – so it was goodbye to the Land Army.

Laura Waterman, who now lives at Eccles, told me – "When I was eighteen, I volunteered for the Women's Land Army. After I had passed a medical, I was given a choice of going on a dairy farm or to a piggery and general farm – I chose the piggery, which was at the top of Hollingbourne in Kent. I lodged in the cottage of the tractor driver and his wife; I remember that there was no gas or electricity – only oil lamps and candles. It was very desolate; there were just two cottages across the road as well as an old manor house.

On my first Monday there, I was shown how to mix the pigswill up in a bucket and then hook them onto yokes onto my shoulders, then take them to the pig stye. The old fellow who showed me how to do all this was called 'Chappie.' The first stye I went into, the pig tipped the bucket over with her nose – 'a poor start', I thought. The worst one to feed was the boar – he was a terror and I always had to be careful he didn't catch me unawares! I had to feed them twice a day, as well as cleaning out all the pens. Other jobs we had to do on the farm included, hedge brushing with a hook, like a small scythe. Also we had to go 'thistle dodging' in the fields, hooking out all the weeds – by the time you got to the end of the field, you couldn't see where you had been!

The best time on the farm was haymaking. We even had prisoners of war from Italy helping with this busy and enjoyable time of the year – that was from 1943 onwards, I think. I had the job on top of the stack – pitching to the stack builder. Later on I had to drive the horse with the hay rake over any loose hay and gather it in. I found it was hard to do at first, but Chappie helped me and showed me how to do it properly.

When it was harvesting time, a threshing team came over from Detling – two land girls and a man called Bob – and that was very hard work! We walked round the field stooking the oats. After thy had dried, they were pitched into the thresher. We worked 'till late into the

191

evening, until the light had gone – I thought my arms were going to drop off, but I got through it.

Another job I had to do was lead the horse up the rows, to weed the 'wurzels;' that was quite easy, but I remember that when we got to the top of a row one day, I said – 'Oi!' – the horse thought I said – 'Whoah' – and stood still, on my foot, it made me hobble around a bit – but would have been a lot worse if I hadn't been wearing boots!

I remember the winter of 1944 was really awful, with snow and rain and freezing cold icicles hanging from the trees. Sometimes I had to dig my way to the styes and pull the pigs food to them on sledges; some of the pigs had farrowed and had as many as 12 piglets – they were a pedigree herd of Wessex Saddlebacks. Before they got too big, they had their ears clipped and numbered – I used to have to hold them while the vet did the work.

The whole thing was an experience for me. We had a few bombs dropped near to us, but not too near – we were close to the airfield at Detling though and, of course, that was a prime target, but much earlier in the war."

The country's other harvest; the harvest of the sea, had been badly restricted from the beginning of the war – with many of the fishing boats, either just not used or used for other purposes. Also, many of the younger men, who had normally earned their living working on the boats of localised fishing fleets, had by this time joined up. It meant, mainly, that the 'older hands' were left to do what fishing they could, in heavily restricted waters, with a complete night time ban on all boating activities. However, the boats did get around many of the coastal areas, and some of the boats crews, even made up with younger men, only too willing to help out – lads not yet old enough for the forces, with some of them still at school.

One such keen young volunteer was Fred Palmer of Herne Bay, in Kent. He remembered that, apart from the fishing, that they quite often rescued pilots or other air-crew shot down by aeroplanes, from the sea. He told me. "One day, with three local fisherman – Alf Priestly, Frank Holness and Harry Scott, after a 'dog fight,' a plane had been shot down. I wasn't supposed to be on the beach, so before we had left off , I got up in the for'ard locker and kept out of sight until we were out at sea. Apparently a German pilot was brought down into the sea and we tried to find where he was – the pilot would release a green dye from a bag that was attached to his survival gear – so we particularly looked out for this, as a guide to where he might be. Before long we found him, and hauled him aboard – his jaw had been shot away and his knee had been shattered; in those days we didn't carry first aid gear, all we had on board a swab we used to wash the boat down with. One of the men held this to what was left of the German's jaw, while another of the crew stemmed the flow of blood from his knee; which looked terrible because, of course, his clothing was wet. At this time, we were about one and a half miles from the shore, and we started for home, on the way back though, we came across another pilot in the sea – this one was British and turned out to be the one which had shot the German down! He was uninjured, just wet of course! Soon after this we reached the shore to find members of the army there to help, with first aid equipment and everything, and also a local doctor who immediately attended to the German and there and then started to sew his jaw up! After this he was taken away in an ambulance – the British pilot returned to his unit."

On another occasion, a Wellington bomber came down in the sea, not far from the pier, and the crew had bailed out just beforehand – except for the gunner, who was killed. Fred remembers that one of the crew landed on the pier, which had three sections cut away from it as anti invasion precautions earlier in the war. The man had to stay 'stranded' on the pier for about twelve hours before he was rescued, by the fire brigade. Fred also used to spend a lot of his time, as did his friends, collecting money for the local 'Spitfire Fund.' There was Spitfire Funds set up throughout the country – all run by volunteers and all extremely useful to the war effort.

As far as the fishing supplies, most shops would only stay open for a couple of hours on the days that there were some fish, and hopefully, you might be lucky when your turn in the queue came up!

With the American services all over the country now, the W.V.S. had also helped by the American Red Cross. Charles Graves, writing in his book 'Women in Green' says, " – When the W.V.S. were originally asked by the American Red Cross if they would state their maximum clothing needs, Lady Reading offered to return seventy/five per cent of the stocks remaining at the end of hostilities. The arrival of American troops, however, meant that a good deal of clothing was returned to the American Red Cross for immediate issue to U.S. army, air force, rest homes and British wives of American servicemen.

Assistance given by the W.V.S. to U.S. troops, particularly those in the air force, were of a very practical nature. The member in charge of a mobile canteen at Lewes in Sussex, was driving up to her house at the end of a morning round when she saw three parachutists land in a field. She drove the canteen straight towards the men, the least injured of whom looked up and said with a broad American accent: "Say, I guess this is real service." The trio were members of a crew of ten, who were forced to jump from a Flying Fortress immediately south of Lewes – they were provided with light refreshments and blankets until the ambulance arrived!

The service given by the W.V.S. to the Americans was by no means one-sided. Nothing could have afforded greater pleasure to the small inmates of the W.V.S. hostels than the appearance on December 25th of a number of Father Christmases in jeeps and even tanks. Few things have contributed more to the lasing good of Anglo-American relations than the enthusiasm with which the American Army and Air Force entertained the children, both local and evacuee. Very little of the candy ration allotted to troops in the reception areas can have been eaten by the men for whom it was intended. Most of it was saved up to delight the British children, who also acquired such a taste for chewing-gum that they became a positive pest to their kindly visitors."

During 1942, unknown to the general public, the plans to try an experimental raid on a German occupied port on the French coast; to test out strength against fortifications – a sort of trial invasion. 'Operation Jubilee,' the raid on Dieppe – was described as a full scale allied disaster! Thousands of Canadians died on the beaches, in this brave, but hopeless raid, which left the German defences – 'hardly ruffled!'

However, the raid was to have its uses in what was learnt from the mistakes made, and this would be 'helpful' nearly two years later when the largest invasion force of all times would land on the beaches of Normandy.

Michael Butcher, at Fletching, with some friends, had got to know quite a few Canadian soldiers who were 'camped' at Sheffield Park – nearby to them. They saw that after the raid, all the troops were very solemn, and many of the normally cheerful faces were now, sadly – not there any more.

On bringing the wounded home to the various ports along the south coast, the voluntary services such as the Red Cross and Women's Voluntary Service, did everything possible to help in any way they could. It was thought that none of the troops would return to Newhaven after the raid – many of them having embarked from there for the raid as well as from Portsmouth, Southampton, Shoreham and

Gosport. But after the disaster plans changed, and immediate accommodation, medical and food supplies had to be found for thousands of the returned troops.

Penny Summers of the Auxiliary Fire Service, who I have written about in chapter eight, was attending an officers training course, O.C.T.U. at the Ocean Hotel at Saltdean – which later in peacetime, would become one of Butlins Holiday Camps. Not far from us in Brighton and a place we used to explore, as children, when it was empty for a time during the war years – one day, whilst she was studying, she happened to look out of the window and saw a lot of Canadian soldiers – many of them wounded, who just happened to return from the Dieppe raid and were being billeted temporarily at Saltdean – where there were already other Canadians billeted. Penny and her colleagues were asked to help organise a dance which, was laid on for the troops by the fire service, to cheer them up. Penny later passed her course and returned to her station.

After Dieppe, the atmosphere even amongst the most optimistic of those with views, on how the war might progress, took a nose-dive and everything seemed rather gloom ladened!

However, a little later that year, came the news – 23rd/24th October 1942 – of the victory at El Alamein, and everyone's spirits uplifted – it was a major breakthrough and a very important turning point in the war. I remember that the next day, my father, was suffering from a rare hangover; there had been a lot of celebrating in the Rock Inn in nearby Rock Street, as well as at a hurriedly arranged 'Victory' party in Sussex Square, later on that evening – one that went on through to the early hours!

With so many servicemen from other countries, including of course the Canadians and the Americans, the ENSA and troop concerts, with many famous artists – helping such as – Gracie Fields, Tommy Trinder, George Formby and, of course – 'our Vera Lynn.'

Also, there were many who volunteered with helping to entertain the forces. One lady, Mrs. Lucas, her stage name was Sheila Ryan, was just nine years old and was living with her mother and father in Preston in Lancashire – her father was an actor in the town's local repertory company. Unfortunately he had heart trouble, caused by repeated attacks of rheumatic fever and he had died in October 1939.

She says – "I had become well known in the town – as the daughter of 'that actor fellow' and I played at entertaining the forces, never dreamed that one day it would be true.

195

Mother had opened a guest house for touring theatricals, but they began to disappear, as they went into ENSA which was an entertainment unit run by the British Army, and of course a lot of the artists went into the forces themselves.

The theatres were temporally closed for a few months because of the bombing, but they began to re-open and camp concerts became very popular. By this time, mother was having officers billeted upon her, they heard me singing around the house and asked me if I would like to do concerts at camps – I earned the princely sum of a guinea a time. I worked up a nice little act, with impressions of popular figures and film stars. I sang and tapped danced; it always went down very well. Two years later, by the time I was twelve, I organised a little concert party – the money went to buy spitfire aeroplanes.

By the time I was thirteen, I decided to go into the theatre full-time, so I went to London for an audition at the Windmill Theatre.

Never having been to London before, I was astounded by the size of the place and the uniforms that were milling around in Piccadilly – Army, Navy, Air Force, Polish Forces, Free French, Land Girls etc. – all passing a big place called 'Rainbow Corner,' which was a huge club for the American forces – it was a real revelation to a girl from a small country town!

When I first approached the Windmill Theatre, I was astounded to see the queues of soldiers, sailors and airmen at least half a mile long, I had to walk past them to get to the stage door; I did the audition, lied about my age and got the job.

That was in the June of 1943, I stayed for two years; we did six shows a day and on Sundays travelled all over England doing concerts for the forces completely voluntary. We went through air raids and ack-ack guns and watched the dog fights with planes – we were often in personal danger, but we still went on and did the shows."

The Christmas was very quiet in 1942 and the winter of 1943 was milder than the previous years.

On 19th February 1943, in Sussex Square, and other areas around Brighton, the Lake Superior Regiment became billeted in various empty houses and school buildings.

In Brighton in 1943, the Eighth Canadian Infantry Brigade, which the Lake Superior Regiment was one of the newly authorised Fourth Canadian Division, "were for training and not for garrison," my father said. He also said "I believe that this the is hope for – before long – the coming of the invasion on France and Europe." My father, as an ex-regular officer, quickly made friends with many of these soldiers – as did many other people who lived close to us.

By this time, the raids were quite a lot less than the early years – however on 25th May 1943 there was one of the worst raids, and I was caught outside, when it happened! Also during the raid, many of the volunteers were from the Canadian Soldiers. I have this incident in my book, about a childhood in wartime Brighton – "The Tree Climbers":

'Up until that time in my life, my visits to the dentist had been for routine visits check-ups only, but for a couple of weeks I had been getting some pain in one of my back teeth and now faced my first 'necessary visit,' which had been fixed for the early afternoon, on May 25th 1943. Our dentist, Mr. Elliot, had a practice in Old Steine, in Brighton, and had been the family dentist for quite some time. I wasn't looking forward to this at all and it was with some trepidation that I got up that morning to start the day – but quickly put this to the back of my mind when I remembered that I had to get to school a quarter of an hour earlier than usual, to play a very important game of marbles with an arch rival of mine – each of us putting up our largest and best marble as the prize for this special match.

The lessons that morning seemed to go more quickly than usual, but my concentration wasn't particularly good, as I was now somewhat preoccupied again with the thought of the dreaded dental appointment that afternoon. At mid-day I was allowed to get ready to go home for lunch and an afternoon off school because of this appointment. Before I left off, my form master gave me a talking to about not getting my 'prep' done correctly the night before – calling it a 'poor effort' – which I suppose it, was! He told me to do it again, as well as doing another 'prep' set for that night. I then spent a few minutes watching another 'important' marbles match, and then started on my walk home along the Eastern Road – the time was approximately 12.15 p.m.

I was nearly as far as The Sussex County Hospital when everything seemed to happen at once. First the siren went; this stopped me in my tracks and I hesitated for a few seconds – wondering whether to seek cover in the hospital; an idea which I immediately dismissed because of my fear of hospitals, or carry on and run home; about half a mile away – or run back to school, only about two hundred yards away. Suddenly, there seemed to be explosions coming from all around me, and the sound of aeroplanes was almost deafening. I could also hear the guns on the seafront giving off a heavy barrage. In fact, you could say that – one minute it was nice and peaceful and the next – all hell broke loose! Under these circumstances, my mind was very quickly made up, and with my 'heart in my mouth' and extremely frightened, I ran as fast as my legs would carry me back to school – which was only a few seconds away at the pace I was going! I ran through the arch at the opening of the college on the Eastern Road, and almost ran into Mr. Burstow, the assistant headmaster, who was standing just by the quadrangle outside the entrance to Bristol House; he was shading his eyes with a book, which he held in one hand and was watching a couple of German aeroplanes, flying straight over the college in the direction of the sports ground – another aircraft seemed to circle the school, but then flew off in an easterly direction. We didn't see any bombs dropped by these aeroplanes, but we heard some machine-gun fire, and we both saw the pilot in the one that circled over the school. We later found out that these were Focke-Wulf 190's.

Mr. Burstow, who had already grabbed me by the arm, hurried me into school and down to the basement of Bristol House, which was used as a shelter. For several more minutes we could hear more bombs going off, some of these quite close to us, and the noise from all the Bofor guns along the seafront, was continuous and very loud. The whole air raid was very frightening for all of us, and from what I can remember, the staff and some of the older boys did a very good job in comforting several of the younger boys, who were crying and very distressed.

Eventually, the noise stopped and there was a tense sort of silence. We stayed where we were for about another ten minutes, and then, although I can't remember hearing it, we were told that the all clear had gone and that we could all return to the assembly room on the ground floor. I didn't know quite what to do, and asked Mr. Stokes, the headmaster, telling him about my dental appointment – which at that time was obviously the least of anyone's worries! However; he went off to phone my parents – returning a few minutes later to tell me that everything was alright at home, which was a relief to me, and that I was to start walking back along the Eastern Road where my mother would meet me halfway.

What hadn't been taken into consideration, was that many nearby places had been hit by the bombs, and this included some of the Eastern Road area as well as many other nearby places, so, after I had got just past the Sussex County Hospital, I found that the police and A.R.P. wardens, were blocking the Eastern Road off. I could also see that there was smoke coming from the direction of St. Mary's Hall. One of the policemen asked me where I was heading for – I told him and he said I was to go down Chesham Place, a small road nearby, and then along Rock Street and then up into the square from there. I told him about my mother meeting me, and he said that she would be told at the other end and would probably meet me in Rock Street. There was glass lying on the road and on the pavements in Cheshan Place and there were floating bits and pieces of ash and stuff in the air and a strong smell of smoke and burning everywhere.

I had noticed that Eaton Place, just nearby, had been bombed and that it was now closed by the police. The A.R.P. and an ambulance were there, as well as a small crowd of onlookers. On turning into Rock Street I immediately saw my mother, and quickly told her all that I seen since leaving off from the college; I also told her about Eaton Place being hit – this especially worried her, as she knew some people who lived there, and this included one particularly good friend of hers. So holding my hand, she walked me to the bottom of the road, and, on getting there, she was immediately reassured, because she could see that the house where her friend lived, was undamaged and well away from the houses that had been hit. The damage at the bottom of the road looked terrible. I can remember seeing a woman being carried on a stretcher, holding her hand, and muttering over and over again, "God help us!" My mother, not wanting me to see any more, clutched my hand even more tightly and we turned and walked back along Rock Street – here and there avoiding walking on piles of broken glass, and even walking into the road, just in time to avoid being hit by a pane of glass, that quite simply – 'fell to the ground' – as we passed by. We eventually arrived at number thirteen Sussex Square after stopping briefly to see smoke coming from the Arundel Road area and also that the gas works were once again on fire. Another thing we had noticed after turning up from Rock Street, was that there was a lot of activity going on near St. Mary's Hall, main school, on the Eastern Road, also quite a bit of smoke coming from the buildings. Amongst the rescue parties there, including – A.R.P., Police, Ambulances and a couple of W.V.S. ladies, my mother knew. We also saw several of the Lake Superior Regiment soldiers that we knew – they were in shirtsleeves and covered in dust, and all of them looked very grim and determined.

There have been many varying reports and versions of stories about that devastating raid, to say which were correct and which were exaggerated would be very difficult. The Evening Argus, on 26th May, said that there were probably 20 F.W. 190's and that of those – four had been shot down, and that there were children among the twelve known to have died. Later it was confirmed that there were no less than 24 F.W. 190's and that the death toll was 24. They also said that if it hadn't been for the R.A.F. there would have been another similar raid later that evening, it says – 'An Air Ministry and Ministry of Home Communiqué last night stated – 'Late last evening, enemy fighter bombers attempted to attack a town on the south east coast of England. They were intercepted by our fighters and driven off!'

As far as the rescue work was concerned, including searching for people buried under rubble and clearing up after an air raid – I actually witnessed some of this, and also remember the bits and pieces I was told by my parents. I know that my father had a very high regard for the A.R.P. and had friends and acquaintances who were members of it – he always said that they did 'a hell of a good job' and I remember that every one was praised for their rescue work – British and Canadians alike. Concerning the damage of St. Mary's Hall, back in July 1941, almost a year after they had been closed for the duration, the governors of the school declared their intention to re-open after the war, but the bomb that had fallen on the main school on the Eastern Road, had hit some terraced houses converted for school use, and this had some more far reaching consequences for the school. I quote a short passage which can be found on page 33 of 'A Short History of St. Mary's Hall 1836–1992':

'Fate was to take a final hand in order to make the re-opening more difficult for on the 25th May 1943 a bomb fell on Hervey Terrace destroying the lodge, 227 and 229 Eastern Road and badly damaging the laboratory. This bomb may have been a blessing in disguise in the long term, for the old houses were quite unsuitable to form part of the school that was to arise when peace was finally restored. After the war it was decided to build Elliott House, to accommodate some sixty boarders on the site of the bombed houses. By September 1951 the houses were ready, and to start with, occupied were occupied by 22 boarders. The old laboratory that had also been damaged in the raid, had been converted for the use as a domestic science room, which also came into use that September.'

Of the German aircraft; the most likely account is that two separate waves of F.W.'s 190's came to attack the town, one wave coming in from an Easterly direction and flying low near the cliffs between Rottingdean and Black Rock before making their attack on the Kemptown area, the second slightly larger wave coming in from the sea, close to the Palace Pier, and then for ten minutes or so, circling around the town – bombing and machine gunning various places as they did so.

After this, during 1943, we had another air raid in the early hours of August 16th – When six enemy aircraft were destroyed in raids on the south east coast of England last night.

The Lake Superior Regiment was later to leave Sussex Square, and with the departure of most of the Canadians and various other military units from the Brighton area, the war seemed a bit quieter now on the homefront; also the Luftwaffe, apart from one or two 'sneak raids,' hadn't unleashed any further devastating attacks on us – such as big air raids in May and August.

My father said it was rather like being 'in limbo' and remarked that everyone that he had talked to, were all wondering when the invasion of France would take place. With all the troop movements of the Canadians and others, not to mention our own forces, it was felt that this, so obviously planned for attack, was overdue. These however were the feelings of the laymen – the 'Brass Hats' were the decision makers and, the elements, now became 'The Divine Hand of Providence,' in other words. The weather would obviously play a very important part in crossing the channel was with the onset of another wartime winter, it was no cheer to anyone that the hoped for assault would now almost certainly not to be until the spring at the earliest.

201

(a) Coventry's Market Hall was destroyed, though its
Clock Tower survived the bombing.

(b) W.V.S. making sandwiches 'By the million' in Coventry 'The morning after.'

(a) Albert Fearn talks to the Queen during a visit to Coventry after the big raid.

(b) My big day – Albert Fearn (right) with daughter Barbara and another
George Medal recipient Sgt. Fred Mason outside Buckingham Palace.

(a) Land Girls – gather in sugar-beet harvest to supply Britain's sugar ration.

(b) Red Cross Nurses at the 'Hospital' at Chislehurst Caves Young onlookers.

(a) Fred Palmer aged 12 Helping the Spitfire Fund at Herne Bay.

(b) West of England Civil Defence helpers after bombs –
Refreshments at a W.V.S. canteen.

(a) Blood transfusion – Call for volunteers.

(b) 'Blitz dog'. The British love of animals was evidenced many times during air raids. Men of the Auxiliary Military Pioneer Corps unearthed this dog, which was buried for three days.

Plymouth 28/29th November 1940 – Turn Chapel Oil Tanks.

Destroyed by bomb, Rose Lane, Canterbury – The Cathedral Saved.

(a) Arthur Coleman, Auxiliary Coastguard.
(Arthur, middle bottom of 3 men kneeling together)
the group are farm workers who worked as coastguards.

(b) Arthur Coleman and workers – Collecting the sheaves.
Arthur Coleman nearest to the horses with farm workers –
on top an Italian P.O.W.

(a) City of Portsmouth, Hyde Park Rd./Russel St. Jan. 1941.

(b) Fritz. Some Red Cross nurses first saw Fritz – his master was a
German officer captured on D-Day, instead of being shot,
he became mascot to The Royal Hampshire Regiment and lived to 1949.

Wings For Victory Week. A Drumhead Service at the United Sports Ground, Gillingham.

Chapter Thirteen

A Canterbury Tale.

In the last chapter, I told a little about the ENSA and concerts for the military; in particular about troops all over the country – both British as well as all Americans, Canadians and others from abroad. Now, apart from the many films during World War II, J. Arthur Rank made a film that was about, young and older – just ordinary people – who actually 'appeared' in this particular film. Also there were, famous actors and actresses in the film, as well, in a wonderful, remarkable and unusual film.

The film was called 'A Canterbury Tale,' and recently a book about this film, was written by Paul Tritton. I feel that parts of the book would be ideal and very apt in this chapter. The end of the film shows soldiers in the congregation of Canterbury Cathedral and might have been a commemorable Armistice Day or, perhaps, about soldiers going abroad, and probably might have been just before D-Day.

There were many people who appeared in the film – both from volunteers – such as the W.V.S., Air Raid Wardens, etc. – as well as just ordinary citizens. This though is about the premier of the film, and at the cinema on Thursday 11th May, 1944. The author, Paul Tritton, says, ' – And we are going to the picture, at Canterbury Friars Cinema – a luxurious Art Deco 'super cinema,' towering above the nearby Blackfriars Refectory and Guest Hall, which have stood beside the River Stour for 700 years.

Those of us who walked to the cinema from the suburbs east and south of the city, made our way past buddleia-cloaked bombsites in St. George's shopping and business district – devastated in the Blitz two years ago. Those who came in by bus alighted at the East Kent Car Company's terminus in St. Peter's Place, close to the Westgate Towers and only a three-minute walk away. At this end of Canterbury, we are among relatively unscathed streets, though the scorched brickwork and girders on the site of Barrett & Son's garage in St. Peter's Street remind us that war is not far away – four months ago the building was destroyed by a fire started by a single incendiary bomb.

Among the guests and their friends, are several people who are more at home in Canterbury's countryside than in the city – Robert and Elsie Tritton of Godmersham Park, and Ernest and Olive Holdstock from Elbridge Farm, Littlebourne. The Holdstocks are with their son and daughter, John and 'Bintie' and John's fiancée, Janet. Another well-known local farmer, Frank Montgomery from Wickambreaux, is also here; several of his friends hurry over to congratulate him on the birth two weeks ago of his first daughter, Sheila. Frank's wife Elizabeth is resting at home at Wickambreaux Court and has given her ticket to her maternity nurse, Alice Killick.

Last summer, the film unit whose work is about to be premiered, spent many days on location at Godmersham, Elbridge Farm and Wickambreaux, and the Trittons, the Holdstocks and Frank Montgomery, are keen to swap stories of their experiences. Soon their conversation turns to another topic of common interest – the prospects for this summer's hop harvest. They mull over last years prices (£18 a hundredweight), glumly agree that another outbreak of hop-wilt is almost inevitable, but are confident that although all their best men are now in the forces, the girls from the Women's Land Army will cope admirably with most of the work that has to be done in the hop gardens.

Elsie Tritton, heiress to the Carreras tobacco empire, has heard it all before, and moves away to say hello to the Horton brothers, Neville and Ben, whose wheelwrights' yard at Shottenden was another of the films' locations. Neville's daughter Myrtle is here too, enjoying a rare break from nursing duties at Kent and Canterbury Hospital.

Mr. Overs is animatedly greeting a civic party led by the Mayor of Canterbury, Alderman Charles Lefevre; Churchillian in stature and manner, he did more than anyone else to help the city keep its nerve in the aftermath of the Blitz. Clustered around the Mayor are Councillor A.W. Fowler, the Sheriff of Canterbury; John Boyle, Town Clerk and Civil Defence Controller; Superintendent George Hall, Canterbury's Police Chief, and Mrs. Hall; and Councillor William Chessell.

Police Constable Vincent (Jack) Russell, here with his wife Dorothy, smartly salutes his chief; only a few hours ago we saw Jack on point duty, helping an Army convoy negotiate the Westgate Towers. Jack and Dorothy are soon in conversation with PC George Bugden, Chilham's village policeman, his wife Nora and their twins Denis and Donald – both of whom we will see in the film. Scanning the other familiar faces we notice that Daniel Brice, Chairman of Bridge-Blean Rural District Council and Mayor Deputy of Fordwich, is here with his wife Edith.

Fordwich is Britains smallest town and the film we will soon see has added another chapter to its long history.

A few moments ago Councillor Chessell and his wife Gertrude were chatting to Mr. Brice, but we will see that they have now detached themselves from the mayoral group to talk to a young man whose pronounced German accent is inevitably attracting attention above the general hubbub. He is the distinguished cinematographer Erwin Hillier, befriended by the Chessells while he was working in Canterbury last year.

We were surprised, when we started to mingle with the crowd in the foyer, not to come across anyone from the Dean and Chapter's staff at Canterbury Cathedral, but as we glance around we notice that the Clerk of Works, Anthony Swaine; maybe a precentor or a minor canon or two will join him later.

The film we have come to see has a 'U' certificate, so inevitably there are many small children in the foyer. Some of them are especially excited because they appear in the film. We have already glimpsed Jimmy Tamsitt, David Todd and Len Smith from Fordwich, whose names are on the cast list in our programme. Jimmy is with his brother, Charlie, and their father, James; and David has his parents Cyril and Winifred and his brothers Brian and Peter to keep him out of mischief. Cyril and Winifred were stewards at the Foresters' Hall in the High Street until soldiers of the Buffs were billeted there after being evacuated from Dunkirk. Len Smith is with his mother, Carrie, and his sisters Eileen and Myrtle; Eileen works in a Spitfire factory at Princes Risborough and has taken a day off to come to Canterbury.

Through the glazed doors we can see four young extras – Robert, Tim, George and Ben Tragett – hurrying up to the entrance with their brother Michael and their parents, John and Mildred. Close behind them are three more extras, John Clark, Roy Fisher, and Roy Samson, all from Shottenden. They caught their local no. 31 'East Kent' bus, driven by Charlie Wicks, and changed at Chilham on to a no. 1, on its way from Ashford to Canterbury, or perhaps a no. 67 from Maidstone.

John is with his mother Ella, brothers Allan and Peter, and their aunt, Beryl Attwood. They spent the morning shopping and struggle through the doors burdened with groceries, candles and other necessities. Roy Fisher is with his parents, Albert and Ivy, and his brother Frank, and Roy Samson is with his mother Mildred.

One of the boys is clutching his autograph book, hoping to obtain the signatures of the few members of the cast and crew he somehow missed while passing his book around while on location with them. Several other autograph collectors are circulating around and Erwin Hillier has signed at least half a dozen programmes while talking to the Chessells.

Standing a few yards from some rather boisterous schoolboys is a shy little girl with dark curly hair, holding her mother's hand. We recognise Janet Woodcock and her mother Adelaide from Dover Street. Janet's father, Bert, drives a Rolls-Royce for Arthur Skam's taxi firm, whose depot is in Oaten Hill Mews. For several weeks last summer Bert, with Janet beside him, could be seen driving the film's director and cast to and from their hotels and locations. We suspect that, because Janet and her mother are on their own, Bert is back on film duty today. Sure enough, attention soon turns to the forecourt as a taxi arrives, Mr. Downs the doorman steps forward to open the doors, and Mr. Overs greets film producer and director Michael Powell and his wife Frankie. With them are Eric Portman, Sheila Sim and Dennis Price, whose names have been featured prominently in advertisements and on poster hoardings for the past three weeks.

Mr. Powell and his personal assistant, Bill Paton, have been staying at The George and Dragon in Fordwich, where Michael has made many friends. Bill, standing a few paces behind Mr. Powell, is on leave from active service with the Royal Navy in the Shetlands; it is his chance to resume, if only for a few days, a friendship and working relationship with Mr. Powell that began some eight years ago.

Where, though, is the films' other star, Sergeant John Sweet of the US Army – the amiable GI who made so many friends in Canterbury last year? Word soon gets round that he is under orders to remain with his unit in London. We need not ask why. For weeks the south of England has been buzzing with rumours that a huge force of British, American and Canadian soldiers is preparing to embark from the Kent coast and invade the Pas de Calais. Clusters of fighter-bombers, tanks and army lorries have appeared in the Canterbury countryside and a friend of a friend has heard that a fleet of landing craft is gathering in Dover Harbour. Others say the war machines are only dummies – inflatable rubber tanks and canvas and plywood boats, lorries and planes – but visitors from the coast and the Weald of Kent tell us that in the past few weeks, American troops have set up anti-aircraft batteries and occupied some hastily-constructed airstrips. US Army Air Force Thunderbolt fighters are based there – real 'planes, because they've been seen taking off and landing.

Whatever the truth or otherwise of these stories, the war is obviously entering a decisive phase and John Sweet and his buddies have more important things to do than go to film premiers.

Suddenly, the foyer is empty. The auditorium is now full – and noisy too. The tip-up seats bang about as people at the ends of the rows stand to make way for those with seats in the middle. Peggy Jones guides the Clarks, the Fishers and the Samsons to their places in the middle of the central block in the stalls, and Ella stows her rustling carrier bags. Soon, nearly everyone is smoking – and coughing – and beams of light from the projection box pierce a tobacco haze, like searchlights on a foggy night. The house lights, concealed in cornices and other plaster decorations, throw magical shadows and silhouettes on the walls and ceiling, and fade as subtle colours play on the red plush curtains and gold tassels concealing the silver screen. Conversation and coughing gradually subside and cease completely as three 'Buffs' buglers play a fanfare. The curtains part, the sound system crackles into life, and the screen is filled with the stark black and white images!

Chapter Fourteen

Women In Green – Red Cross And Civil Defence – In Portsmouth And Other Ports, D-Day, Doodlebugs and V2's Then 'Victory Day,' In Europe.

During late 1943, my father was still attending the army officers hospital at Percival Terrace, near the seafront in Brighton. As I have said – after his wounds from World War – he still got treatment on his leg stump and on his left arm, but he also went there to visit fellow officers, who were still recovering in hospital – friends of his.

Their main topic of conversation, by this time, was about when the invasion on France 'would happen.' After the catastrophe of Dieppe, they also wondered whether, perhaps, attacking across the Pas De Calais, but by this, would be highly defended with a fortress – bristling with guns and men.

Early in 1943 – in January, Winston Churchill, President Roosevelt and many of the senior officers, had thought about things whilst meeting at Casablanca in Morocco – but everything wasn't right, they thought they would meet again later. Another conference was agreed to meet at Quebec in August 1943 – but nothing yet was ready. However in early summer 1944, it was thought that May or June would be the time of the invasion – but, of course, this was all very secret at the time.

However, later, it was told, in order to get enough buildings and many more landing crafts – and also perhaps the weather, that June would be the best time.

They had also chosen the beaches of Normandy for the invasion and – not the Pas De Calais. However during the month of the invasion, an enormous plan to deceive the enemy came together – and hoping that the Pas De Calais was the place the invasion the Germans thought. This plan was called 'Operation Fortitude' and became over the south east of the country – in particular in Kent. It was hoped the Germans might photograph from their aircraft, particularly over the fields, showing plywood dummies, or other things made as tanks, aeroplanes and other things, looking part of an invasion, and looking perfect apparently 'alright' from the air – and they thought the real thing!

Also with thousands of troops coming into the country, this is where the W.V.S. helped when large bodies of men required feeding at short notice while in transit. So it was natural, as the armies accumulated in the south, for the volunteers, in particular the W.V.S., to provide food for convoys and arrange halting places – sometimes with only a few hours notice.

In 1944, there was some good hot weather during the May of that year, and on May 29th a temperature of 91 degrees Fahrenheit was recorded at Horsham in Sussex. This was an all time record for May, and that record still stands to this day. However the early days of June became unsettled and we didn't know just how crucial it was at that time for the elements to be kind and certainly for the sea to be calm – or reasonably so!

On Monday 5th June, we were ignorant of the fact, that because of inclement weather, a huge armada, that had been set to sail from the shores of Great Britain that day, had to stay where it was. However by the following day, the weather had improved enough for the invasion of France to take place.

In Brighton, during that memorable day of Tuesday 6th June 1944, we started getting reports of the invasion on the beaches of Normandy – quite early, and the country, including us at school, was kept informed of the situation throughout the day.

The headlines of the 'Argus' that evening were – 'Mighty Air Land and Sea Attack.' It also reported that tanks had been landed in France. All our thoughts immediately went back to all the tanks we had seen on manoeuvres and of the men we had known so well during the months they were training in the Brighton area during 1943. We didn't know even if they were involved as yet – but they were in our thoughts nonetheless. However, the W.V.S. and the Red Cross were certainly involved, with everything to do with D-Day; but before I say about these, I feel I should put a piece about a friend and author, Michael Butcher – who I helped to write his book 'Paraffin Lights – Water From The Well' – in particular a part about D-Day, he says – "In Sussex, we were later to learn of some of the huge amount of work that had gone on in preparation for the invasion – some of it right under our noses, without our realizing. Apart from Sheffield Park and nearby Searles, all the troops that we had seen under canvas in various camps, a lot of the highly secret preparation had taken place in nearby areas – particularly in the Newhaven area. Apparently, at Piddinghoe, not far from Newhaven – and situated not far from the tidal stretch of the Sussex Ouse – a secret project had gone ahead so that it was possible to conceal a large amount of invasion craft from being seen by German

218

reconnaissance planes. A canal had been dug to by-pass a bend in the river, and this had been disguised with various types of foliage, and also large quantities of camouflaged netting. The ships in the harbour, getting ready for the invasion, were also shrouded in the netting.

After this part of the invasion force had left Newhaven Harbour, this area of Sussex was still very much involved, in as much that a large part of the invasion fleet had been installed in a network of tunnels and rooms below the village of Heighton – just near Newhaven. From the corridors and rooms, many of the planners and strategists were able to keep in constant contact with what was going on in a line from Dover to Portsmouth. This was also to see that ships from different embarking ports met at assembly points in the channel correctly – before moving on towards off-shore areas near the Normandy Beaches. These tunnels had been excavated and built in 1941 as an essential part of a naval shore base – in what looked to be a port, which would soon play a significant part in the war, because of its important position on the south coast and nearness to the French coast. The base was called H.M.S. Forward.

However before the invasion, artificial harbours – coded 'Mulberry Harbours' – in order to keep the huge forces – would need to be supplied.

In 1942, Mr. Churchill had said, when first thinking that building harbours would be necessary, that they must be – up and down with the tides – and the 'anchor' problem must be mastered.

Concrete Caissons would build various places around the coast, and many of these were also built around the Thames Marshes. A lot of these were eventually at Tilbury and managed by tugs – and the very big tugs were for towing around the coast.

One of these tugs, *Challenge*, I have written about in 'Esacpe From Catastrophe,' and told how she assisted in the berthing at the east mole and took small craft into tow – vital and valuable work!

Challenge also helped to tow the Maunsell Towers in 1940 for defences in the Thames Estuary. Also before and during D-Day helped to tow some of the Mulberry Harbours in the Thames.

Michael Butcher also says in his book – 'In the early hours of the morning 6th June, it was immediately noticeable to us, that the whole area seemed quieter than usual – there seemed to no troops about at all. This 'eerie' quiet was quickly shattered by the sounds of hundreds of aircraft flying overhead, in the direction of the channel. I remember I got up much earlier than usual that morning – as did many of my friends, and we quickly cycled to a viewpoint just outside the village, in time to see aircraft towing gliders on their way towards the channel and France – the invasion had begun!

The aeroplanes seemed to passing overhead 'forever' – like a swarm of giant bees! It seemd that every type of aircraft that could tow a glider, was doing so. There were Stirlings, Dakotas, Halifaxes and many others as well – it seemed a wonder that they didn't collide.'

In Women in Green – Charles Graves said – 'Then came D-Day. W.V.S. took food by mobile canteen to numbers of beaches, so that the men loading the landing crafts could work continuously. Other members had the dramatic job of feeding the marching troops in pitch darkness as they made their way down to the embarkation points. Absolute silence was demanded, and only the clink of mugs would have been heard by any enemy agents present.

Although security measures prevented W.V.S. from doing much that they would have wished to do for the men, in the crafts which were taking them to the Normandy – the south coast port centres were called on to give help with the return of the first of the wounded. Thus in Portsmouth W.V.S. held highly confidential consultations, with the authorities of the local Emergency Medical Service Hospitals, together with the officers of the joint war organisations of the Red Cross and St. John's, to discuss how to provide the help likely to be needed in the event of wounded men being brought to the city, and the W.V.S. undertook to provide domestic as well as clerical helpers. They were then asked by the Port Authorities if it would be possible for the W.V.S. to maintain a twenty-four hour special canteen service in the dockyard to service small ships and landing craft bringing in survivors from the invasion beaches. With one mobile canteen borrowed from the British Sailors Society and their own, they found they were able to keep up a rota.. Within an hour of the request being made, a member and her crew of helpers had the first canteen out and were serving tea, cakes and biscuits, later on that day, to a queue of hungry and weary sailors recently from the Normandy Beaches. It took a day or so to become familiar with the routes to the various jetties, and to get 'bearings' in the vast dockyard, while canteens were switched from one jetty to another to meet these small ships, sometimes at night – which made driving over 16 narrow dock bridges, both difficult and hazardous.

The twenty four hours were divided into five shifts of four hours each, with the night shift being of longer duration – this, of course, was unavoidable. Later the request was extended to ships bringing in the wounded. This taxes the resources to the utmost (especially mugs) and many hundred cardboard ones were quickly obtained and pressed onto service. All walking wounded were served by the W.V.S. – either in the ambulances or coaches, or as they were waiting to enter them – with free tea, cocoa, chocolate, cake and cigarettes (the latter given by the wrens and people of Cosham). Numbers of the men were cold and shivering from sea-sickness and wounds, and given sweet tea and kind ministering. Later, stretcher cases were saved, and attention had to be given to the weary sick-berth attendants and R.A.M.C. personnel – including, stretcher bearers who, having been on duty for twelve hours at a time, more than appreciated the food and drink!'

Naina Cox, who I told about being at school at the time of the biggest raid on Portsmouth, at the end of chapter eight, had, at sixteen years, become a member of Hants. 28th Red Cross Division. She said – "I became a member of this division of Red Cross – this was at Cosham, on the outskirts of Portsmouth, and near an old military hospital – Queen Alexamder Hospital. From the day I joined the Red Cross, I, with a few others, worked hard for the basic certificates – first aid, home nursing, child welfare and an extra in wartime – 'gas warfare'. Voluntary work in hospitals – mainly menial tasks, were a 'must.' If you didn't do this you were asked, to leave- thankfully my reports were good!

At about 2 p.m., on 6th June, 1944, a senior commandant of The British Red Cross Society came into my Cosham office, where I was a clerk, and said – "Miss Beaver (now Mrs. Cox), you must get permission to leave at once, go home, put on your Red Cross uniform and report to the matron at the Queen Alexander Hospital. I did this, and, as I walked up to the gates, it was obvious that a very long stream of army lorries were wending their way to the hospital. The matron, after checking my credentials, soon told me what was going on – she also told me that this was D-Day! The men loaded on stretchers, were the first casualties from the Normandy Beaches. Within seconds, I was taking off their wet clothing and removing emergency dressings, washing dirty faces, hands and feet. Drinks in feeding cups were given to those able to lift their heads. Many fell asleep – these were the first exhaustion cases. They had been fighting from at least 3 a.m. that day! A day later, hardly keeping awake myself, I helped a senior nurse dress the first bullet wounded I had ever seen. I also worked on a German P.O.W. ward; mainly grey – frightened teenagers, who cried a lot! The matron said to me –"Do you have any objections working on a German prisoners ward?" She had asked one of the other girls – who

221

said she had a brother who was fighting abroad and would like to think that if he needed help, someone would give it to him, no matter what the circumstances, and this made up my mind for me, and I said I would!

We were escorted to the further hut, where two armed soldiers, standing by the closed outer door, stopped us. After checking our names, we went along the passage to the inner doors of the ward – also closed with an armed guard outside. They called the army sister, who took one of us on the ward with her, and the other with an army orderly.

By this time, we were quicker at changing soiled sheets and washing perspiration off dirty faces and bodies. The main difference in the ward was atmosphere, so still, scarcely a word spoken – long, long staring looks from pathetically young grey faces.

My small contribution to D-Day was unpaid – but what a wealth of inspiration it gave me for the future. When I was old enough, I joined the Navy as a full-time VAD, and was then sent out to work in Hongkong."

Niana has also said – "both before, during and after D-Day," she says – "a lot has been written about the heroism of our invasion troops at D-Day, and quite rightly so. We have also heard about pipelines under the sea, and Mulberry Harbours and such like. However, little has been said about the vital work of the support services, which helped the provision of the vast armada.

This was indeed a tremendous task, for it involved not only feeding the crews of the assault vessels, but also the embarking of the troops. So, full credit must go to the men and women employed in support establishments; like the Royal Clarence Victualling Yard at Gosport.

This important task by the yard, was not carried out solely from Gosport, for, three years earlier, in 1941, the site was a victim of the Blitz and, on one terrible night, it seemed that the whole place was engulfed in flames. This confirmed the old adage that it is not wise to 'put all your eggs in one basket' so, much of the depot was dispersed to several subsidiary depots around the south of England.

Although the headquarters were moved from Gosport to Thatcham, near Newbury, The Royal Clarence Yard was responsible for victualling ships afloat, while the subsidiary depots provisioned most of the shore establishments in Portsmouth Command.

With D-Day imminent and the invasion fleet assembling in large numbers, the task facing the yard was daunting, and in the week prior to the historic day – more than 1,000 tons of meat, potatoes and bread as well as vast quantities of dry goods had to be distributed to the

222

ships. To maintain supplies to the assembled craft, the yard fleet of 10 vessels was augmented by eight motor fishing vessels. The MFV's were manned by a somewhat motley bunch of crewmen recruited by the Admiralty in desperation. They comprised civil servants, company managers, salemen, clerks, retired admirals and even members of the aristocracy!

On being confronted with having to skipper a 90 ft boat, one alarmed recruit pointed out that he had never handled anything bigger than a 14 ft sailing dinghy – but this fell on deaf ears and he was ordered to 'get on with it.' – to his credit, the chap did and made a success of it.

The men on the Yard vessels maintained a continuous provisioning service for the invasion – fleet night and day – with each vessel assigned its own area, in which to sail back and forth issuing fresh provisions to any ship flying the appropriate flag.

Of course, water supplies were vital, and for this, two 10,000 ton oil tankers were cleaned out and prepared to hold fresh water for the fleet. Once a week, the tankers put in to Southampton to be replenished – on returning to Gosport, the water was transferred as required to the smaller water tankers.

To provide this 24-hour service, the Yard craft and MRV's had to be kept moving, and to this end, men from the New Barracks were enlisted to boost the labour force.

A word of praise must also be afforded to the women workers, for during the war around 150 women were employed at the Yard to take on such formidable jobs as trucking goods and loading and unloading stores. In addition to this, many of the ladies volunteered for nightly fire-watching duries and ARP work as well as W.V.S ladies.

After the hostilities, the headquarters moved back to Gosport and recognition of the Yard's services to keep vital supplies flowing during the war was shown through medals being awarded to various officials and individuals."

In chapter eleven I have written about Margaret Hall and Mary Cooke who were nurses in the Red Cross and worked on the 'Blood Transfusion'. I think that a little more about this, in particular at the time of D-Day, from the official account of the blood transfusion service, 'Life Blood' which says:

'When, on the morning of the 6th June 1944, the news reached every home, office and factory in Britain that the invasion of France had begun, three questions came to our minds. How will it turn out? Will the casualties be very high? Will 'he' come through all right?

There were many casualties; but far fewer than had been expected. One fact stands out – many wounded men were saved on the Normandy beaches who would have died in similar conditions in the last war. One of the chief reasons for the low death rate among casualties was that the men in the landing craft, the ships, the transport planes and the gliders, took with them blood given by men and women in towns and villages all over Britain. Strapped into the equipment of the medical units of the paratroops and other assault units, were bottles of the blood product, plasma, with transfusion sets in waterproof boxes. Transfusion Officers with the assault troops carried waterproofed instruments and dressings, so that, without waiting for their special lorries to be beached, they could set to work dripping life blood into wounded men.

Soon after the transfusion teams had waded ashore, came Field Transfusion Unit lorries, equipped with refrigerators. In the refrigerators were 1,100 pints of fresh whole blood. Blood plasma was also carried in other military vehicles – slung on the underside in containers which in the ordinary way hold trench mortar shells; four bottles and two transfusion sets took the place of three shells.

So not only the thoughts and hopes of those at home went with the fighting men to Normandy, their gifts of blood went too. Here are two of the first messages telling how that blood was used, the first from a field transfusion unit officer: "We arrived at the appointed time without mishap, we were running our resuscitation ward in the local Mairie within an hour of our arrival. My two orderlies proved themselves extremely efficient. We were too busy to keep any records the first forty eight hours, but at the end of that time I had about a hundred empty bottles which had contained blood or plasma – rather more of the latter. The refrigerator is running well. One of the first casualties I saw was an old friend with a penetrating wound in his chest, he was doing quite well when I last saw him."

The second message came from an Advanced Dressing Station: "A Highlander who had been lying in a field for three days with a shell splinter in his chest, was pulse less when admitted. At first the doctor despaired of his life – a blood transfusion officer decided to give him a transfusion. After he had been given four pints of blood, he revived and started to relate his experiences. A lance-bombardier, who had had both legs shattered by an 88 mm. shell, was given a transfusion within fifteen minutes of becoming a casualty."

As the troops fought their way inland, supplies of blood and blood products followed them, and continued to follow them day-by-day.

More plasma in round wicker baskets was dropped by parachute to airborne troops and isolated units.

The invasion force's first reinforcements of whole blood, carried in insulated boxes on landing craft, began to cross to France a few hours after the invasion. On D+14, daily air transport began, blood given by civilians in England one day, had sometimes been used on the battlefields the next. Plasma was still sent by sea. Before D-Day, blocks of maintenance supplies had been built up at an army medical store in England. Each block represented the estimated daily needs of plasma for the whole invasion force. Every day after D-Day, one of these blocks was transported to the beaches; and all the way to Germany, supplies of blood and plasma followed the fighting men.

All over the country people have given their pints of blood. In every one of the fighting forces and in all the bombed towns and cities, there are men and women who owe their lives to these gifts. Not only that, in many towns in Britain men and women are walking about and doing vital war jobs who, though not war casualties, would certainly be dead but for the Blood Transfusion Srevices.

Mary Verrier was telling, in chapter eight, about the biggest air raid at Portsmouth, during Friday 10th January 1941 and was a nineteen years old, then working at St. Mary's Hospital as a Red Cross nurse – later she went on to the Queen Alexander Military Hospital and Southern Hospital General Command. She says: "At the time of D-Day, the area was under 75 Southern General Army Command, and the navy under Admiral Sir Bertram Ramsey, who was so brilliant as chief at Dover during the days of Dunkirk.

In the days leading up to the invasion of Normandy, very tight security was in operation in and around the Portsmouth and Gosport area. Unnecessary movement was forbidden – all identity cards frequently checked by police/army. Police carried loaded rifles and civil defence personnel and air raid wardens also contributed to the vigilance required. No one could have misinterpreted that something 'was on' for prior to this day – some roads in the city and elsewhere had been widened and infilled with rubble from bombed buildings to take heavy traffic.

Military Provost and personnel were shepherding the incoming army vehicles and tanks, which would eventually snake back 16 miles from the sea front. No leave was allowed; military men to remain in barracks or tents, and naval men to remain aboard ship or in the naval base. Hospital and medical staff had no leave, – fraternisation and speaking to any army personnel, by civilians, was forbidden; although people did speak to some of the men waiting by vehicles (gave them cups of tea). Men by their tanks/vehicles brewed up; kept busy – some helping with 'repair' jobs needed by civilians. Hospitals were on alert, all available beds made ready; dining rooms were taken over – the chapel and every available space!

Mary remembers and laughs about one thing that happened in the later days, she says: "An Army Sergeant Dispatch Rider turned up at the hospital, seeking directions to General Eisenhower's Headquarters – he said he had an urgent dispatch. I said, 'Come this way' and took him to a long cupboard where all the stretchers were kept. I said, 'If you would like to wait in here, I will get someone to see to you' and locked him in. Then I got so busy that I forgot all about him. It wasn't until the early hours of the morning that someone happened to hear him bashing on the door and let him out. It turned out he was genuine and had some dispatches for General Eisenhower." As a result of the delay, the sergeant lost his stripes and Mary Verrier got a severe reprimand from the Matron.

The incident may seem quaint now, but in those security conscious days it was a matter of deadly seriousness. The entire south coast of England was one huge sealed camp, and while most people could guess that an invasion was imminent, the big questions were – where and when?

The packing of equipment, dressings and stores was of intense activity. Matron divided hospital staff into groups and spoke to each group with words of advice. We were led very well by example – although several of us worried if we would be able to rise to what was expected of us.

Schools, Churches and church halls were commandeered and made ready to receive those whose need was not for hospitalisation, but for compassionate and supportive care – including those who were shell shocked. Two of the big stores sent blankets and other goods to men waiting on the Common. There was the noise of movement and marching feet of hundreds of soldiers – some sitting on the beach waiting for departure, some attending Drumhead Service on the beach. The two Beach Masters at Southsea were an English and an American Major. The Mayor allowed children to speak to the troops, which was good for morale – although some men cried at seeing little ones. Soldiers gave money and items to the children and, as usual, there were one or two comedians who received a rebuke from Senior Matron, for familiarity.

Then, at last, all aboard and this huge fleet of ships, some with barrage balloons and Mulberry Harbour Section, was off! For unknown reasons, at the time the proceeding six weeks our Allied Air Forces had taken on and defeated the Luftwaffe with huge loss of life and planes on both sides. Then, the horizon was clear, and a peculiar silence settled down on us all – the long wait began, a most unforgettable experience. Chaplains moved amongst us to give us encouragement. Soon, over the horizons came the battered hospital ships and wounded to R.N. Hasler and Camber (not allowed in the early stages into the dockyard because of security). Then we collected up these tired and seriously wounded men. Next day brought hundreds in, laid on stretchers in St. Mary's Hospital grounds, and a triage team sorted out those in urgent need (all were to a degree). As a junior nurse, I and one other had to go ahead of doctors and medical team to look for lads marked with H(He), T(Tourniquet), B(Burns), S(Shrapnel – Spinal) injuries. A most horrendous and heartbreaking task. They were moved to ward 12, Queen Alexander Military Hospital. Hours passed, and still they came, ladies from churches who came to sit, to wash, to watch, very well supported us. The W.V.S. now Women's Royal Voluntary Service and Salvation Army all rallied round and helped.

Troops, trains, everything you could think of still were being ferried out, rumours and stories of what was going on had circulated. Our casualties were a mixed bag – P.O.W.'s, Free French, Allied forces and some French civilians, which made life very difficult and our interpreters were hard pressed. But it is amazing how you can communicate by sign language, expression and touch. We should always be grateful for our City Planners and Medical Officers of Health for their foresight and forward planning – although no really expected saturation and the amount of work to be undertaken by all.

As the days wore on, some semblance of order arose and transfer to P.O.W. camps and hospitals – wherever possible, was undertaken, the populace moved with a lighter heart and step, although tired out, and I do mean tired! But we should not forget the young boys, who on their bicycles, acted as messengers; a brave and very reliable service they gave.

I cannot end without mentioning the fiercest German Prisoner captured on D-Day. He was a magnificent Pyrenean Mountain dog named Fritz. Taken with his German Officer, he was doomed for execution, but leading Wren Elgar undertook to pay quarantine fees.

227

Captain Thomas, who was in charge of the platoon arranged for when the dog was released – he became the Royal Hampshire Mascot.

Fritz was no easy prisoner, he gnawed through zinc-lined door. But he soon became used and responded to Army discipline and became an obedient member of the Regiment. He weighed 122 lb and been trained for service in the field – he could clear a six foot barbed wire fence with ease! He would make short work of any intruder. His army number was H1157, he was groomed and dressed with a beautiful velvet jacket – he died in 1949.

I add this little story to show, that without humour and compassion and a sense of what is right, we could not have survived.

Soon the city returned to its usual busy routine and the time for re-building lives began.'

Mary added – "Just a few thoughts on D-Day – most of which I did not know until sometime after that date. On the evening before 5th June, General Dwight Eisenhower, with his comrades, gathered at Christ Church, Portsdown, for a short service of dedication. This church, being about four miles away from Southwick House – some years later a commemorative plaque was placed in the church.

The weather on June 6th was quite nice – though hardly sunny. There was an unmistakable atmosphere, but it was later in the day before the official news broke. When I walked home, late in the evening, from working at the Queen Alexander Hospital, the evening was absolutely brilliant, dry and warm – the remains of a bright sunset.

The drawing room at Southwick House still contains the original operations wall, set for 'H. Hour' of D-Day (now H.M.S. Pryad). Droxford always was a small village – in 1944 it had a tiny railway station. Winston Churchill has a train set up in a siding there – it was there that he received a visit from General de Gaulle, who was told of the allies proposal to liberate his country. The railway is now disused and the station a private house."

During the next few days, we heard mainly encouraging bits of news about the allied advances into Normandy – and these reports led to many people thinking that peace could be just around the corner and that, in any case, the Germans would be so busy fighting rearguard actions in France in their retreat, that, we, at home would be left in peace at last! The assumption proved to be incorrect, because on June 13th 1944 – weeks after D-Day – the Germans unleashed a new terrifying weapon on the south of England. It was the day the enemy sent over the first of their unmanned aircraft – the V1 rocket, or 'Doodlebug,' as it quickly and unaffectionately became known to us!

Dot Weedon, who I talked about in Chapter Four, about helping the soldiers at Chatham Railway Station, at the time of Dunkirk and who worked at Short Brothers at Rochester – as well as helping in the A.R.P., said – "About a week after D-Day, with one of my colleagues, standing at the entrance of our 'post' about one o'clock in the early morning, all was quiet, not a sound in the sky, the moon was shining bright and we thought that we would soon get the all clear, and be able to go home. However, suddenly, we heard this peculiar noise coming from the direction of Essex; it nearly passed overhead – we couldn't understand what it was; it had flames coming out of the back, but no wings. While we were discussing if it was a plane that had been badly shot up, when the sky lit up and there was a loud bang! We later learned that it had dropped near Swanscombe, just a few miles away.

Soon we were getting these Doodlebugs every night – sometimes every ten minutes. We soon learnt that if you heard the noise of the engine stop, and the lights go out, you dived on the ground – luckily for us, we didn't get one explode very near to us, but even to this day, I have not forgotten that first night of Doodlebugs."

In Brighton, we had quite often seen them going over while we were in the Sussex Square gardens playing, and if we were climbing a tree at the time, we would very quickly scramble down! We were fortunate that they always missed us and flew to some less fortunate area – making their unmistakable deep engine noise, and showing their fiery tails as they disappeared from view.

As I said, in Brighton we just saw the doodlebug on its 'journey' – the nearest one to drop was at Cuckfield, just a few miles away. Although many did drop in country areas and towns in the Home Counties, Hitler had ordered that London was to be the prime target – and it certainly was!

By the end of June, approximately 2000 of these devastating weapons had been sent across the channel, and this set a big problem for the Air Force and those on the ground manning the guns, who were trying to shoot them down before they could do much damage. In trying to work out the best way of destroying these machines, it was found out that they flew over at a height of between 2000 and 3000 feet; this it made it difficult for the gunners – because it was too high for the light guns and too low for the heavy guns. They could also reach speeds of up to

400 mph, before the engine suddenly stopped – then a silence – then a whooshing sound, and then the inevitable explosion.

It was decided that by using new kinds of shells and positioning many more guns in a line, from just near Newhaven, to just beyond Dover, that this would give the guns unrestricted field of fire at the V1's coming in from the channel, destroying them and falling harmlessly into the sea – this would also give the R.A.F. a better go at them as they flew from the coast to the North Downs – where they would run into more defences, in the shape of large numbers of barrage balloons.

The pilots of fighter planes soon discovered that it was hazardous to shoot down one of the missiles from too close behind; the safe distance being about 200 yards – certainly no less!

Some pilots though, if they had run out of ammunitions, would fly close to the doodlebugs, and place one of the fighter's wings against one of the missiles – and 'tip it over' – always bearing in mind where it was likely to come to earth!

Towards the end of July, the ground and air defences against the V1 were enormous, and the threat from this horrific type of warfare lessened considerably!

Babs Davies, who I wrote about in chapter ten, and was a Red Cross nurse at a hospital in Erith, Kent. She said – "A lot of doodlebugs were brought down by the anti-aircraft; nearly all the factories were near the Thames in this area. One day, I saw one passing over the Belvedere Marshes, when a Spitfire chased it – the wing of the plane tipped the doodlebug and dived straight into the marshes, the pilot did a victory roll – it was great to watch!

Later on in September one night on my way home from the hospital, I thought I would go and visit my sister-in-law who lived nearby, and see her and her new baby. Just behind her house a rocket crashed down just as I was arriving there – everything was silent, then a whoosh, then an awful flash. There was rubble everywhere, including her home that had the roof gone! However when they found that her mother-in-law, who had also come to see her – she had found that they were alright, except that the baby had a piece of glass in one ear – which her mother-in-law had managed to get out.'

Reviewing this subject, it was thought at the time, and still is thought, that if Hitler had started using these weapons a couple of weeks beforehand, and if it had targeted the Portsmouth, Southampton and similar areas, instead of London, D-Day, the invasion of France wouldn't have taken place when it did and Operation Overlord would have been delayed at least – changing the history books!

On the 9th September, the news came through of another type of flying bomb – the V2 – which was far more devastating than the 'Doodlebug' – the V1. The first of these was exploded in England the day before, but thankfully, we in Brighton, never saw anything of these horrific weapons – but many had been seen in many places – and were apparently powerful enough to demolish a whole street. (See front jacket of book.)

In each of the months of 1945, apart from the news of continuing advances into Germany, on the radio on Thursday 12th April, the news came through of the death of President Roosevelt.

On 30th April, two days after it was reported in Italy, that Mussolini had been 'executed' by partisans, the news also came through that Hitler was dead. After this, everyone's hopes were raised, in the expectancy of an imminent announcement of the end of the war. When on 2nd May, it was announced that the Germans had finally capitulated in Italy, and that the Russians had taken Berlin, our wireless set was left on for most of the time, and we eagerly awaited the overdue news of the end of the war – which would probably be made by Winston Churchill.

On Tuesday 8th May, Mr. Churchill announced that 'hostilities in Europe would officially end one minute after midnight.'

On 8th May, V.E. Day, in Brighton, I went with a friend and his mother, to see all the celebrations in the town.

We noticed that the crowds on the streets were getting larger all the time, and now and again we stopped to watch impromptu 'turns' performed by merrymakers and intended as general entertainments. Red, white and blue rosettes, scarves or hats or a combination of them, were worn by practically everyone – including us. The streetlights came on just as dusk was descending, and this was the first time this had happened since the beginning of the war. The blackout of course had been over for quite some time, but with this added light, the normally darkened streets became brightly lit from a myriad of lights of varying intensity. The pubs, with their doors open and their customers flowing out onto the streets, were all doing a roaring trade, and here and there, people took to dancing on the pavements and on the roads; through which, no cars could pass. Snake-like lines of people wearing funny hats and grasping each other's waists, did the 'Hokey-cokey' – winding their way through the shoulder to shoulder thronging crowds, who readily made way for them to go unimpeded in their revelry.

231

The fireworks soon started, with rockets zooming into the air from all over the place, and screams coming from excited young ladies, as penny bangers exploded – sometimes perilously close to them. Some of the more agile and adventurous ones from the huge crowd even climbed up the clock tower – a few actually reaching the top!

After passing the crowds that had gathered on the seafront, near the Palace Pier, we walked past the Aquarium and then went to our house in Sussex Square. On arriving, after saying goodbye to my friend and his mother, I made my way to where my parents and their friends were – there was a full party going and I listened to the loud talk and happy laughter of celebrating adults – with their cups running, who, without reserve, were letting their hair down and having a whale of a time! Once again the drinks flowed generously – a bit too generously in some cases – including my father's, as was to be very evident the next morning!

At well past midnight, we made our way back to number thirteen, and very quickly to bed and instant sleep. The night had certainly been one to remember, but what I remember the most about it was the conviviality between everyone – wherever we went, it was as if we were all part of a huge family party, and, I suppose, in a way – we were!

Epilogue.

I have put those who helped me in the acknowledgements, but I feel I have to say just about a few people in the book – as well as some of boats.

I have written about Dunkirk in my book, 'Escape From Catastrophe – 1940 Dunkirk.' In 2000 and have written also some pieces about this time in chapters three and four, but in writing about the UK – the home shores – I feel certainly that some pieces deserved to be written about again, and therefore there were parts that were across the channel – at Dunkirk.

I have told about Albert Barnes, in particular, who in chapter three, at the age of fourteen and a half, was the cabin boy on the Thames tug, '*Sun XII.*' On the day that Albert left for the hellish beaches of Dunkirk, his mother had expected him home for tea that afternoon – but didn't see him again for nearly two weeks. Albert keeps well and recently phoned me.

During the book, about Dunkirk at the launching of the 60th anniversary, at the Imperial War Museum in May 2000, I sat next to Ernie Leggett, who is again in the book – he was editor of the Dunkirk Veterans Association. Unfortunately Ernie died recently. I miss him and all his help in the past – farewell good friend.

In chapter five, I wrote about Maureen Andrews and her twin sister Joyce, who told me about their mother – Alice Rawlings in the A.R.P. at Shoeburyness in the war. Later that year, for her bravery, Alice was awarded the Defence Medal. Maureen told me she never collected this medal. However, many years after her death, her daughter Maureen, after enquiring whether it was still possible to claim it, was delighted to receive it, just a few weeks after making her request – they got Alice's medal.

Also in chapter five, I told about the George Medal received after a terrible raid during the night of 8th/9th September 1940. Joan Goodyear, of the British Red Cross at Horsham, sent me information about 'Nanny White' for the book; she has also written about her – "When Dorothy White got the George Medal, she was the first V.A.D.

nurse to do so, when a reporter told her of the award, she said – "Are you sure you haven't made a mistake?"

Her war work was not over; she collected for a National Savings Group as well as the Spitfire Fund. Dorothy loved life and people and, though her name has been recorded with pride for her heroism during one night, those who knew her closely, remember her life as a record of small everyday acts of healing and devotion, interlaced with plenty of fun."

One person, in chapter six, unfortunately I haven't found any relatives about Grace Rattenbury, of the W.V.S. When this particular air raid, happened in the Bermondsey and Rotherhithe area, in London. For her bravery received the George Medal. The following later appeared in The London Gazette:

Awarded George Medal.

Miss Grace Rattenbury, London Women's Voluntary Services and organiser, Invalid Children's Aid Association.

'Miss Rattenbury, of the Invalid Children's Aid Association, who is also a member of the W.V.S., volunteered to assist in the evacuation of people from a dockland area during an extensive fire caused by enemy bombs.

With a W.V.S. van, she commenced a 'shuttle' service from a wharf, to a first line rest and feeding centre. With great determination and courage she continued driving until the last woman and child had been evacuated from the danger zone. All the time, the enemy aircraft were continuously dropping bombs over the area. The fire threatened to cut people off from the mainland, and there was only a single span bridge left open. The road was extremely dangerous on account of the fires, bomb craters and delayed action bombs, yet Miss Rattenbury continued her work without hesitation. She remained calm and confident, and by her example steadied everyone. On more than one occasion, whilst assisting wardens to evacuate families, she had to throw herself down to escape the blast from bombs, which fell a few yards away, and her car was blistered by the encroaching flames.'

I have thanked Paul Tritton, the author of 'A Canterbury Tale' the book of the film, which has helped so much with the atmosphere of the war years – in particular 1943/44 – an odd, but beautiful film, and, to many, prophetic at that time.

I also thank another author, my friend Michael Butcher. He and I worked together for a year on 'Paraffin Lights – Water From The Well'

234

about his younger years in the village of Fletching in the beautiful Sussex countryside. I have included several pieces of his book, and Michael has helped by reading my manuscript.

Some years ago Michael contacted Parkinson's Disease. Although he doesn't play golf any more, he still has plenty of other hobbies, including attending creative writing at the 'centre' in Newhaven and is now chairman of the Eastbourne Parkinson's Society.

I should also like to tell of some of the small ships. In chapter three I told of the '*Sylvia*', one of the boats that went to Dunkirk. She is berthed on the river Medway – not far from where I live in Rochester. She is a houseboat and home for A.D.L.S. member, Ian Pearson and his wife, now renamed the '*Wendy Ken*.' Her adventures might easily have been forgotten under her new name, had it not have been for Lt. Commander Maynard who was harbour master at Ramsgate and recognised her when she entered the port one day – "I would have recognised her anywhere." He said, and went on to tell of what he knew of the rescues she had done at Dunkirk.

The other boat is a tug; her name is '*Challenge*.' At the time of the 60th anniversary of Dunkirk, I was told that '*Challenge*' when fully restored, would have been offered a berth close to the *Cutty Sark* and Sir Francis Chichester's *Gypsy Moth* at Greenwich, where it would be able to provide the public with a memorial to the evacuation of Dunkirk. Unfortunately that hasn't come to be. However things have changed, and *Challenge* is now berthed at Southampton. One of the people who still help with the restoring of *Challenge* is John Puplett – and I feel that his words are better than mine.

He said:

"*Challenge* has been extensively replated, had gun decks fitted and a total repaint. She is now back in the water and currently lies at Marchwood, Southampton undergoing the second stage of a major refit, due for completion in October 2002. It is now hoped that she will, along with the British Military Powerboat Trust and the Southampton Hall of Aviation, form part of 'Solen Aero-Nautica' – a major new attraction proposed for the area."

Finally, I thank meeting, speaking and writing to all the volunteers in these stories, which have become the backbone and heart of this book.

Index.

237